VAN GOGH
THE ASYLUM YEAR

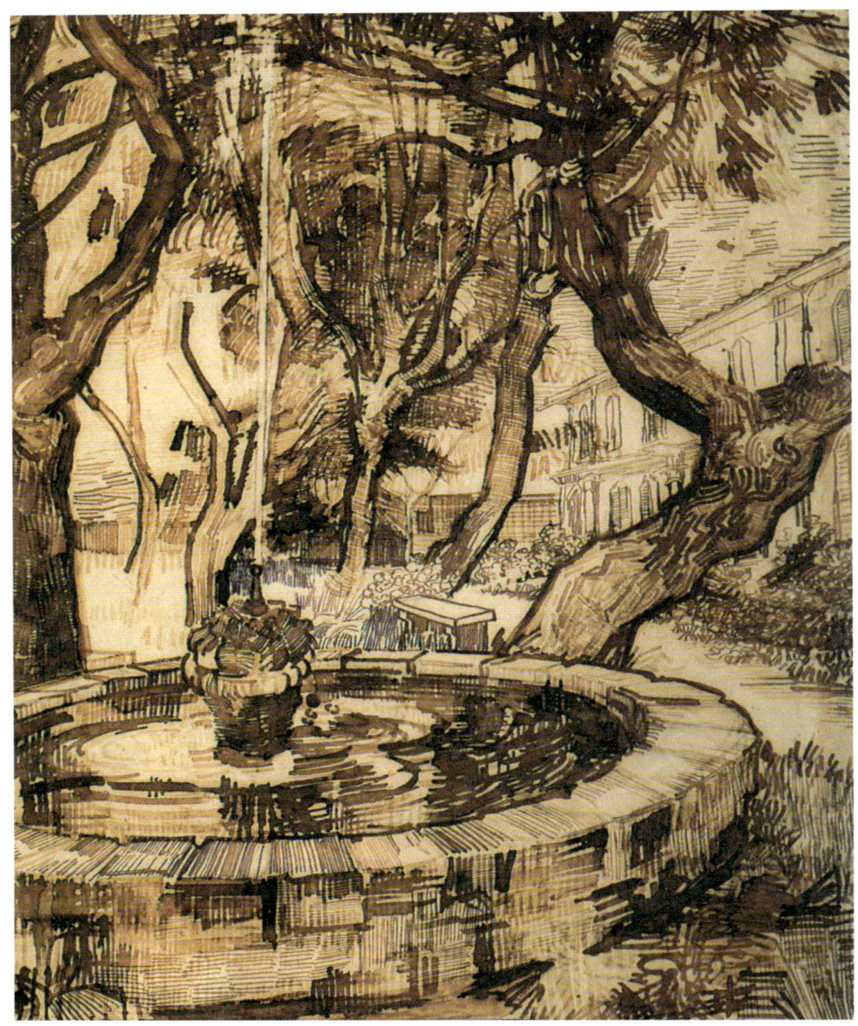

Fountain in the Asylum Garden (detail)
Saint-Rémy-de-Provence, May 1889

VAN GOGH
THE ASYLUM YEAR

EDWIN MULLINS

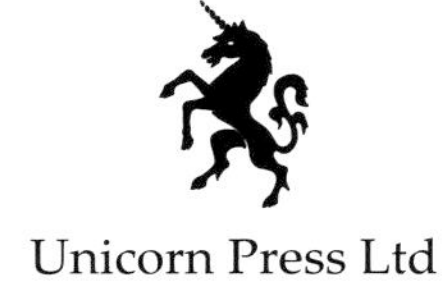

Unicorn Press Ltd

Unicorn Press Ltd
66 Charlotte Street
London
W1T 4QE

www.unicornpress.org

Published by Unicorn Press Ltd 2015
Text Copyright © Edwin Mullins 2015

ISBN 978-1-910065-53-2

10 9 8 7 6 5 4 3 2 1

Book design by Felicity Price-Smith
Printed in Spain by Graphycems

CONTENTS

PREFACE

On May 8th 1889 Vincent van Gogh was admitted to a mental asylum near Saint-Rémy-de-Provence. He remained there as a voluntary patient until May the following year, before moving to Auvers in northern France, where he took his own life (possibly in an accident) a little over two months later.

The asylum in Provence is a former 12th century Augustinian monastery, Saint-Paul-de-Mausoleo, named after the Roman triumphal arch and funerary monument which still dominate the landscape. The monastery still stands, with its massive Romanesque tower and secluded cloisters. It was closed down during the French Revolution and converted into a private mental hospital early in the 19th century. Altogether the place remains much as Van Gogh would have known it, with its stark corridors and the enclosed garden where he painted irises and roses. His small bedroom on the first floor still overlooks the mountains and a wheat field which he depicted repeatedly in all seasons whenever he was forbidden to work outside the asylum grounds because of his mental state.

Van Gogh had been treated at the hospital in Arles, twelve miles away, since late December the previous year. This followed the celebrated incident when he cut off part of his left ear after a dispute with his fellow painter Paul Gauguin, with whom he had shared the

Yellow House. From this moment it had become increasingly clear to the medical authorities and eventually to Van Gogh himself, that his mental instability made it inconceivable that he should live freely in the outside world. Furthermore, public hostility had built up against him following his self-mutilation, culminating in a petition being

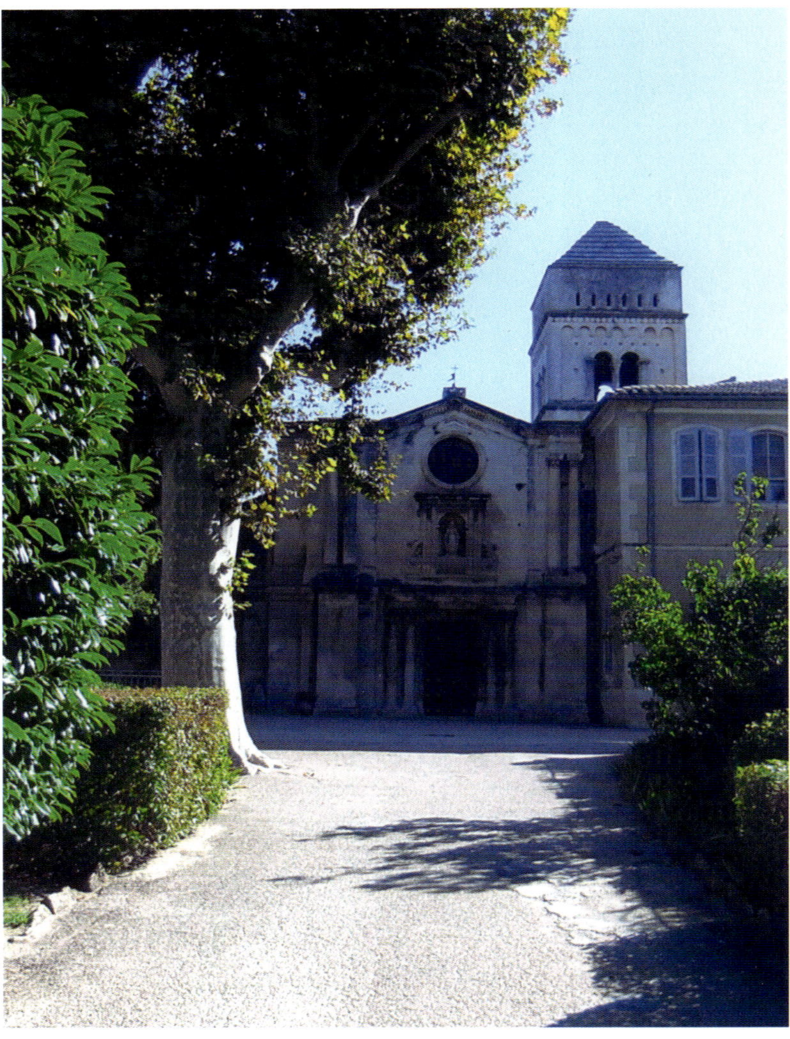

The Asylum at Saint-Rémy

drawn up and presented to the local mayor. As a result, while leaving his furniture and a number of canvases with friends in Arles, he agreed to become an inmate of the Saint-Rémy asylum until his mental health improved.

So on a May morning in 1889, the local Protestant pastor accompanied the artist from Arles and duly delivered him into the hands of the asylum's director, Dr Théophile Peyron. Dr Peyron, a former ship's doctor with no training in mental illnesses, was described later by Van Gogh as 'a little gouty man with very black spectacles'. The following day the painter was entered in the register, with the added comment by Dr Peyron that he was 'suffering from acute mania with hallucinations…which have caused him to mutilate himself'. Peyron then offered his opinion, based on information passed to him by the doctor who had treated the artist in Arles, that 'M. Van Gogh is subject to epileptic fits (so that) it is advisable to keep him under prolonged observation in this establishment.'

The crisis which brought Van Gogh to the asylum has been attributed to an imaginative variety of causes besides epilepsy, including excessive quantities of absinthe, foxglove poisoning, syphilis, schizophrenia and manic depression. It is also known that his family had a history of mental disturbances. One of his grandfathers is said to have died from some form of brain disease. An aunt suffered from epilepsy all her life. An uncle committed suicide. Another uncle suffered epileptic fits at the same age as Van Gogh was first struck down. At least two cousins are believed to have become mentally ill.

Van Gogh's own initial breakdown is also likely to have been related to the collapse of an overpowering dream that had drawn the artist from Paris to Provence little more than a year earlier. This was the dream of making this sun blessed region of France the inspiration for the art of the future. It was to be his Studio of the South, where painters would congregate and work, inspired by the light and colours of the region, sharing their thoughts and discoveries in a spirit of creative harmony. The romantic dream collapsed. In reality there had been only disharmony. Gauguin, Van Gogh's one recruit to his enterprise,

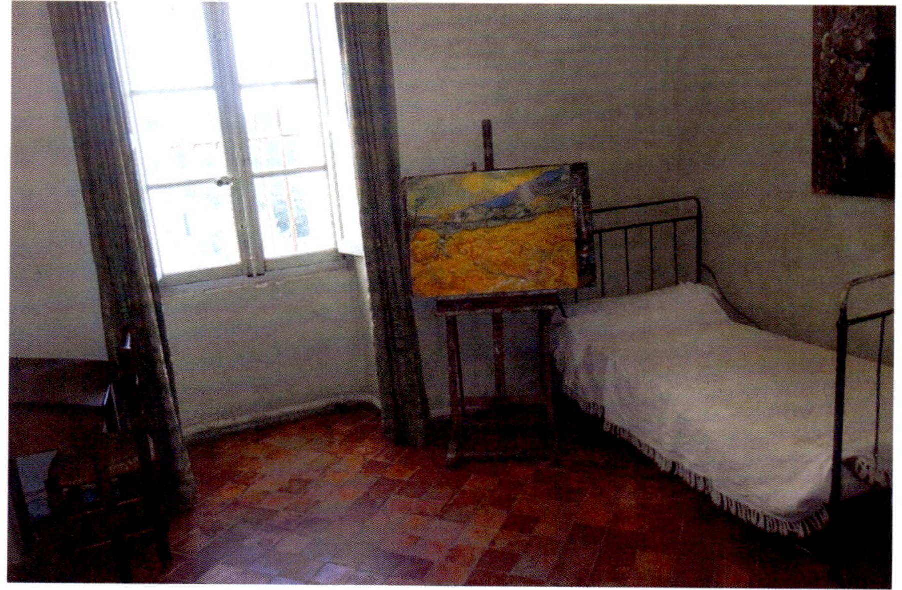

Van Gogh's Bedroom at the Asylum

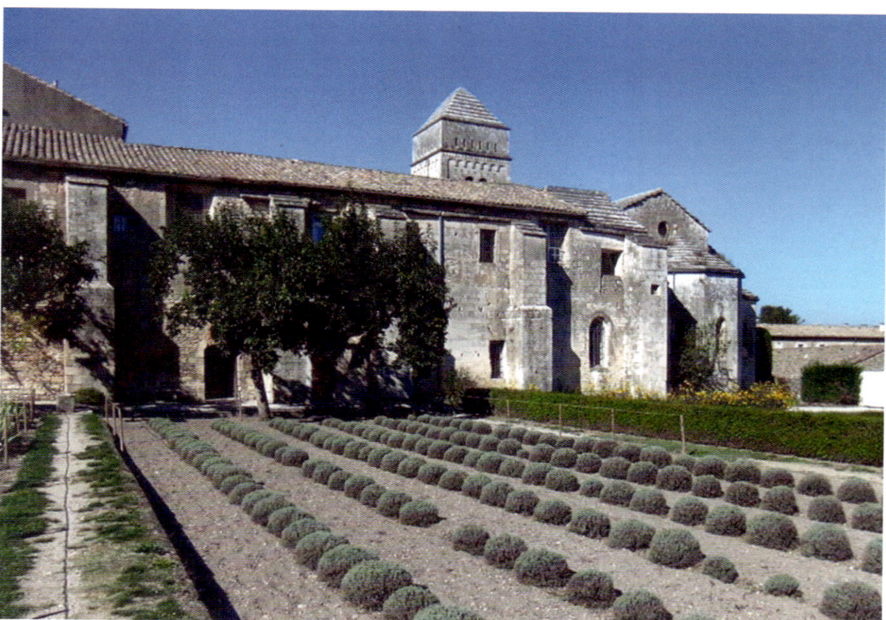

View of the Asylum from the Gardens

soon made his rapid departure in a major clash of personalities. The only member of his longed-for Studio of the South was himself, by now disillusioned and sick.

Van Gogh arrived in Saint-Rémy with the shattered remnants of this lost idyll. The burden of failure continued to haunt him throughout his year in the asylum and periodically it overwhelmed him. In that year he suffered four further mental breakdowns, rendering him incapacitated and confined to his room for months on end. On at least one occasion he tried to poison himself by swallowing paints he had been using for his canvases. Yet, characteristically, he was driven to paint more intensely than at any time in his life. Painting was his best therapy and his only salvation. His letters to Theo, his art-dealer brother in Paris, are as lucid and perceptive as at any time since he came to Provence. There were lengthy periods when he was too depressed and ill to write at all; yet between those dark months the letters contain repeated flashes of hope, even belief, that he might be able to begin an undisturbed life again and all in the end would be well. His life at the asylum was a volatile blend of creativity and despair, as if he spent each day dancing in the sunlight on the edge of an abyss; the abyss which of course finally claimed him.

The Asylum Year, fraught and dislocated though it was, nonetheless became the most intensely productive chapter of his short life, producing some of his best and most celebrated paintings, among them *The Starry Night* and the *Olive Orchard* series. In the course of that year Van Gogh despatched one hundred and thirty canvases by train to Theo in Paris in seven batches, four more than he had sent during the previous fifteen months in Arles. Even this impressive number does not represent his total output. Van Gogh is known to have given paintings away; also his letters record that he sometimes made two or more versions of a composition, particularly of portraits, giving one version to the sitter (all these are now lost). In all it is estimated that he produced a total of about one hundred and fifty canvases while at Saint-Rémy. Since for about one-third of the time he spent there he was too ill to work, or forbidden to do so, each painting must on average

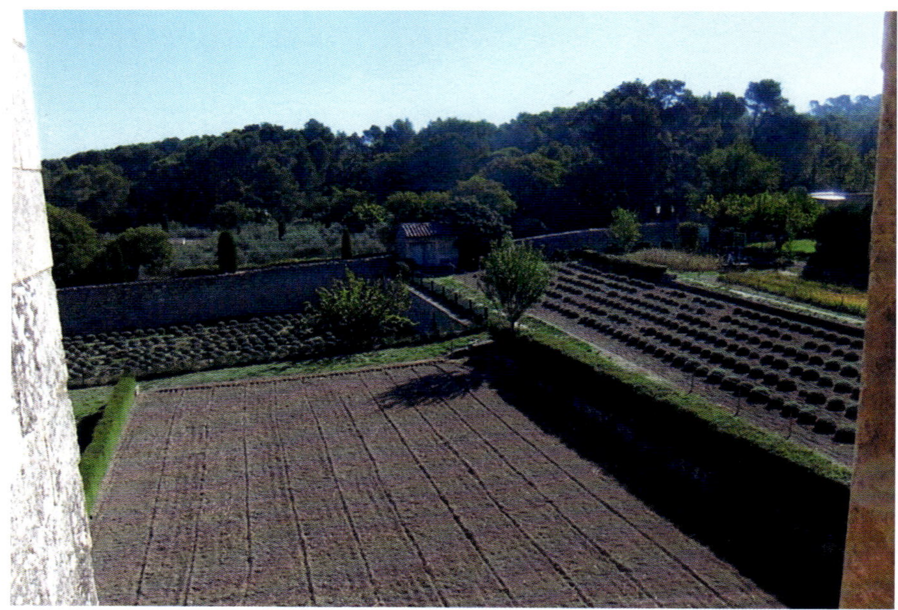

View from Van Gogh's Bedroom Window

have been completed in little more than a day – a truly astonishing work-rate; and by way of a reward, during that year Theo managed to sell just one painting.

The circumstances of his illness conditioned to a large extent how and what Van Gogh painted at Saint-Rémy. For the first month after his arrival in early May he was never permitted to leave the grounds of the asylum and only given permission to paint out of doors in the enclosed monastery garden. Here he was restricted to painting flowers and shrubbery at close range, even to observing blades of grass very closely. Alternatively, he could choose to paint the view from his bedroom window, which faced east over the jagged Alpilles peaks and onto a small wheat field in the foreground enclosed within a stone wall.

His letters reveal the calming effect these restrictions of movement had on him. Painting was always his most effective cure: besides, the asylum provided the shelter and order he needed. There were two periods during that year when he was permitted to work outside the walls – from June to mid-July and again in the autumn through to early winter. The two spells of freedom were separated by a massive breakdown lasting six weeks, while the second period of freedom was followed by a sequence of further breakdowns lasting until the spring, close to his final departure for Auvers. It was during these two extended spells of mental calm that Van Gogh embarked on several series of paintings on new themes which came to dominate his thoughts and ambitions. These new motifs were the cypress trees which abounded in the region, the olive orchards just beyond the walls of the monastery and the dramatic scenery of the Alpilles mountains.

In all three series the trees and rocks are described in a frenzy of agitated whorls and loops of the brush which Van Gogh claimed to be his search for the true character of the subjects he was painting. It is hard, though, not to see the frenzy of these late landscapes as an ever-more-perilous mental dance. Theo clearly believed as much: on receipt of these canvases he continually urged his brother to stick to describing what he saw and not indulge in contortions of nature. His faith in Vincent and belief in his exceptional gifts were touching; and his joy was unbounded when he received one of Van Gogh's last paintings from Saint-Rémy, a branch of an almond-tree in blossom against a vivid Provençal sky which the artist had sent in celebration of Theo's newborn son.

The Asylum Year saw Vincent at his most raw and needy. Letters flowed, especially to Theo. He identified totally with his brother, constantly writing of 'us' as if Theo was an essential spiritual element in his life and career as a painter. In turn Theo paid the bills for Saint-Rémy; he did what he could to show off the batches of paintings that kept arriving; and he offered support and guidance where he could. Vincent's state of mind constantly perturbed him and his letters convey an appealing blend of concern and reassurance, culminating in the search he made for a way to bring his brother back nearer Paris where he could be looked after with greater understanding than the untrained care offered at the asylum.

This book offers an account, month by month, of that penultimate chapter in Van Gogh's life, treating his letters, his paintings and his illness in parallel. It is a chapter separate from the others that make up the artist's life because it is nonetheless a self-contained episode, a play within a play, with a shape and dynamic of its own. Van Gogh's 'Asylum Year' is unlike any other year in the history of art.

*

I came across Van Gogh's monastery-asylum in the course of quite a different venture. I was preparing a book on Roman Provence and was keen to visit the ruins of the Graeco-Roman city of Glanum, the Pompeii of Provence, tucked dramatically into a cleft of the Alpilles mountains near the town of Saint-Rémy. The former gateway to Glanum is a striking though somewhat battered triumphal arch; and next to it stands a second monument built in honour of the Roman dead, generally described as the Saint-Rémy Mausoleum. A short distance from these twin 'antiquities', beyond an avenue of pine-trees, lies the complex of monastic buildings still known as Saint-Paul-de-Mausoleo, even though the place had been a mental asylum in the early 19th century. It was here, behind these protective monastic walls, that Van Gogh spent a year of his life.

The environment Van Gogh knew so intimately has not changed very much. A stroll through the asylum's enclosed gardens, then a longer circuit beyond the perimeter wall of the monastery grounds, takes in most of the subjects he painted and drew during the course of that year. Today reproductions of appropriate canvases are set up here and there to remind us of where and what he painted. These reminders also point to some surprising omissions in his work. Though Van Gogh recorded the exterior and the inner corridors of the asylum and the view of the grounds from his bedroom, he only once included the monastery church, at a distance, and never the beautiful and intimate Romanesque cloister through which he must have walked

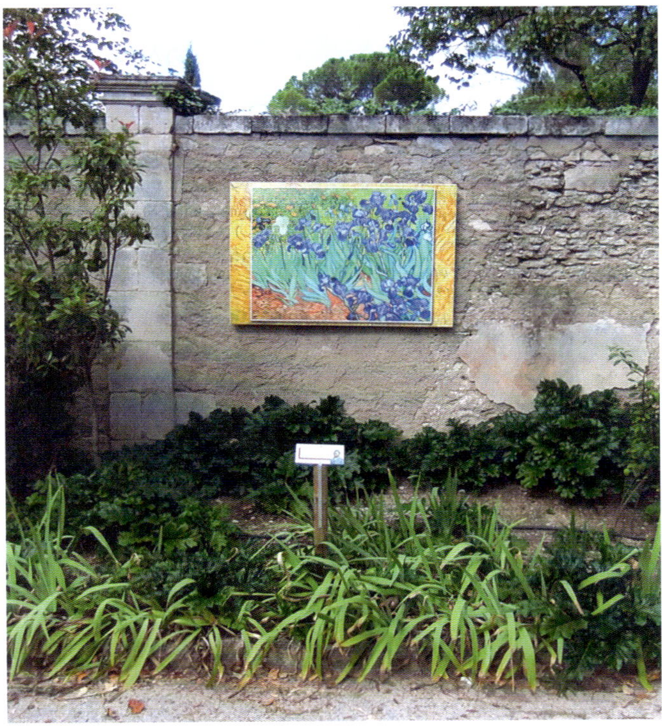

Reproductions of Van Gogh's paintings marking the locations where he painted them.

many times a day. These surprising omissions remind us of his early apprenticeship to become a pastor in the Protestant church. Van Gogh was certainly not interested in glorifying a Roman Catholic institution, or in celebrating the beauty of mediaeval architecture.

Equally surprising is that he never seems to have been tempted to draw or paint the monumental Roman antiquities, the triumphal arch and mausoleum, which stood so prominently only a few hundred yards beyond the asylum gates. Just about every visiting artist for the previous hundred years had faithfully (and often fancifully) recorded these twin monuments in order to satisfy Parisian collectors' romantic taste for the picturesque. But again, Van Gogh was not interested in history and certainly not in the picturesque. What always concerned him most was the true character of a place or a person. The word 'character' occurs repeatedly in his letters to his brother in Paris explaining what he was constantly searching for in his paintings. His whole two-year stay in the south, first in Arles and now in Saint-Rémy, was envisaged by him as a portrait-study of the region. Provence to him was the undiscovered country he was driven to introduce to the world. To present the 'true character' of Provence became his mission and clearly in his view that true character did not include the Roman conquest of the region by Julius and Augustus Caesar.

The one unavoidable omission from his work at Saint-Rémy was the ruins of the ancient city which were yet to be excavated – archaeological work only started there in the 1920s. All he would have been aware of were the two Roman monuments which originally stood at the entrance to the now-buried city and the massive stone quarry close to the asylum from which Glanum had been built. Van Gogh was attracted to the convoluted rock-forms of the deserted

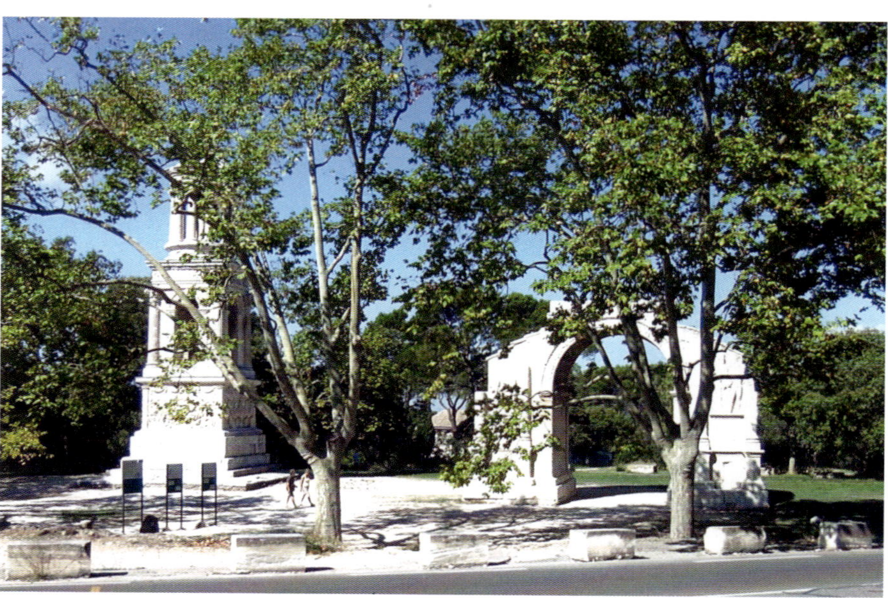

The Roman Monuments at Glanum

quarry and painted it several times without having any idea of what the place was for. He also painted a vigorously dramatised view of the ravine that stretches southwards between the enfolding walls of the Alpilles mountains, beneath which the city of Glanum lay buried. Photographs taken early in the 20th century show precisely what Van Gogh would have seen, with just the occasional fragment of stone wall or arch protruding above the surface and the stream gushing from the rock-face which he mentions in his letters. He could not have known this was the famous sacred spring round which the ancient city was created.

Van Gogh's footprints stretch across this landscape. In the lengthy periods between mental attacks when he was permitted to work outside the asylum walls, he would explore the mountain tracks and lowland fruit orchards tirelessly in search of fresh subjects to paint. We can trace those footprints everywhere – through the olive groves, the clusters of dark cypress trees, the wheat field (now a lavender garden) which he recorded in all seasons, the almond trees which he painted in full blossom as early as February during his only winter here; and of course the ever-present curtain of the Alpilles mountains whose wild and jagged shapes so caught his imagination and which seem as we gaze at them, to reflect the turbulence of the artist's mind during these last months of his life.

Familiarity with this vivid and varied landscape so little changed in one-and-a-quarter centuries brings the reality and pathos of Van Gogh's life and work here sharply in focus. Equally moving is the experience of being at the Saint-Rémy asylum itself, the place which both sheltered and trapped Van Gogh during that year while he clung to sanity by the finest of threads.

The letters from Saint-Rémy are especially rich. They flow like a fast river that is continually bursting its banks. These letters, mostly to his brother Theo, offer a refreshing and intelligent account of the artist's thoughts and passions, hopes and disappointments, as well as a personal account of his work-in-progress. Through these letters we feel we know Van Gogh better than any other artist of recent centuries – know him,

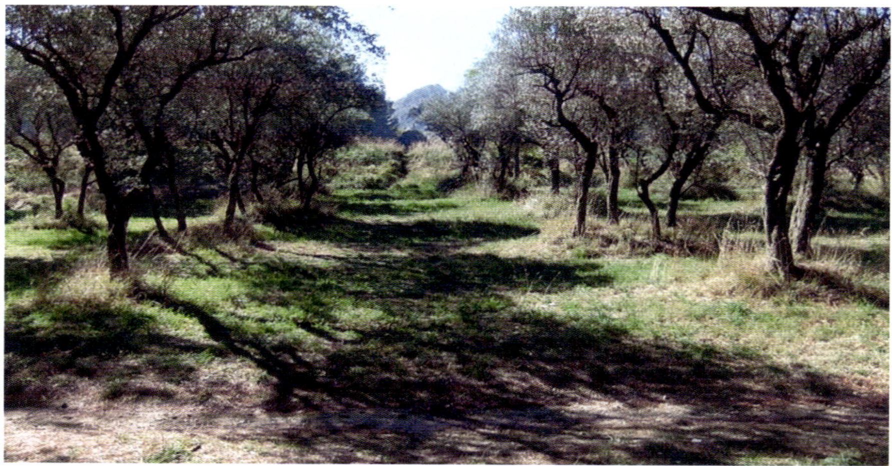

The Olive Orchard

warm to him and despair of him. Such lucid intellect; such volcanic gifts; such resourcefulness in the face of failure and illness, yet such an utter human mess. He is a man repeatedly in torment, perpetually on the brink of suicide. There are lengthy gaps in the correspondence when he is simply too ill to write at all. At other times letter writing feels like a lifeboat he clings to, a sister-ship to his paintings. There is nothing else he can do but write and paint, write and paint. All other human activities are unavailable to him. He is trapped – within the asylum and within himself.

Regularly, often day by day, those letters to and from Van Gogh and others – Theo, Gauguin, Emile Bernard, his mother and sister, a few friends – chronicle an urgent dialogue with the wider world beyond the sanctuary of the asylum walls which he could no longer inhabit. That dialogue, embracing his painting, his thoughts and fears, his illness and his friendships, has provided me with the basic material for this book.

Edwin Mullins
Saint-Rémy-de-Provence
2015

On the morning of Christmas Eve 1888 Van Gogh was taken to hospital in the Provençal city of Arles where he had been living since February, in recent months sharing a rented house with fellow artist Paul Gauguin. This was the celebrated Yellow House, lovingly portrayed in Van Gogh's paintings. The artist had been found, seemingly by Gauguin although accounts vary, lying in his bed bleeding and in a coma. Police transported the injured man to hospital where he was attended to by a young physician, Félix Rey. Dr Rey continued to treat the patient and monitor his condition through a succession of mental crises over the course of the next four and a half months. During that time the two men developed a certain friendship and a mutual respect, as a result of which Van Gogh came finally to accept that he needed a sustained period of medical help free of the strains of day-to-day living in Arles with which he had proved unable to cope. Accordingly, he agreed to be transferred as a voluntary patient to an asylum some fifteen miles away at Saint-Rémy-de-Provence.

The day before his admission to hospital, December 23rd, Van Gogh had suffered a severe mental breakdown sparked off by mounting disagreements with Gauguin. A confrontation had taken place between the two artists that evening, resulting in what has become one of the most richly publicised acts of violence in the story of art.

Van Gogh cut off part of his left ear and presented the gory trophy to a local prostitute. Gauguin meanwhile had taken the precaution of spending the night in a nearby hotel, unaware of these events until he returned to the Yellow House the following morning to find a crowd gathered outside. Inside the place was smeared with blood and the artist was lying semi-conscious in his bedroom. After police had taken the injured man to hospital Gauguin telephoned Vincent's brother Theo in Paris, urging him to take the train to Arles urgently, which he did, arriving on Christmas morning. The two men visited Van Gogh in hospital, discussing the case with a bemused Dr Rey. Later that same day Gauguin and Theo took the train back to Paris.

Gauguin never returned and his departure marked the end of an intense and claustrophobic relationship between two creative spirits which had begun promisingly only two months earlier, when Gauguin

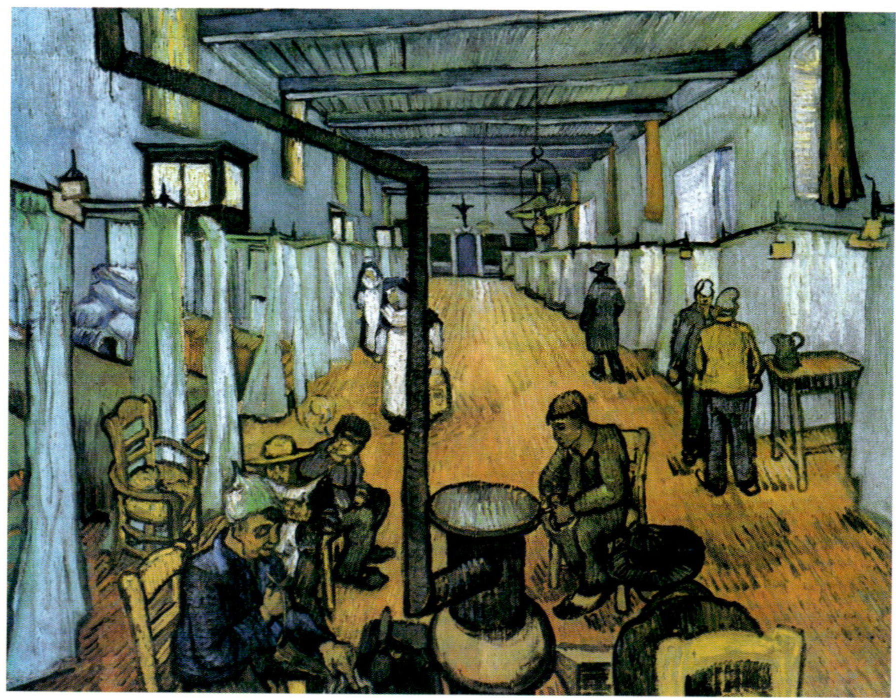

Ward in the Hospital in Arles Oil on canvas, 74 x 92 cm
Oskar Reinhart Foundation, Winterthur, Switzerland

arrived and they shared the Yellow House. Gauguin's departure also shattered Van Gogh's idealistic dream of establishing a Studio of the South, a kind of artists' cooperative which was to have been the fountainhead for the art of the future. Gauguin had been the only recruit to the venture; but it seems clear that after little more than two months he had experienced more than enough of living and working with a utopian fanatic and so he fled. Yet during the following year the two artists continued to correspond warmly at a safe distance and Gauguin never wavered from being a strong admirer of Van Gogh as a painter, even proposing a year later that they try a joint venture a second time, a suggestion which came to nothing.

The violent events of December also signalled the end of Van Gogh's ability to live freely in the outside world. His mental breakdown before Christmas was to be the first of many; and they would recur persistently, rendering him helpless for weeks on end and confined to his room for his own safety. From now on he would live and work perpetually under the dark threat of another attack. In Dr Rey's view it was some form of epilepsy and the form it took could be violent and was invariably self-destructive.

The nature of the dispute with Gauguin, which prompted this first mental attack and self-mutilation, is somewhat hazy and has inspired some fanciful scenarios, the most implausible being that it was Gauguin himself who cut off his friend's ear. Van Gogh himself never described what happened; he invariably had a mental blackout on such occasions as though all painful memories became airbrushed from his mind. Besides, there was no witness, except possibly a group of young boys who promptly disappeared (an invitation to yet more theories). The only account we have is from Gauguin himself as reported back in Paris to his artist friend Emile Bernard and the art critic Albert Aurier, who was later to write the first serious appreciation of Van Gogh's work. According to Bernard, Gauguin described Van Gogh as mad, believing himself to be some kind of god, prone to visions which encouraged him to believe that Gauguin was trying to murder him, which was why Gauguin had fled the house on that fateful evening, with Van Gogh in pursuit, perhaps brandishing the weapon which he subsequently turned on himself.

Merely a week before these violent events, Gauguin had made it clear in a letter to Theo that he would have to return to Paris because he and Vincent could no longer live and work together. During one argument Vincent had apparently hurled a glass of absinthe in Gauguin's face. Undoubtedly Gauguin's uncertainty as to whether or not to leave Arles contributed to Van Gogh's erratic behaviour and breakdown. The picture is made even more unclear as letters to and from Van Gogh in the weeks following the violent incident before Christmas give little impression of anything serious having occurred at all. In his first letter to Theo written in hospital on January 2nd, just one week after the incident, Van Gogh merely expresses the hope that he 'didn't alarm' Gauguin and hopes that his friend will soon write to him. He added that he will soon be allowed back home to the Yellow House feeling 'very calm'. Two days later he wrote directly to 'My dear friend Gauguin', wishing him well and 'prosperity in Paris', concluding 'with a good handshake'. Gauguin duly responded on January 8th, making no reference to the violent incident less than two weeks earlier, but expressing his enjoyment at seeing Van Gogh's *Sunflowers* in Theo's house, which he described as 'the essential Vincent'.

Van Gogh's behaviour in hospital was at first unpredictable and disturbed. He took to climbing into other patients' beds and chasing the nurses in his nightshirt, even trying to wash his face in the coal bin. He became confined to an isolated cell with shackles to restrain him if necessary. On January 8th Van Gogh was allowed to leave hospital and return to the Yellow House, going back each day to have his wound dressed.

For a while a semblance of normality seemed to be returning to his life. Without the challenging presence of Gauguin he felt lonely; yet he had friends, the amiable postman Joseph Roulin and the nearby café-owners M. and Mme Ginoux, all of whom sat for him. Van Gogh had a considerable gift for friendship and those who regarded him merely as an eccentric foreigner often warmed to him and enjoyed his company. Furthermore, as was to become a regular practice with Van Gogh's breakdowns, once his balance of mind returned a period of calm set in as if nothing had happened; and this mental peace would be accompanied by a volatile burst of creative energy. Between sessions of being treated by Dr Rey for his wound Vincent now returned to his easel and portrayed himself quite dispassionately smoking his pipe and with his head swathed in bandages as though he was merely suffering from a bout of earache. (Thereafter, once the bandages were removed he never again painted the left side of his face; only the right profile – which ironically, being a mirror image, looks like his left side.)

But the period of calm was brief. In the first week of February Van Gogh suffered another attack and returned to hospital. Here he explained to Dr Rey that there were people in Arles trying to poison him. It was to become a familiar pattern: paranoia combined with self-destructiveness was soon to be a regular feature of these breakdowns. Two weeks after this second breakdown he was writing to Theo announcing that he had just left hospital, 'I hope for good'. The attack, in his view, was no more than some local malady, something he might have caught and most unlikely to return. The self-deception must have sounded hollow even to himself because he then added that it might be wise for him to seek some form of psychiatric treatment. Now that he had suffered a second attack a sense of reality was beginning to erode his optimism. He was beginning to feel he was walking a cliff-edge and recognised that he might slip again.

In fact he had only half-left hospital: he was still returning at night. By the third week of February he was at least taking walks in the town during the day and was beginning to paint again in the Yellow House. Yet his return was not entirely welcome: there were signs that his behaviour in December had provoked local hostility. He was becoming harassed and mocked by children as he came and went to the house. Matters came to a head at the end of the month when a petition was drawn up and delivered to the mayor of Arles demanding that

Van Gogh be interned. Arles was a tight provincial community little used to foreigners or artists, least of all to foreign artists given to strange behaviour and violent outbursts. Disturbed and angry, he returned to the safety of the hospital.

A man who began to figure prominently in Vincent's life at this time was the local Protestant pastor, the Rev. Fréderic Salles. Van Gogh's early apprenticeship with a view to becoming a cleric and preacher in the Protestant Reformed Church in Holland brought him naturally close to the man who was its local representative here in Arles. Salles made efforts to take Van Gogh under his wing, besides acting as a link between Vincent and his brother Theo in Paris, especially in periods when Vincent himself was too stressed or unwell to write letters. One such interval occurred during the first weeks in March, when it was left to the Rev. Salles to inform Theo of Vincent's new misfortunes. 'I learn that you are not yet better, which causes me much grief,' Theo wrote on March 16th after hearing from Salles. The letter prompted Van Gogh to break his silence; and over the following weeks letters to his brother follow one after the other in rapid succession in a positive lava-flow of his thoughts and fears.

Reading this painful outpouring to his brother it becomes clear that it was at this time, in the wake of his second mental breakdown, that Van Gogh's life had reached a turning-point from which there could be no retreat. His days as a free and independent human being were over; and it becomes ever more obvious that an asylum beckoned. The letters show a man desperately trying to harness his intelligence to understand the kind of person he has become. He tells Theo of the petition claiming him to be 'a man not worthy of living at liberty', which he finds 'a hammer blow in the chest'. Under pressure from the local police chief he is confined to an isolation cell in hospital: 'Here I am shut up day after day under lock and key.' He knows he must resist getting angry about it, aware that he would otherwise be judged 'a dangerous lunatic'. He writes about 'feeling calm', while aware that at any moment he could 'fall back into a state of over-excitement'.

In dozens of letters over the months, to become 'calm' is forever the

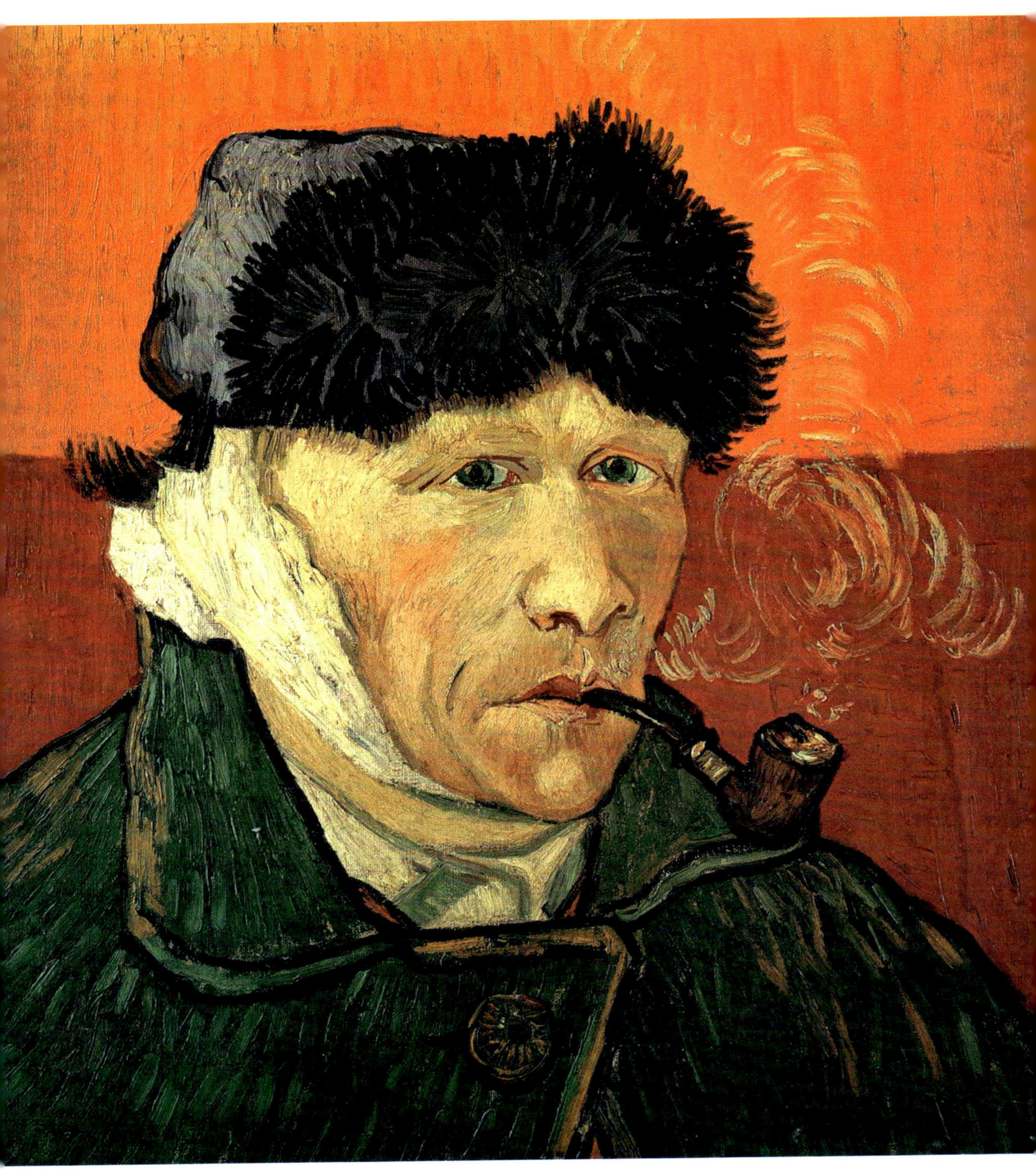

Self-portrait with Bandaged Ear and Pipe Oil on canvas, 60 x 49 cm
Private collection (Stavros Niarchos), on loan to Kunsthaus Zürich

mantra Van Gogh reaches for, knowing 'calm' itself to be quite out of reach.

He had now been unable to work for several months and something needed to be done urgently to regenerate his life. He longs most of all to be given back his 'fresh air and his work', both of them essential to him. Meanwhile frustration has set in: 'my house has been shut up by the police,' and he is unable even to send any of his earlier canvases to Theo because they too are under lock and key. He perceives more than ever that work is the best cure for his mental condition; yet he is not permitted to draw or paint. All he can do is write letters to his much-loved brother several hundred miles away, which he now does almost daily and at great length.

The fatalistic tone of the letters lightens just a little towards the end of March as a glimmer of optimism returns. He begins to reconsider the possibility of living a normal life, mentioning to Theo that efforts are being made to find him an apartment in a distant part of Arles far from hostile neighbours. 'As far as I can judge I'm not mad strictly speaking,' he adds; and once his new home is established he may discover 'a more peaceful path'. Then he almost immediately backtracks, suggesting that he may become 'really mad' again, but that at least he now knows himself well enough to understand that there will be intervals of normality between such bouts. In this assessment of his condition he was absolutely right, as the year he was shortly to spend at Saint-Rémy would prove. Those 'intervals' would also become intensely productive, as if the knowledge that they might offer only a brief remission concentrated his mind and fed the creative flow of his imagination. Almost in the same breath he acknowledges that he might prefer to live permanently in a madhouse rather than impose himself on another person (presumably reflecting on his disastrous attempt to set up house with Gauguin). He even considers that, were he a Catholic he would like to become a monk.

Another stabilising influence at this time was a visit to him in hospital of a fellow-painter whom both he and Theo liked and respected. Paul Signac, ten years younger than Van Gogh, had come to Arles specially to see him on his way south by train from Paris to the Mediterranean. Vincent had seen no-one from the art community since the departure of Gauguin three months earlier and Signac seems to have brought a youthful breath of fresh air into Van Gogh's claustrophobic life, filling him with renewed hopes of returning to work and to something approaching a normal life. Vincent even managed to obtain access to the Yellow House where he presented his visitor with a still-life.

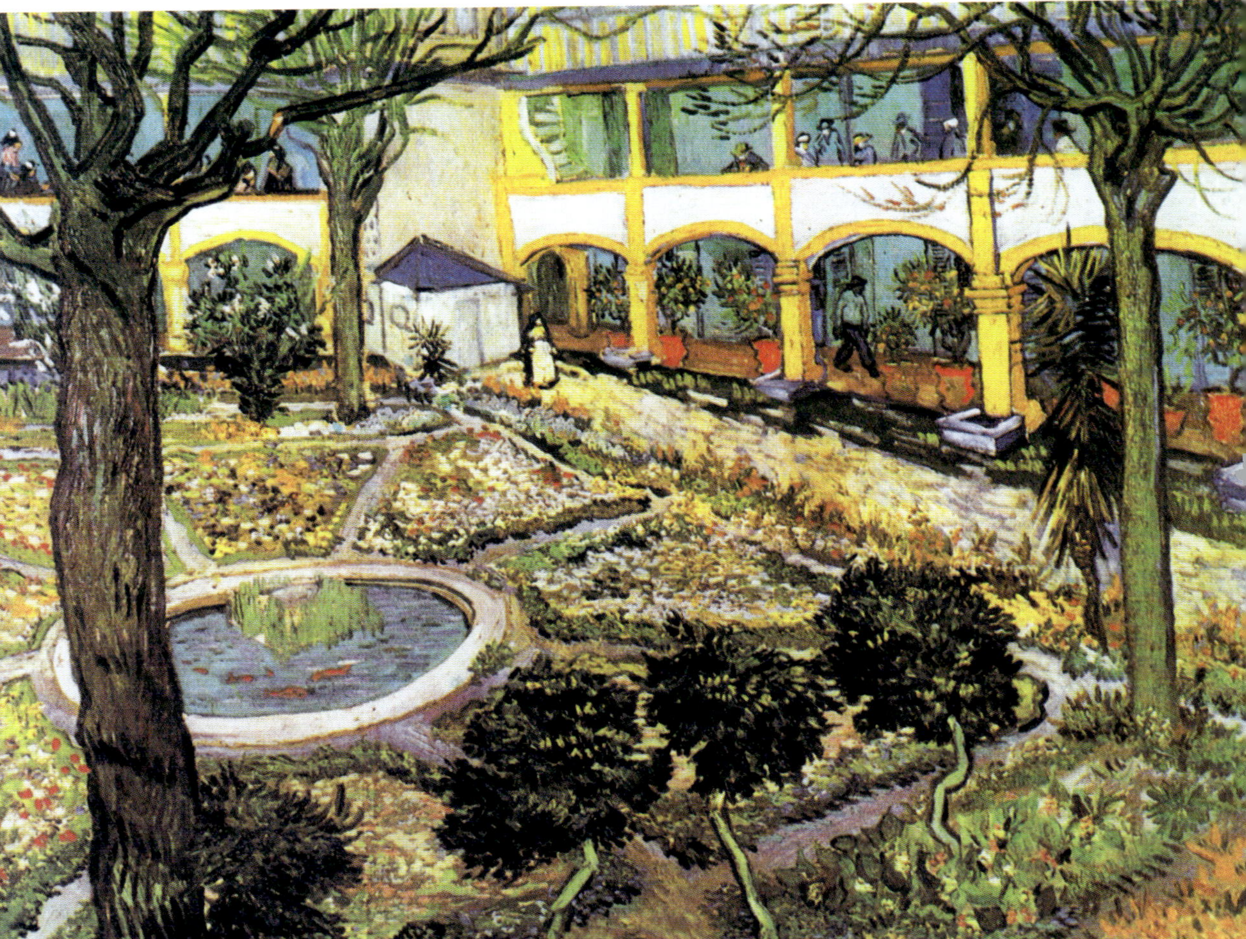

Garden of the Hospital in Arles Oil on canvas, 73 × 92 cm
Oskar Reinhart Collection, Winterthur, Switzerland

Signac reported back to Theo that he had discussed Van Gogh's requirements with Dr Rey and they had agreed that it was essential for Vincent to live in a controlled environment in which he could be regularly supervised and not be left on his own. At the same time Signac assured Theo that he had found Van Gogh in a perfect state of health.

Everything now pointed even more strongly to an asylum of some kind, in which his daily life could be regulated and protected from outside interference while at the same time providing him with the opportunity to work, which was essential for him. As Vincent himself wrote in his next letter to Theo, 'I must have my freedom in order to practice my profession.'

He seems to have been allowed a measure of that freedom by Dr Rey and the police authorities. At the end of March he wrote to Theo that he had been shopping for painting materials in Arles and had also been able to revisit the Yellow House and meet friendly neighbours who had not signed the petition against him in February. He was looking back on the 'moral anguish' of the past three months with dismay and now intended to 'throw myself back into work which has fallen behind'.

After such a long period of inactivity April awakened a remarkable surge of creative activity, of a kind which would soon become Van Gogh's customary behaviour after recovering from bouts of mental illness. On April 4th he described to Theo, almost casually, what he had been painting. 'Just now I have on my easel an orchard of peach trees beside a road with the Alpilles in the background.' He then changes the subject. But one week later in a follow-up letter he waxes more enthusiastically about the same painting, offering Theo a longer description accompanied by a quick sketch of it. After months of isolation and dark despair Van Gogh was able to go out and produce one of the most radiant and well-loved landscapes in art, *La Crau with Peach Trees in Blossom*, a reproduction of which has since graced a million living-room walls around the world, as eloquent a demonstration of Van Gogh's particular genius as one could find.

To be painting spring landscapes again would have taken him back to the previous spring when he had just arrived and became overwhelmed by the light and the colours of the south. A golden sunlit future seemed to lie ahead. For a while his hopes that he might after all be able to live and work freely again seem to have revived; and in the same letter to Theo he writes of the possibility of finding an apartment that might be affordable (since Theo would be paying for it). Then, as so often in these rambling letters his flow of thought leads him to contradict himself. He is now accustomed to being confined, 'and if I had to remain in hospital for good I would get used to it and would find subjects to paint there.' Yet next we hear that he has actually rented a small apartment and hopes to stay in Arles for at least four more months.

This see-saw state of mind persisted throughout most of April. By the third week of the month he appears to have moved into the new apartment, although in a letter to Theo of April 21st he expresses a wish to go to 'that mental hospital in Saint-Rémy'. It was his first mention of the place where he was soon to spend a year. Evidently the Rev. Salles, as ever Vincent's local guardian and mentor, had sent Theo a prospectus of the asylum, including the cost (since Theo would be paying for it, as with everything else in Van Gogh's life). Reading between the lines of Vincent's letter it becomes evident that he has already abandoned the idea of living in the new apartment, finding the responsibility of coping on his own impossible to bear. 'I CAN'T DO IT,' he writes in capital letters. 'For the time being I want to remain confined, as much for the sake of my own tranquillity as that of others.' The last dream of independence had vanished. Now Saint-Rémy was the only answer.

Once reconciled to going into the asylum he immediately began to envisage the advantages of such a move. He imagined being allowed to go out into the countryside to draw and paint once he was at Saint-Rémy, without the hazards of being in a town and having to cope with intrusive or hostile people. 'It's a matter of no longer causing scenes in public,' he concludes.

While still making plans to leave Arles within a few weeks he introduced a new fantasy. On April 28th he wrote to Theo that he was toying with the idea of enlisting in the French Foreign Legion for five years. It would do him good, he thinks. Then, almost in the same breath he begins to look forward to working at Saint-Rémy. 'Ah, my dear Theo, if you could see the olive trees at this time of the year.' Even before setting eyes on his new environment he is already anticipating one of the major themes which will dominate his mind throughout his Asylum Year. An olive grove has a special beauty and meaning to him, possessing 'something very intimate, immensely old about it'. His search for the 'true character' of Provence, which was to preoccupy him throughout his year at Saint-Rémy, is already feeding his imagination. Yet, on the very same day he writes to his sister Wil in Holland of his thoughts on committing suicide and how close he is to it, 'at moments all but…' and he leaves it open. Olive trees and suicide were keeping company in his contemplation of the future.

The fantasy of joining the Foreign Legion still persisted. On April 30th he bent Theo's ear with the thought that he might enjoy 'going to Arabia as a soldier' and perhaps finding it easier to paint in a backroom than in an asylum; straightaway following up this fanciful thought with a down-to-earth list of paintings which he was proposing to send to Paris in two crates. These included the celebrated exterior of the night café in Arles and 'several sunflowers', all of which had been locked up in the Yellow House until recently.

Two days later, on May 2nd, he harboured doubts that the Foreign Legion would accept him due to records of his recent behaviour. The following day, even as 'I am packing my trunks' Van Gogh is still writing about wanting to enlist 'soon'. Fantasy is keeping pace with reality to the last. There follows a sad reflection about himself as a painter – 'I'll never count for anything important.' Then immediately he expresses his delight at starting to draw with a reed-pen once again and is greatly looking forward to being productive once more in the asylum.

Fantasies finally gave way to practicalities. There was no further talk of the Foreign Legion and Van Gogh's last undertaking before leaving Arles was to despatch a final large consignment of about 125 paintings to Theo in Paris. These represented the majority of canvases he had produced during the previous year, no longer under lock and key in the Yellow House. A small number of spring landscapes he had painted within the last month he left behind, planning to return to Arles later and send them on to Theo once they were dry.

On the morning of Wednesday May 8th the faithful Rev. Salles collected Van Gogh from the hospital and together they took the local train on the short distance of some fifteen miles to Saint-Rémy and thence to the asylum of Saint-Paul-de-Mausoleo – where he was to remain until May the following year.

After so many changes of mood and changes of mind over the past four months Van Gogh finally made the move from Arles to Saint-Rémy with surprising ease, even with a feeling of relief. From his demeanour on arrival it was evident that he was turning his back on a life in which he had felt victimised and with which he could no longer cope. He was now looking forward to a new life, even at the price of being caged. The asylum walls would confine him, but also protect him and regulate him. He was a willing prisoner.

The Rev. Salles, the Protestant pastor in Arles who had become Van Gogh's self-appointed 'guardian', accompanied the artist to Saint-Rémy on May 8th. Afterwards Salles returned to Arles and reported to Van Gogh's brother Theo in Paris with some relief that 'M. Vincent was perfectly calm and explained his case…himself to the director as a man who is entirely aware of his situation…As I left he thanked me profusely and appeared somewhat moved by the prospect of a completely new life that he was about to lead.' Salles had been assured by the director, furthermore, that Vincent would receive all possible help at the asylum.

The director of the Saint-Paul-de-Mausoleo asylum was Dr Théophile Peyron, a former naval physician who seems to have been a kindly disciplinarian well-disposed to helping Vincent, but possessing no training or qualifications in matters of mental health. What he was doing running a mental institution can best be explained by local nepotism. Van Gogh later described him as 'a little gouty man with very black spectacles'.

At their first meeting Dr Peyron listened to Vincent's calm statement about himself. The next day he entered his new patient in the asylum register. 'The patient is suffering from acute mania with hallucinations of sight and hearing which have caused him to mutilate himself by cutting off his ear…At present he seems to have recovered his sense of reason, but he does not feel that he possesses the strength and the courage to live independently…It is my opinion that M. Van Gogh is subject to epileptic fits at very infrequent intervals and that it is advisable to keep him under prolonged observation in this establishment.' Dr Peyron's opinion of Vincent's condition was evidently formed to a large extent by a medical report sent to him by the conscientious Dr Rey at the Arles hospital where he had been observing the artist for the past two months.

Vincent was allocated a bedroom on the first floor of the old monastery building with a view through a barred window of a wheat field which lay within the walls enclosing the asylum grounds. A short distance beyond the wall rose the dramatic peaks of the Alpilles mountains. Today his bedroom is kept as a modest shrine to the artist, the prospect from the window unchanged except that the wheat field is now a lavender garden. At the time of Van Gogh's arrival here the asylum had only ten male and twenty female patients. There were plenty of empty rooms and Dr Peyron allowed Vincent the use of a second room as a studio overlooking the former monastery garden (or park), now severely neglected and heavily shaded by pine-trees and shrubs. Beyond were stone benches and an elegant fountain and circular pool, all of which were soon to feature prominently in Van Gogh's paintings.

The complex of buildings and the surrounding gardens had originally been an Augustinian monastery dating from the 12th century. It had shared the fate of so many monastic institutions during the French

Revolution, falling empty for several decades before being transformed into a private mental hospital early in the 19th century. A spacious new building was added as a clinic and medical centre at the far end of the park beyond the stone fountain and pool, also added at this time.

For the first month Van Gogh's movements were restricted to the monastery complex and to certain areas of the adjoining park and gardens. He was not allowed in the wheat field which he could gaze down on from his bedroom window. There was little for patients to do in the asylum. There seems to have been little in the way of regular treatment and occupational therapy had not been invented. There was a library and a billiard-room and not much else. Boredom and gloom ruled in the place; Van Gogh found it dispiriting and avoided the other patients as much as possible. But at least the environment was not threatening and few demands were made of him. Most of all it was safe. As for his own medical treatment, this was minimal and fairly rudimentary, a regime consisting principally of a controlled diet with not too much meat and a little wine, regular dosses of bromide to calm him and two-hour baths twice a week.

Unlike other patients in the asylum Van Gogh had come here with a driving need to work. Painting was his profession and his passion. It was also, as he was constantly to remind Theo in his letters, the best possible cure for his mental illness. He took just two drawings with him to Saint-Rémy and no paintings; these had been sent in the large batch to Theo in Paris just before his departure from Arles. All that remained were the fruits of his final weeks in Arles and these were left behind to dry until he could return later. Perhaps the two drawings he brought with him were intended as proof to Dr Peyron of his seriousness and skill, though the director would already have been appraised of his new patient's abilities by Dr Rey. At any rate Dr Peyron was entirely sympathetic to Vincent's needs and in the very first week here Van Gogh set to work painting in the asylum garden. There was hardly a generous range of subject-matter in this restricted wilderness, but for Vincent, as always, the important thing was to paint. He lived to paint and if there was only a flower, a patch of undergrowth, a moth or a cicada available, or a stone bench or an empty corridor, they would suffice if there was nothing else.

His first painting in Saint-Rémy was a study of irises, a dense cluster of vivid blue flowers and sword-like leaves which he depicted life-size and exactly as they grew in the asylum garden. The dazzling quality of the painting lies in the way he has expressed the rich variations of blue and violet in the flowers. He managed to convey the swordlike nature of the leaves through equally subtle variations of green with dark outlines, all set off against the contrasting red of the soil and the orange of the marigolds in the background. This was not a subject Vincent had tackled before and with his love of the Dutch Old Masters he might have been expected to follow the still-life tradition of carefully composed bouquets of flowers in a vase. But Van Gogh instinctively painted them as nature offered them up to him. The vigorous tangle of flowers and leaves clearly appealed to him and the painting is a precursor of so many other swirling and entangled forms that he was to find in nature during his year at Saint-Rémy and which characterised his style in this late period of his life.

Irises was the very first of the one hundred and fifty or so paintings Van Gogh was to produce in the densely-packed months to come. It was the pilot pointing the way ahead. If there is personal symbolism in the painting it rests in the solitary white iris among the cluster of violet-blue. Is this Van Gogh, isolated in the world? Psychological interpretations of his work are irresistible because of the nature of the man and the traumas of his life; also because, due largely to his letters, we feel we know so much more about him than we do about most artists. He is everyone's favourite mad genius. Van Gogh himself is said to have called *Irises* a 'lightning conductor of my illness'; and indeed the sharpness of those iris leaves does suggest an electric charge could pass through them. But Vincent's description is even more appropriate. The irises are earthed: there is no danger. His 'illness' has been dealt with. Throughout his Asylum Year Van Gogh constantly wrote that the only cure for his illness was to be working with nature. In absorbing his state of mind like a lightning conductor, his irises, like the olive trees and cypresses to come later in the year, have been transformed into art. The lightning and the lightning conductor had done their job.

(*Irises* was a painting which especially pleased Theo when he received it in July and in September Theo arranged to include it in the annual Salon des Indépendants in Paris, where puzzlingly it was entitled *A Study of Geese*.)

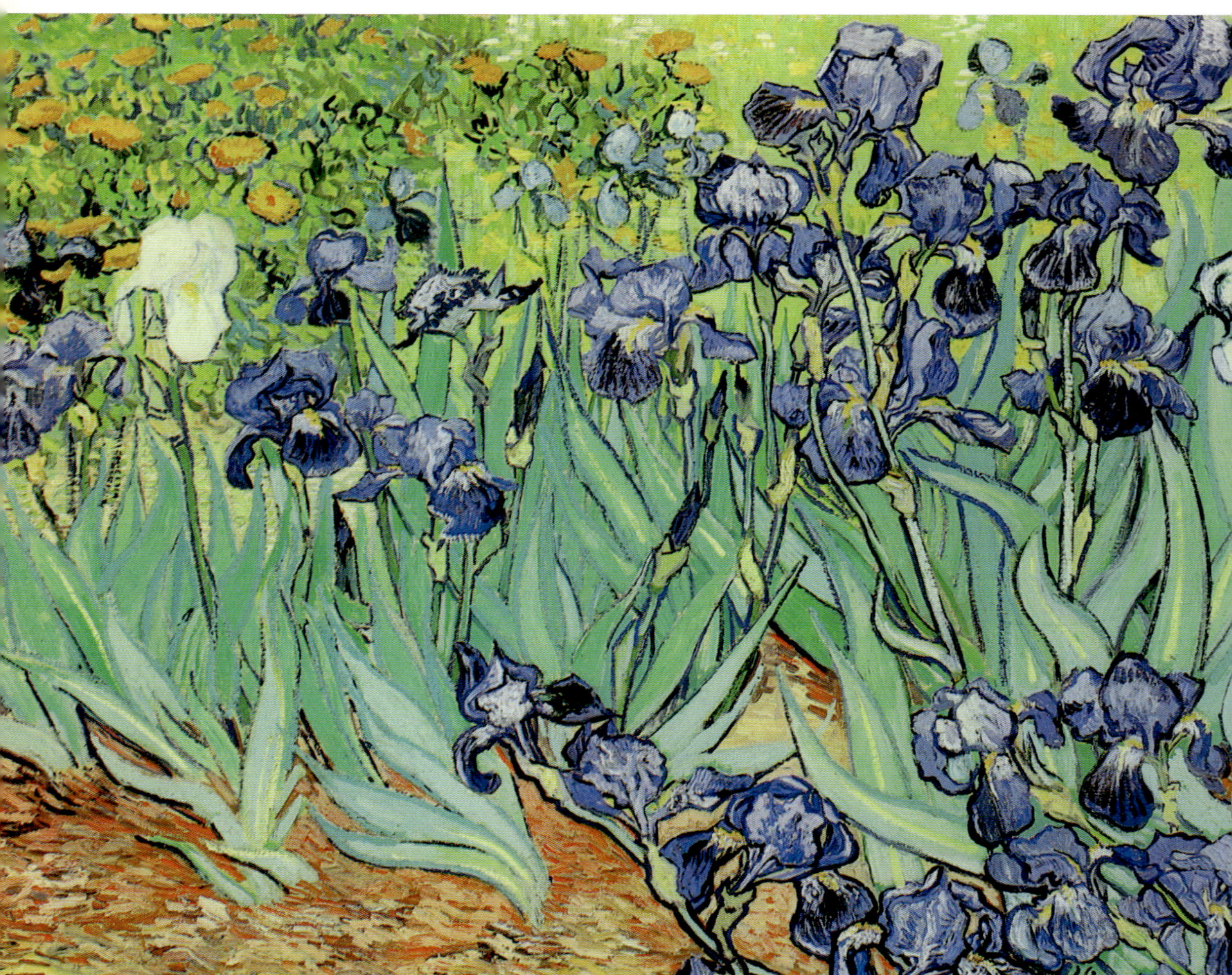

Irises Oil on canvas, 71 x 93 cm
Getty Centre, Los Angeles

In that same first week at Saint-Rémy, Vincent also made a number of large drawings of the asylum garden with its trees and undergrowth, stone benches and circular fountain. Some of them were enhanced with watercolour or gouache and generally executed in pencil, black chalk and his favourite drawing implement, the reed pen. This pen was ideal for the short stabbing strokes which he preferred and which characterise his drawings of this period. True to the tradition of the Dutch Old Masters who invariably valued drawings for their own sake, all these new drawings of the asylum garden were conceived as finished works in their own right, not as preparatory studies for a painting or (as so often) a record of a painting to show Theo what he had been doing. He was also keen to show his brother the sort of place in which he was now living. Theo, after all, was paying for it all – not just for the asylum and Vincent's upkeep there, but for his paints, brushes and rolls of canvases. In addition he was also trying, with limited success, to interest clients of the Goupil Gallery where he worked, in Vincent's paintings, as they arrived in repeated batches at his Paris apartment. It must have seemed a thankless task. Brotherly love was mutual between Vincent and Theo, but brotherly support was heavily one-sided.

Vincent wrote to Theo during that first week in the asylum. The letter was uncharacteristically brief; nonetheless it was a fairly cheerful one. 'I want to tell you that I think I've done well to come here,' he says. He goes on to tell Theo how glad he is to see 'the reality of mad people's lives' though he is beginning to think of madness as 'an illness like any other'. He mentions the irises, ending on the need he feels to be able to work and how it totally absorbs him when he is painting, blotting out all dark thoughts. On the same day in a much longer letter to his sister Wil, Vincent expands on what it is like living among mad people, how he continually 'hears shouting and terrible howling like animals in a menagerie'. On the other hand he notices how the patients help each other at moments of crisis and when they stand around watching him paint in the garden they are discreet and polite unlike the people in Arles. He intends to remain here quite a while, he assures her, 'never having been so tranquil' and glad 'to be able to paint a little at least… I shall consider myself very happy,' he concludes, 'if I manage to work enough to earn my living, because it makes me deeply anxious that I have done so many paintings and drawings without ever selling a single one.'

On May 21st Theo replied to Vincent's letter with an air of obvious relief that his brother appeared to have settled in at Saint-Rémy. Words like 'tranquil' must have been music to his ears after the discordant meanderings of the letters from Arles. Now Theo was anxious to know more about the asylum he was paying for. What were the other patients like? What kind of medical treatment was Vincent receiving? What about the food? And had he yet been able to enjoy the countryside which he would soon be painting? Meanwhile the latest batch of canvases sent from Arles had just arrived and among those Theo liked most was the portrait of Vincent's friend the postman, Joseph Roulin. It is not hard to understand why. Vincent's picture of the jovial postman with his vast beard parted in two is a portrait that exudes warmth and affection. Theo always preferred Vincent's work when it was a straightforwardly true to nature. It also seems likely that he enjoyed being reminded amid the traumas of recent months of his brother's very real gift for friendship.

Theo was also keen to know which paintings Vincent might wish to include in the next Salon des Indépendants. He was allowed to submit four. (It was to be Van Gogh's paintings of Provence in the next Salon des Indépendants in Paris which were to win him some of the first acclaim to come his way, especially from fellow-artists.) Then, towards the end of the month letters to and from Theo began to flow in a torrent. On May 23rd Vincent responded to Theo's request for information with a lengthy and detailed account of his day-to-day life at the asylum, describing the conditions in which he was living, as well as his hopes and plans for working here once he was free to do so. The letter gives the impression of a man who has come to terms with the new regime and is now bursting to get on with his work. It reads like a testament; a statement of faith in himself as he takes stock of his new life, restricted and yet settled, after the traumas of the past months. Arles has been put behind him.

Now there was so much he was anxious to tell his brother. There was the place where he was permitted to work, the asylum park. 'Since I have been here the deserted garden planted with large pines under which the grass grows tall and uncontrolled, intermingled with various weeds, has provided me with work and I have yet to progress outside.' Later in the letter he gives Theo a list of the paints he needs for the time when he is eventually allowed to explore beyond the asylum walls. Meanwhile, until Dr Peyron gives that permission he has embarked on an intensive drawing 'campaign', using pencil and chalk, reed pen and ink and sometimes water-colour or gouache. From what he can see

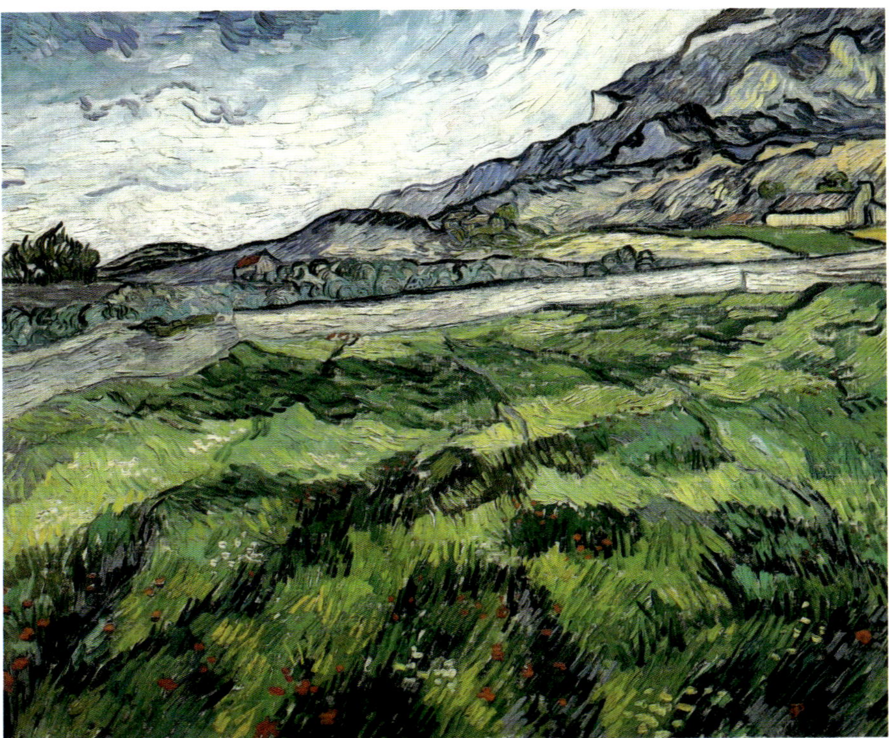

Green Wheat Field Oil on canvas, 73 × 92 cm
Kunsthaus Zürich

tantalisingly from his bedroom: 'The landscape of Saint-Rémy is very beautiful and little by little I am probably going to make excursions into it. There is an iron-barred window,' he explains, from which he can 'make out a square of wheat in an enclosure…above which I can see in the morning the sunrise in all its glory.'

Since Theo had asked what the asylum was like to live in, Vincent gave him a description of his room. 'I have a little room with grey-green wallpaper and two water-green curtains with designs of very pale roses enriched with thin lines of blood-red, probably some former inmate's leftover…Probably from the same source comes a very worn armchair covered with a tapestry.' As for the food, 'It smells naturally a little musty, as in a cockroach-ridden restaurant in Paris or a boarding-school.' Most of the other patients are bored out of their minds and have nothing better to do than 'stuff themselves with chickpeas, haricot beans, lentils and other foodstuffs in regulation quantities and at fixed times…And so they fill their days.'

In spite of his discomfort at having to live with patients who 'shout' and 'howl' like wild animals and who do nothing all day except scoff beans and lentils, Vincent makes it entirely clear to Theo that he is 'very well here and that for the time being I see no reason at all to come and board in Paris', which Theo had suggested as a possibility in his previous letter. 'My hope would be that at the end of a year I'll know better than now what I can do and what I want. Then, little by little an idea will come to me for beginning again.' The letter soon returns once more to his art and what he has been drawing. 'Yesterday I drew a very large, rather rare night moth,' he explains – and includes a rough sketch between the lines of a death's-head hawk-moth – 'its colours astonishingly distinguished…To paint it I would have had to kill it and that would have been a shame since the creature was so beautiful. I'll send you the drawing of it with a few other drawings of plants.'

At about this time Vincent made three studies of the asylum interior which he proposed to send to Theo. One is of the arched entrance with a door opening onto the garden. Another shows a long corridor, while the third is a section of his studio with its tall window. Why he chose

Corridor in the Asylum Black chalk and gouache on pink ingres paper, 65 × 49 cm
The Museum of Modern Art, New York

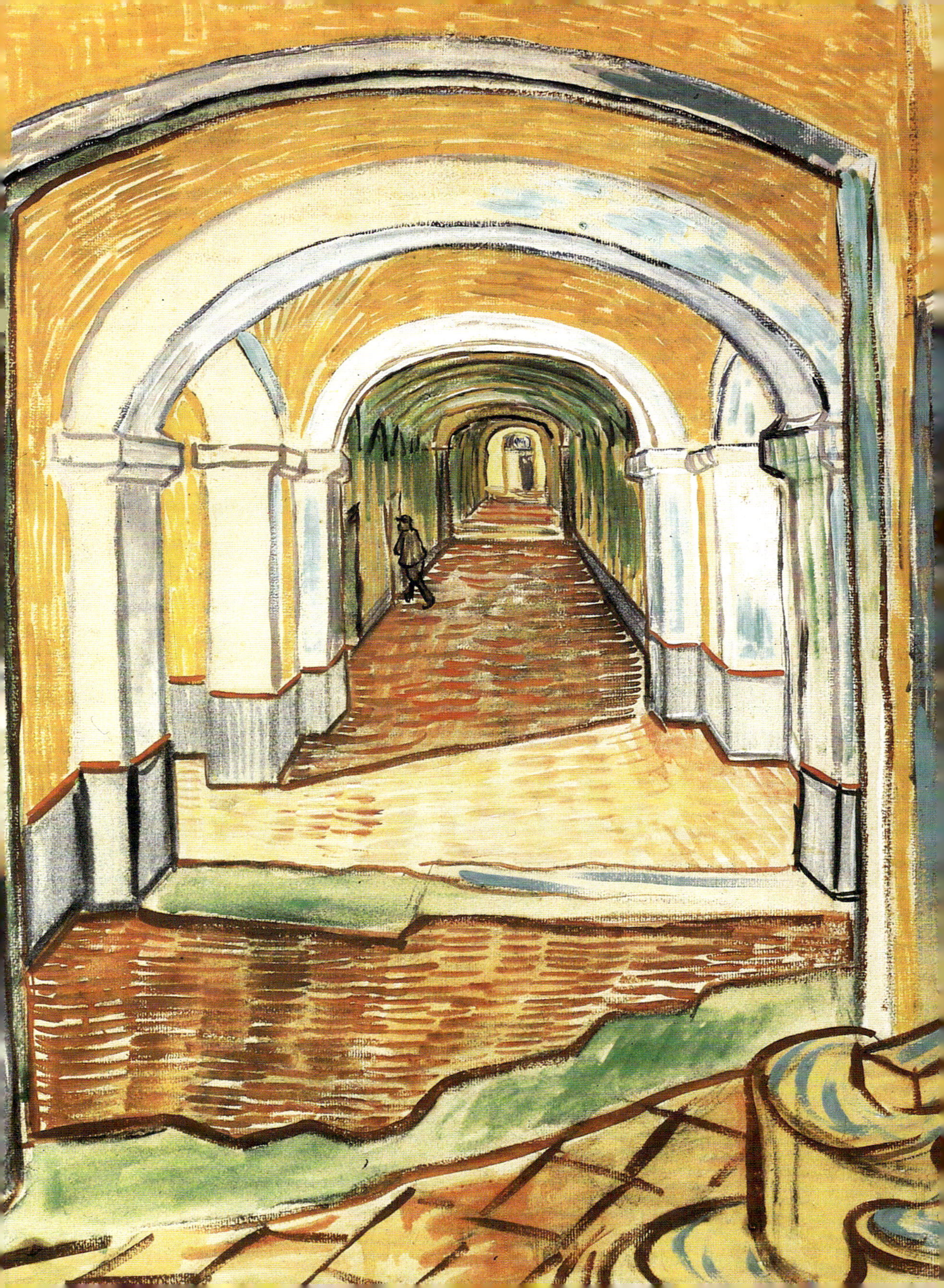

these subjects he failed to say; but all three are executed in gouache and in radiantly bright colours. One might imagine this to be the most joyful place on earth: certainly they must have borne little resemblance to the gloomy corridors of the old monastery where Vincent walked many times a day endeavouring to avoid mad fellow-patients. Either they were designed to cheer himself up, or perhaps to avoid giving his brother a depressing image of the place. Had Vincent been a Roman Catholic he might have offered Theo a view of the intimate and delightful Romanesque cloister; but his Calvinist upbringing must have rejected any such concession to popery.

Two weeks after Dr Peyron's first comments on Van Gogh in the asylum register the director added a further brief note on May 25th, stating that his patient 'has shown a notable improvement in his condition, but must be kept in this establishment to continue his treatment.' The official entry in the register may have been promoted by a request from Theo for information about his brother's health following Vincent's own letter describing life in the asylum. The next day Dr Peyron replied to Theo, expanding his cautious entry in the register. He was pleased to report that Vincent was calm and that his health was improving day by day. The 'painful nightmares' he used to suffer had lessened and his appetite had also improved. 'He spends all day in the garden here,' the doctor continues, 'but as I find him entirely tranquil I have promised to let him go out so that he may find subjects to paint outside this establishment.'

It was a giant step – and a huge relief to Theo and above all to Vincent himself. At last he could enjoy the prospect of exploring a new and exciting landscape which he had so far only glimpsed from behind bars. On the last day of May he began a long letter to Theo beginning with an urgent request for more brushes now that he was about to be allowed out of the asylum gates to explore and work in the countryside for the first time. He even added a drawing to show exactly what kind of brushes he needed – three of them, and he wanted six of each!

He could scarcely contain his excitement at being about to venture into a new world and a new landscape. 'This morning,' he continues,

'I saw the countryside from my window long before dawn with nothing but the morning star, which looked enormous. What a beautiful land.' It was now the season of spring flowers, he reminds Theo; and the thought prompts him to suggest that 'it will perhaps be wise to send me another five metres of canvas in addition…The flowers will be short-lived and will be replaced by the yellow wheat field. The latter, above all, I would like to capture better than at Arles.'

Vincent seems to have dragged out this long letter to Theo, whiling away the time until the asylum gates were finally drawn aside and he could take in a new world.

In the first week of June Dr Peyron lifted all restrictions on Van Gogh's movements and allowed him to venture outside the walls of the asylum for the first time. On June 9th Vincent wrote to Theo thanking him effusively for the canvas, paints and brushes which he had been 'pining for' now that he was able to go out and paint in the countryside. What he omitted to mention was that patients were only allowed outside the gates at certain hours accompanied by a trusted attendant and never after dark. It may be that these cramping conditions deflated Vincent's buoyancy at being awarded a freedom he had been patiently looking forward to for nearly a month. It may also be that the prospect of being exposed once again to the outside world rekindled old fears. Certainly his first reaction to this freedom was far from the ecstatic embrace of a new landscape one might have expected. Of the two canvases 'on the go', he told Theo, one was a view of the enclosed wheat field he had been gazing at from his bedroom window ever since his arrival.

The second canvas was painted outside the asylum walls: a rather low-keyed *Field with Poppies* which has none of the wild energy that was soon to characterise his Saint-Rémy landscapes. It is almost a reversion to his earlier Impressionist landscapes from his Paris days. Significantly it was a canvas that particularly appealed to Claude Monet when he attended Van Gogh's posthumous one-man exhibition held in Paris in 1891, one year after his death.

The long letter of June 9ᵗʰ to Theo offered a rambling account of his state of mind at this key moment when a new and challenging world was opening up before him. The early days of 'freedom' were far from easy, overshadowed by fears and unhappy memories of the outside world. He described a disturbing incident when he had recently ventured into the small town of Saint-Rémy barely a mile from the asylum, accompanied by the regulation attendant; the mere sight of people going about their normal lives made him feel ill and he had to flee. 'I wouldn't have the courage to start again in the wider world,' he assured Theo. What the Saint-Rémy episode seems to have made painfully clear to him was that he needed to find subjects to draw and paint which did not bring him directly in touch with people. In consequence he concludes in his letter: 'In the face of nature it's the feeling for work that keeps me going.' This realisation set the tone for what was to follow, both in his choice of subjects and the fierce intensity with which he set about painting them.

Van Gogh loved to work in series, each variation on a single theme adding a fresh aspect of the character of the subject he was painting. The word 'character' recurs frequently in his letters: he proclaims it to be his mission as an artist to portray the true 'character' of Provence, this newly-discovered land in the sun which had become his artistic terrain. His search, now that he was free to explore, was to discover those motifs which would symbolise that region, engaging his imagination as powerfully as the sunflowers and blossoming fruit-trees had in Arles.

Van Gogh discovered these subjects in the first weeks of his freedom. The first of them was revealed in a letter of June 16ᵗʰ, not to his brother but to his sister Wil back in Holland. 'I have just finished a landscape of an olive grove with grey leaves somewhat like those of willows, casting violet shadows on the sun-baked earth.' From his description the painting is clearly identifiable as the first in a prolific series on olive orchards which was to occupy him on and off throughout his time at Saint-Rémy, becoming one of his favourite subjects and symbolising the true character of Provence which he was determined to depict. The picture is delightfully fresh and vigorously painted, probably in a single day, in light Impressionist tones of green, blue and pale yellow, and rapid brushstrokes, all of which would have pleased Claude Monet as much as the study of a poppy field which preceded it. Van Gogh, it seemed, had identified a theme which would engage him and become the successor to the sunflowers and blossoming fruit-trees.

Yet there were surprises ahead. Only two days after informing his sister that he had just finished the olive orchard painting Vincent wrote to brother Theo, 'At last I have a landscape with olive trees...' But this was not the painting he had described to Wil forty-eight hours earlier. What the two letters reveal is that in a burst of creative energy that was to be characteristic of his working method here, Van Gogh had managed to produce not only another version of the olive trees painting but also 'a new study of a starry sky', as he went on to explain to Theo. (The latter picture was the celebrated *The Starry Night*). The two canvases are linked together in Vincent's letter and seem to have remained linked in his mind as a pair, perhaps because they were painted one after the other within a very short span of time, but more particularly because they have stylistically so much in common. In both canvases the style is restless and disturbing, almost hectic, quite unlike the sunlit landscapes that immediately preceded them. The change is startling, as if something dramatic has occurred and his letter to Theo suggests as much. He does not just tell him about the two paintings; he writes 'At last...', as though he has made an important discovery, and found his new direction forward.

The first of these two new paintings is *Olive Trees with the Alpilles in the Background*. Unlike the earlier canvas of an olive orchard as described to Wil just two days earlier this is a wild painting. Stylistically it feels closer to German Expressionism of the early 20th century than to the late 19th century Post-Impressionism with which Van Gogh is normally associated. The olive trees that fill the centre of the painting seem on the move, their branches twisting and contorted in a frenetic dance described in swirling brushstrokes of dark colours. The soil around them looks liquid and unstable, as if it were invading floodwater, and the air of turbulence extends to the distant Alpilles mountains. Their contorted shapes are darkly sinister; while overhead a ghostly cloud hovers menacingly. Nothing is still. Nothing is at peace. Every natural form in the landscape is exaggerated for dramatic effect.

This was not a style Van Gogh had employed before and it is intriguing to speculate on why he should have chosen to do so now.

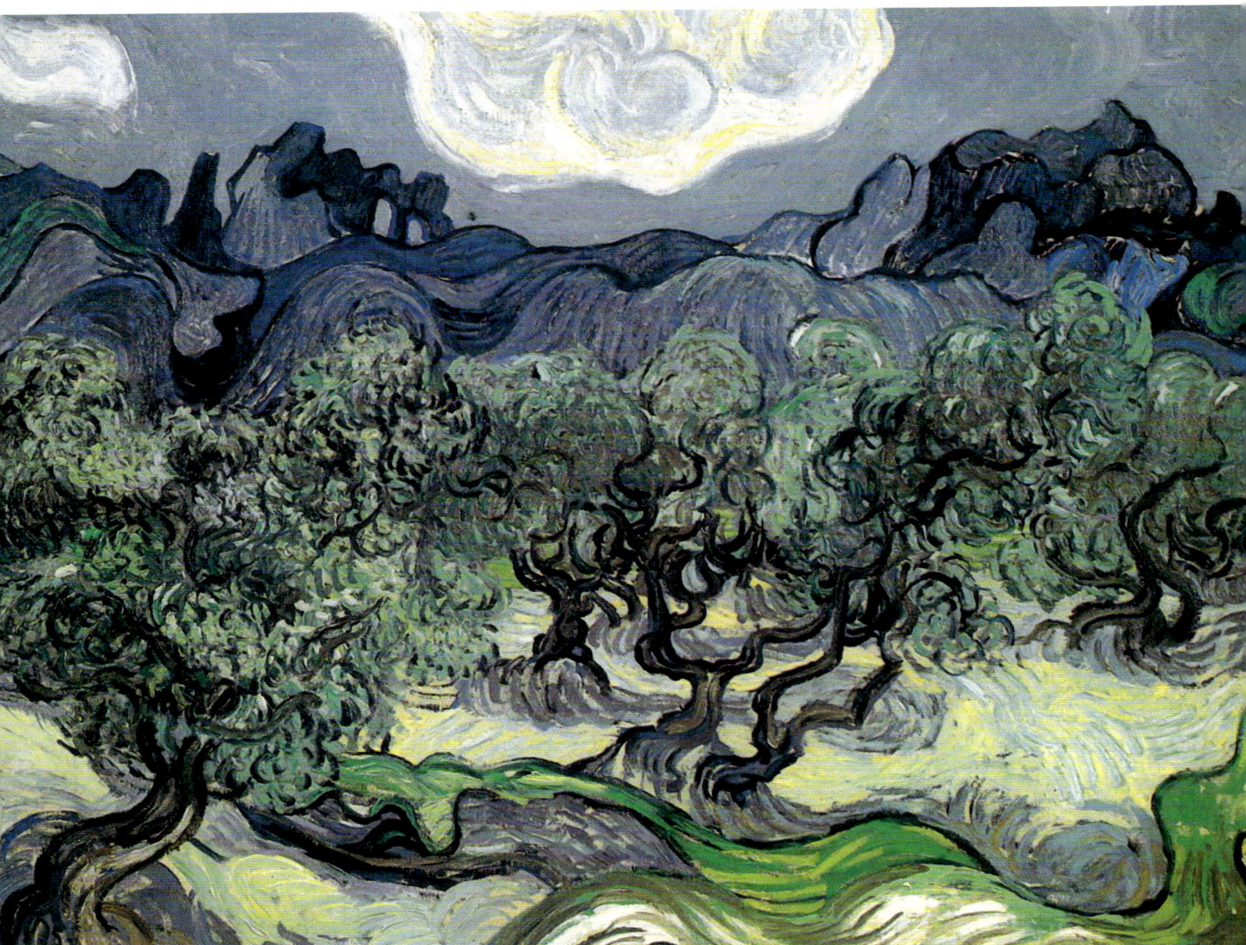

Olive Trees with the Alpilles in the Background Oil on canvas, 72.6 × 91.4 cm
The Museum of Modern Art, New York – Mrs. John Hay Whitney Bequest

Van Gogh's vigorous liberties with the subjects he was depicting have been ascribed to the influence of his fellow-artists Paul Gauguin and Emile Bernard, with whom he was frequently in touch and whom he greatly respected, even admired. Yet even if there may be an element of truth in such a claim it would seen more appropriate to ask why Van Gogh, in one of his first major paintings since being allowed out of the asylum, should suddenly have embarked on such a turbulent and disquieting style – one that he had never employed before.

A clue lies in a personal credo he presented to his brother in the letter he wrote only a short while before, on June 9th, when he was about to embark on this painting. He offers his opinion in the form of a question, as if asking for his brother's approval: 'When the thing depicted is absolutely in agreement with the way in which it is described, isn't that what creates the quality of a work of art?' Touchingly he then gives as an example of that ideal relationship between artist and subject a loaf of bread painted by the 18th-century still-life and genre artist Chardin. (And those familiar with Chardin's calm and intimate still-lives of fruit and flowers will know precisely what Van Gogh meant.)

His aim, as he made clear, was to find a perfect harmony between nature observed and nature interpreted – between 'the thing depicted' and 'the way of depicting it'. A harmony between subject and style, was what he felt he had achieved 'at last', in the pair of new paintings he announced to Theo in his letter. He had taken a leap forward. It is as if he was proclaiming that the Impressionist style of his previous landscape was no longer appropriate for him. In interpreting nature he had now adopted a style of painting that was volatile and turbulent, one that emphasised that nature was unstable even when it seemed most solid and governed by dark forces as much as by the warmth of the sun. Essentially it was a style of painting akin to his present mental condition and which reflected it. He had found a way of projecting the turbulence of his mind on to his chosen subjects. His so-called 'madness' had become creative.

From this point onwards the ability to project his mental disturbance on to the subjects he chose to paint was to become a characteristic of much of Van Gogh's work at Saint-Rémy, giving his paintings of the Asylum Year a distinctive and troubled quality that is unlike anything he had achieved before. Paintings of the eye had become paintings of the mind.

Van Gogh informed his brother of the two new paintings in a brief phrase: only the words 'at last' might have given away how important the breakthrough was in Vincent's mind. He would have been aware that the exaggerated style he had employed was exactly what Theo was urging him not to use. Vincent had received a letter from his brother that day advising him 'not to venture into mysterious regions', in the interests of his recovery. 'If you could be content to give merely a simple account of what you see there are plenty of excellent qualities in what you do for your paintings to last.'

For Theo it was firstly an issue of Vincent's health and wellbeing: he believed instinctively that straying from a direct response to nature into 'mysterious regions' of the mind would impede his brother's recovery and even provoke another breakdown. This view brought him into direct conflict with Vincent who was convinced that he needed to interpret nature as he perceived it, not merely record it. What Theo regarded as a danger to his brother's mental health Vincent saw as his best chance of a cure. For Theo commercial considerations also came into play. As a Paris art dealer he was witnessing the growing success of the Impressionists, Pissarro, Monet and Renoir in particular; and he was confident that Vincent's work would soon become saleable if his brother continued in that direction: whereas artists such as Gauguin and Emile Bernard who were pursuing 'mysterious regions' were remaining unsalable.

Furthermore there was beginning to be a glimmer of interest in Van Gogh's work by influential critics. In the same letter to Vincent he mentioned a Dutch art critic by the name of Isaacson who 'likes your latest consignment very much', the consignment being the paintings from Arles in the sunlit days before Vincent's mental breakdown. If only, Theo seems to be suggesting, Vincent would go on painting sunflowers and peach blossom in the Provençal sunshine his

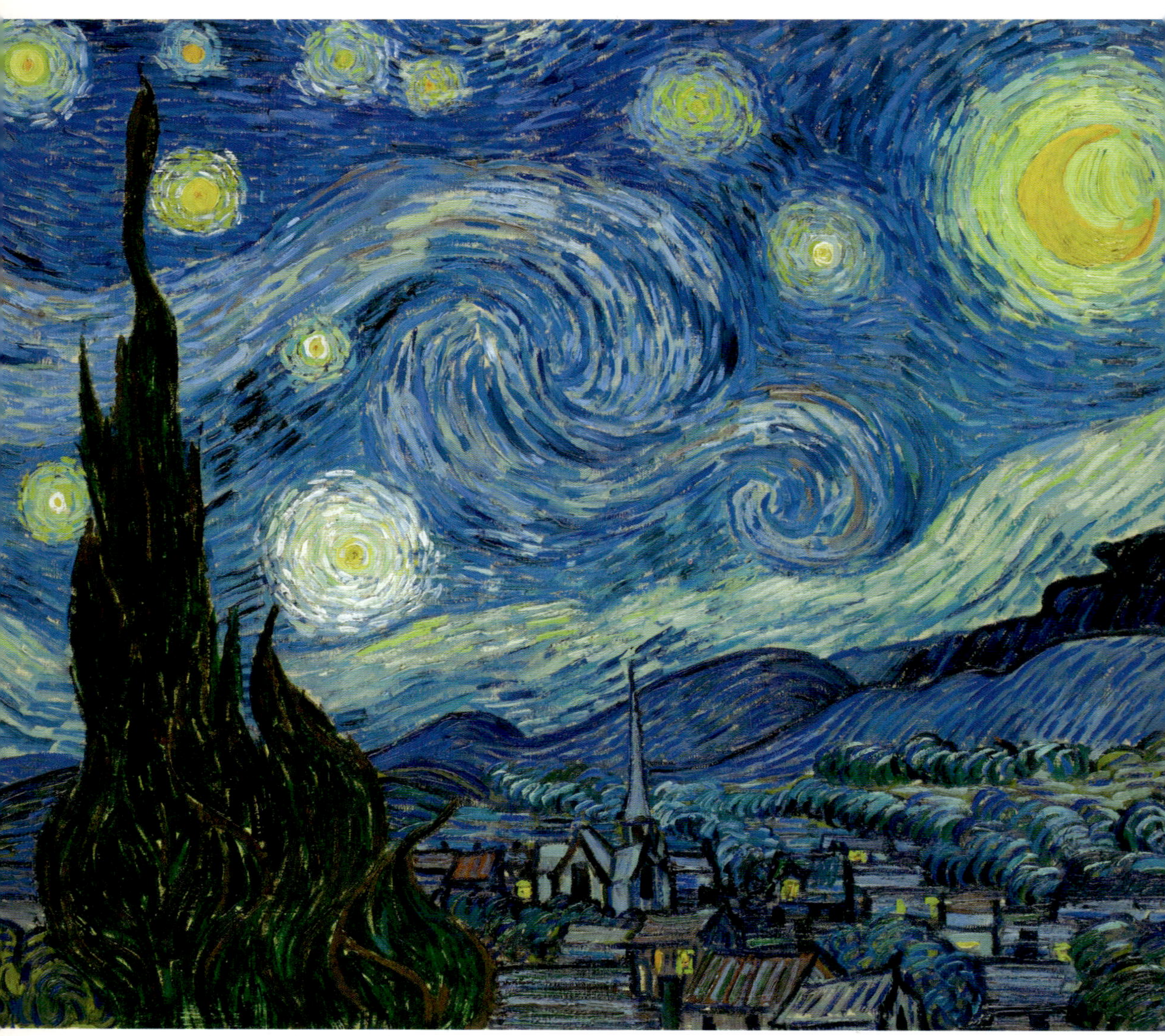

The Starry Night Oil on canvas, 73.7 × 92.1 cm
The Museum of Modern Art, New York – Acquired through the Lillie P. Bliss Bequest.

future would soon be assured. Instead Van Gogh had painted what he describes to Theo as 'a study of a starry night'. How welcome this must have sounded to Theo's ears: yet it is hard to imagine a painting that conformed less to Theo's request for nothing more than 'a simple account of what you see'.

No other artist has painted a night sky quite like this and understanding it poses a problem. Had it been an account of a dream, or a vision born of the imagination of William Blake or Hieronymus Bosch, it would have been easily acceptable on those terms. But Van Gogh's night scene was presented as real: this was how the artist saw it one night from his bedroom window, or so we are asked to believe: it was simply 'a study of a starry night'. It seems to be a tranquil rural scene. A sleeping village clustered round a church with a tall spire rests among low hills. In the foreground a pair of cypress trees thrusts upwards into the night sky. At this point we enter a quite different world. A soft veil of light is draped across the hills. An orange crescent moon glows within a golden halo and across the vast night sky a wild ballet of stars is being performed. Constellations spin like illuminated Catherine-wheels in a vortex generated by some gigantic force of nature belittling our humble existence down below.

Needless to say stars do not spin like this except in the mind. So, what kind of vision is this? *The Starry Night* is the best-known of all Van Gogh's paintings from Saint-Rémy and theories about the meaning of its celestial ballet have gathered momentum for more than a century. Among them has been the familiar claim by art historians that Vincent was emulating Gauguin – a view hard to substantiate: stylistically the picture has remarkably little to do with Gauguin and a great deal to do with what was going on in Van Gogh's head. More fanciful interpretations include a supposed debt to the Old Testament (Genesis), the New Testament (the Book of Revelations) and to the writings respectfully of Longfellow, Walt Whitman, Emile Zola, Alphonse Daudet, Charles Dickens and Uncle Tom Cobley and all. A recent biography evokes scientific evidence to suggest that Van Gogh's night sky represents a mental firework display of a kind created by electrical impulses in the brain as a result of epileptic fits. Add to the list any number of Freudian and Jungian interpretations and it is clear that *The Starry Night* has become an adventure playground for writers of all descriptions drawn to comment on Van Gogh.

The artist himself remained largely silent on the painting. All we know is that in the first weeks of being permitted to venture outside the asylum walls, Van Gogh felt the need to interpret the natural world as composed of elements constantly in motion, restlessly twisting and spiralling. It would seem undeniable that this perception of nature was a projection of whatever possessed his mind during those few short weeks, sandwiched as they were between his release from the asylum walls and a second major mental breakdown which was to overtake him early in July. Those few weeks in June were an interlude between crisis and crisis – an interlude of intense productivity when the demons ruling his mind, whatever they were, drove him to create paintings that possessed a new and disturbing dynamic.

The Starry Night was not a straightforward view from his window. It would have been painted in his studio on the ground floor where neither the Alpilles mountains, nor the cypress trees and certainly not the distant village, would have been visible. Contrary to his usual practice the images which make up the painting were put together from other paintings that were drying around him as he worked. The wild sky would have been painted in daylight from memories of the night observed from his bedroom window, the stars choreographed by his imagination into a whirling dance across the heavens. Even the peaceful village may derive from a distant memory rather than from a study of Saint-Rémy. A drawing he made of the painting makes the houses thatched and therefore more likely to be a memory of a Dutch village. Vincent's letter to his sister Wil, written at exactly the time when he was painting *The Starry Night*, opens with a nostalgic confession that he has been away from Holland far too long and that 'my thoughts often stray involuntarily to those parts'. A yearning to return to the north was soon to become an impassioned plea, culminating in his ultimate departure to Paris and Auvers the following spring.

Throughout the month of June, Van Gogh's energies continued to be at bursting-point. Only a week after telling Theo about the olive orchard painting and *The Starry Night* he wrote another long letter to his brother announcing 'some glorious hot days' as a result of which he now has twelve new canvases 'on the go'. These included two studies of cypress trees. He then expands on his new fascination for these trees, jotting down his thoughts as they spin round his head, interrupted by other matters that concern him, such as how work 'distracts' him from thinking about his health and how being away from Paris has liberated him from Parisian ideas about art and enabled him to throw himself into 'the heart of the country'. At the same time he was desperately keen to know from Theo what was going on in the Paris art world, particularly anything that involved Gauguin, while remaining determined to stake out a path of his own in Provence.

The fascination for cypress trees emerged within weeks of his first study of olive trees. Hence, within a very short time after being released to paint outside the asylum walls Van Gogh had discovered two of the major themes that were to dominate his mind during his remaining months at Saint-Rémy. His love of working in series had already expressed itself in Arles with his paintings of sunflowers. They had come to symbolise the south that he had discovered, the region of sunlight and brilliant colours in which he had invested so many of his hopes and ambitions. Sunflowers stood for the sun itself. But now he needed different, darker, symbols of the region; images that reflected a very different state of mind following the collapse of his dreams of a Studio of the South in Arles and most of all the collapse of his mental health. The twin themes of olive trees and cypresses answered that need for symbols of a darker Provence: olive groves with their 'grey foliage' that cast 'violet shadows' as Vincent related to his sister; cypress trees standing as 'a splash of darkness in a sun-baked landscape'. Nor would it have eluded Van Gogh that in Provence the cypress tree was a symbol of death, just as the sunflower was a symbol of light.

'The cypresses continue to preoccupy me,' he explained to Theo in the same long letter. He would dearly love to do something with

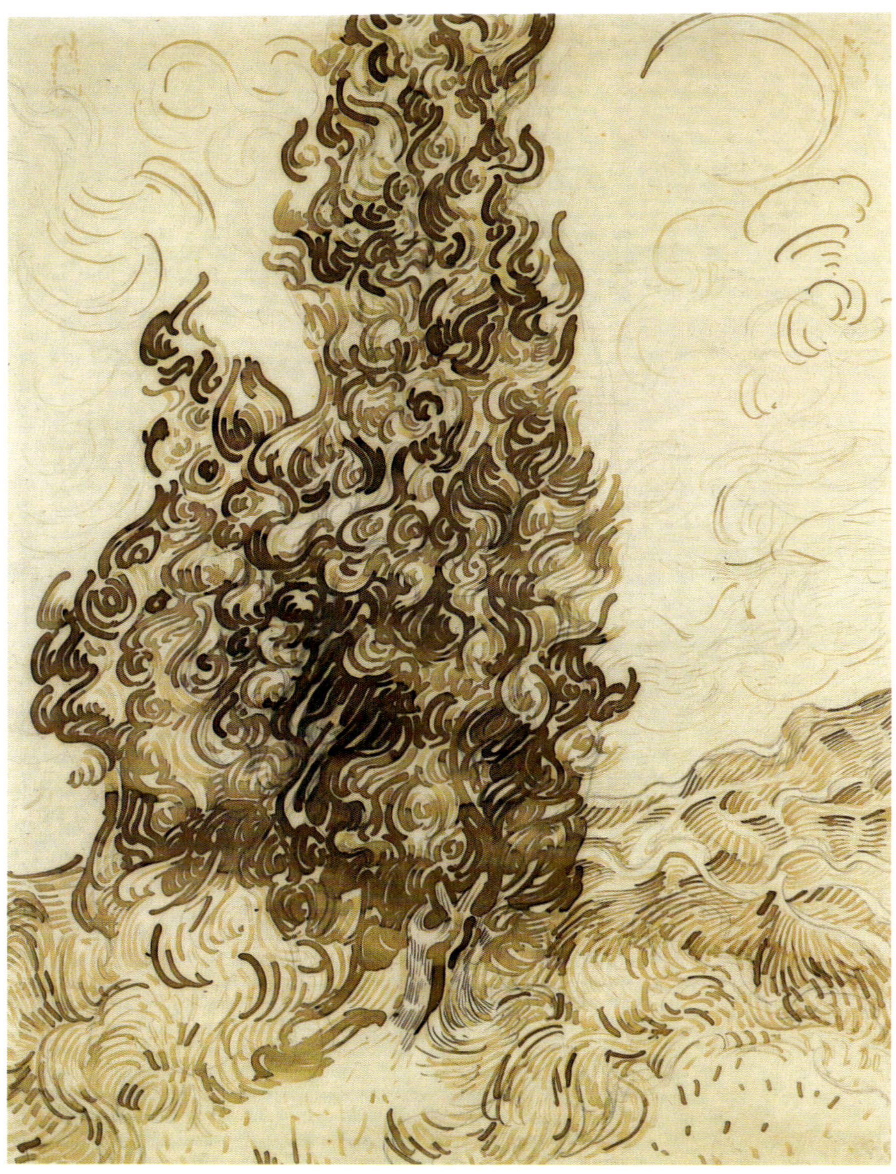

Cypresses Reed pen, graphite and ink on paper, 61.9 × 47.3 cm
The Brooklyn Museum, New York

them 'like the sunflowers', he goes on: and it astonishes him that 'no one has done them the way I see them'. In a particularly revealing passage he then explains to his brother in some detail what cypress trees mean to him and how he has set about painting them. He finds them 'beautiful both in line and proportion,' he says, 'like an Egyptian obelisk.' Choosing exactly the right colour to describe them he finds particularly hard – 'that difficult shade of bottle-green…But you must see them against the blue, in the blue, rather.' When it came to painting them he stressed the importance of making the foreground extremely firm and solid to support the massive shape of the trees rising from it. He does so by applying a heavy impasto, 'thick layers of white lead which gives firmness to the ground…On top of that I can then put on the other colours.' Then he adds nervously – 'But I do not know whether the canvases are strong enough for that kind of work.'

It is rare to find an artist so precise and open about his working method; and these lines, written when the paint on the canvas was still wet, are especially valuable in trying to understand Van Gogh at one of the key moments of his life. While he explains carefully why he uses heavy impasto in these paintings to give them solidity he makes no mention of the way he has painted the cypresses themselves, other than referring to 'that difficult shade of bottle-green'. Van Gogh's solution to the difficulty lay not so much in the choice of suitable dark colours as in the shapes his brush creates. He has given the trees an extraordinary density of textures by describing the blackness of them as a mass of whirling shapes which catch streaks and specks of light as they appear to spin. The same spinning shapes fill the sky in the background; furthermore they are an echo of those Catherine-wheel shapes that fill the sky in *The Starry Night* painted only a week or so earlier. The spirals and whorls of the visionary night painting have come down to earth.

Van Gogh included a thumbnail sketch of one of his two cypress paintings in his letter to Theo. He also made two large drawings of the two canvases in reed pen and red ink, which he sent separately. Here the whorls and spirals no longer sink into the blackness of the foliage but dominate each drawing, rendering the cypress trees even less naturalistic. Theo's comments when he received the drawings were cautiously disapproving: 'The last drawings give the impression of having been done in a rage and are rather far removed from nature.'

Vincent's awareness of his brother's disapproval of these stylistic innovations may be why he kept silent about them and his reasons for adopting them. Or maybe he felt unable to explain a way of working that was largely intuitive. How convenient it would be if one or more of the innumerable theories about Van Gogh's style and imagery at this period of his life were to be proved correct and the impulses of his creative mind could be demystified and explained away. How convenient and how banal. All we can accept with confidence is that on this fragile raft of sanity between storms a turbulent dynamism guided Van Gogh's art, steering it away from naturalism and rendering his paintings as much an art of the mind as an art of the eye.

June was a pivotal month in Van Gogh's year at Saint-Rémy. It was a period in which he found fresh bearings again as an artist after the catastrophes of the final months in Arles and the first severe onset of mental illness. He rediscovered the confidence of being able to work outside the confines of hospital and asylum. In doing so he found the direction he wanted his art to take, identifying two series, the olive orchards and the cypress trees, that would continue to focus his mind in the months to come. Such was his buoyancy that he even expressed the wish to his brother, only half in jest, that the large number of empty rooms and vast corridors in the asylum might usefully be transformed into an exhibition centre for his paintings.

Perhaps one day such an exhibition might even be shown, a selection of the 150 canvases he produced in the course of his Asylum Year, displayed in the very place where he painted them.

JULY

Van Gogh's energies were restored once he was allowed to paint in the open countryside again and this creative burst continued unabated well into July. One effect of this buoyant mood was a flurry of letter-writing to and from his sister and mother in Holland, his brother and sister-in-law in Paris, to friends and even to Gauguin, now in Brittany, with whom Vincent was keen to rebuild a friendship after the disastrous events of the previous December. The length and scope of Vincent's letters are frequently a guide to the level of his spirits; and now these were clearly high, certainly higher than they had been since before his breakdown in Arles more than six months before.

The letters reflect a growing confidence that his mental attack in Arles had been no more than a passing storm which in all probability might never return, so long as he remained 'calm' while he was in Saint-Rémy and avoided stress; and above all continued to work – which he knew to be the best way of dealing with the demons in his head. In the first of these letters, to Theo on July 2nd, he thanks his brother for the customary consignment of paints and rolls of canvas, but equally for an edition of Shakespeare's plays which he had particularly requested. He intends to start with the history plays, which he has never read: 'This will help me retain what little English I know.' What he particularly loves about Shakespeare, he goes on, 'are the voices of the people, which come to us across a gulf of several centuries'. The only artist he can think of with comparable gifts is Rembrandt, for 'the tenderness in the gaze of the human beings he paints'.

One purpose in writing was to give Theo an idea of what he had been doing since he last wrote. For this reason, he explained, 'I am sending you ten or so drawings today, all of them of canvases I've been working on.' The most recent of these canvases was of a wheat field 'where there's a little figure of a reaper and a large sun'. The subject was the enclosed field which Vincent had been gazing at from his bedroom window ever since his arrival here almost two months ago. He had painted the field before and was to continue to do so throughout his time at the asylum. He never referred to the subject as one of his 'series' like the olive orchards and the cypress trees; nonetheless the field became something of an obsession to him and he painted it in all seasons and weather conditions. It became his record of the changing seasons and the vicissitudes of nature, a theme which always caught his imagination.

In his letter to Theo the subject is described simply as a peasant working in a wheat field. But then, writing to his sister immediately afterwards the scene has already been awarded a spiritual significance, becoming a vehicle for the artist's gnomic thoughts about the human condition and by implication his own condition: 'Are we not very much like wheat to be reaped when we are ripe like the wheat itself?' he suggests portentously to Wil. Subsequently it became a canvas he could not leave alone. Two months later he was working on it again, touching it up here and there, and then stressed to Theo its significance, by now almost biblical: 'I see in the reaper a figure striving in the intense heat to complete his appointed task. I find in him an image of death, humanity being the wheat he is reaping.' The painting had by now acquired a weighty allegorical significance, cut down when ripe and at full strength, as Van Gogh perhaps felt himself to have been. The painting had now become like a memento mori in a mediaeval manuscript, or perhaps an echo of some Calvinist sermon of Vincent's youth in Holland when he was nurturing an

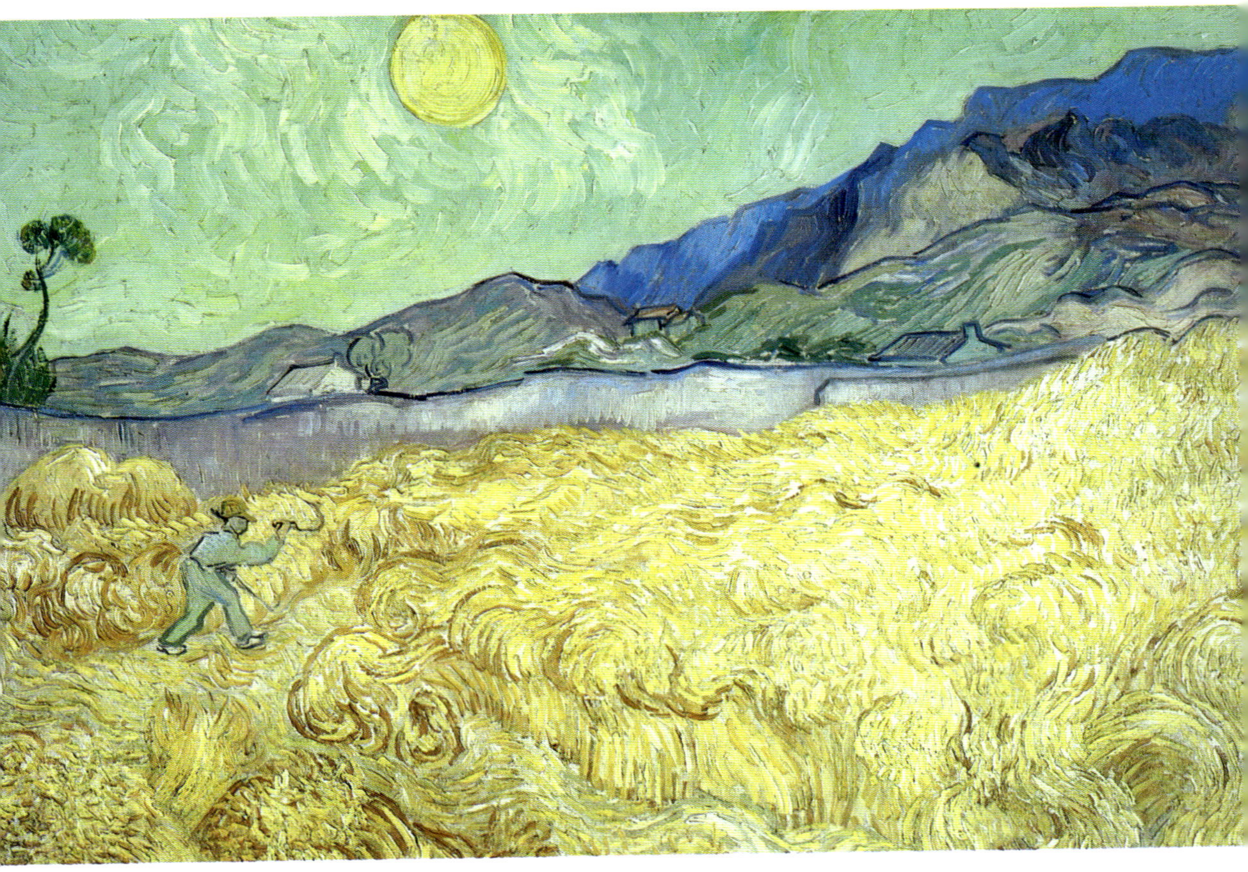

Wheat Field with a Reaper Oil on canvas, 73 × 92 cm
Van Gogh Museum, Amsterdam

ambition to become a pastor in the Protestant church.

Nonetheless *Wheat Field with Reaper* remains a peaceful, lyrical account of a harvest scene in bright sunshine. The ripe corn is described in his familiar whorls and swirls, and the Alpilles in the background are heavily outlined with dark brushstrokes. Yet nowhere are there intimations of death beyond the fact that the peasant wields a sickle. Rather, the painting seems to reflect a new serenity and buoyancy in Van Gogh. Not for the first time his words and his art do not always speak the same language.

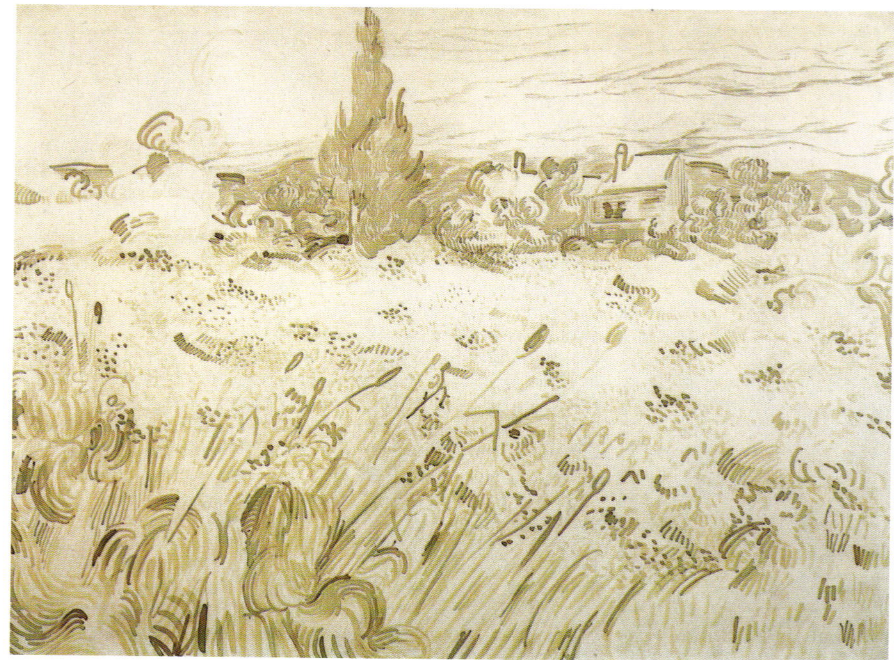

Wheat Field Reed pen and brown ink on cream wove paper, 46.7 × 61.7 cm
Metropolitan Museum of Modern Art, New York

Vincent's revived self-confidence prompted him to announce to Theo in the same letter that he was planning a return to Arles for a day in order to collect paintings he had left behind to dry. These were canvases he had painted in the spring during that last creative burst before leaving for Saint-Rémy and included the wonderful *La Crau with Peach Trees in Blossom*. With memories still fresh of his panic-stricken excursion into Saint-Rémy only a few weeks earlier, this decision would have taken a good deal of courage, supported by his hopes of seeing the Rev. Salles and Dr Rey again, as well as other local friends who had supported him during his time in Arles, especially M. and Mme Ginoux, the café-owners who were now storing his furniture from the Yellow House.

While he was still preparing himself for the visit to Arles he received a letter from Theo's wife Jo telling him she was pregnant. She was sure it would be a boy, she announced, and they intended to call him Vincent. The news prompted Vincent to send a congratulatory reply to Jo in a fulsome letter to her and Theo together. He had recently spoken again to Dr Peyron, he explained, who had suggested he should remain at Saint-Rémy for a further year, by which time he should be cured. Meanwhile 'I'm going to Arles tomorrow,' he stated confidently. Throughout he had an air of a man liberated, proud to announce that he had now been sober for six months while admitting that he used to drink far too much, an admission which casts a light on some of his more excitable behaviour in Arles. Then, with a swift diversion towards his own work he told Jo: 'I hope to go and do the olive trees again,' meanwhile 'the scorched grassland here is taking on beautiful tones of old gold.'

The visit to Arles did indeed take place the following day, July 7th. Since he was never allowed out on his own, Vincent was accompanied probably by the head attendant at the asylum, Trabuc (whose portrait he later painted). As it transpired the day was not the happy reunion with friends he had hoped for. The Rev. Salles, Vincent's mentor, was on holiday. Dr Rey, the young doctor who had treated him at the local hospital the previous winter, was nowhere to be found. Despondent, he spent the day with former neighbours who had not taken against him during the traumas of the previous winter. But at least he succeeded in collecting eight canvases from where they had been left to dry in the Yellow House before he left for Saint-Rémy, and these he was now able to include in the next batch of paintings to be sent to Theo in Paris. The consignment would be made up of eleven canvases in all. In addition to the paintings from Arles, Vincent would include several recent canvases from Saint-Rémy, among them *Irises* (see the May chapter) which he must have known Theo would enjoy, but not *The Starry Night* which he may have suspected his brother would appreciate a great deal less. Instead he included an earlier study of a night sky painted more naturalistically when he was still in Arles.

'As you can see,' he wrote, 'I've been to Arles to collect these canvases,' and he described briefly the abortive attempt to see Salles and Rey.

Yet this was a letter written a week after the actual visit to Arles. That it took him this long to tell his brother suggests that Vincent was too disturbed by the experience to communicate. In fact his agitation was so acute after his return to the asylum that Dr Peyron ordered his ration of meat and wine to be reduced to help calm him. The return to where he had experienced his first attack had revived a host of old fears. The only person he wrote to during this period was his mother. In a long nostalgic account of his thoughts, Vincent drew comparisons between life in Holland and Provence, mostly in favour of Holland, though finally acknowledging the beauty of the olive trees and that 'I never tire of the blue sky'.

The setback was temporary: soon he began to feel 'calmer'. He had also begun to paint again, vigorously, thanks to a new consignment of canvas and paint for which he thanked Theo profusely. 'The latest canvas I've completed,' he explained on July 14th, 'is a view of mountains with a dark hut in the foreground among olive trees.' Vincent's claim to be feeling calmer is scarcely borne out by the painting. *Mountains at Saint-Rémy* is a return to the restlessly agitated style of *The Starry Night* and the landscape of olive trees which he had painted in June soon after being allowed to work outside the asylum for the first time. The lightness and delicacy of *Wheat Field with Reaper* have disappeared, replaced by a scumble of heavy brushstrokes suggesting a landscape in the grip of an earthquake. Dr Peyron's view that the visit to Arles was responsible for reviving Vincent's state of agitation would seem to be borne out by the turbulent style of *Mountains at Saint-Rémy*.

Van Gogh's moods and volcanic temperament were chameleon-like and could change in minutes. He wrote a second letter to Theo on or around that same day, July 14th containing not a hint of agitation. 'Above all, dear fellow,' he addressed his brother cheerfully, 'I beg you don't fret or worry or become melancholy on my behalf.' He explained that he had a special reason for writing a second letter, 'because I'm enclosing a few lines to our friend Gauguin.' It was his first letter to Gauguin since arriving at Saint-Rémy. The letter is lost, but he reports to Theo that it includes a sketch of *The Reaper* which he hopes Gauguin will enjoy. Vincent then offers Theo the thought that with Jo's pregnancy he has to think of himself as 'about to be turned into an uncle,' though he is puzzled that Jo is so confident the baby will be a boy. In the meanwhile he can 'do nothing but fiddle with my paintings'.

There follows one of the interludes which make Van Gogh's correspondence so engaging. He encloses a sketch of three cicadas he has been observing. 'Their song at times of great heat has much the same appeal for me as the sound of crickets in a peasant's hearth at home.' Typically this nostalgic thought leads him to offer his brother

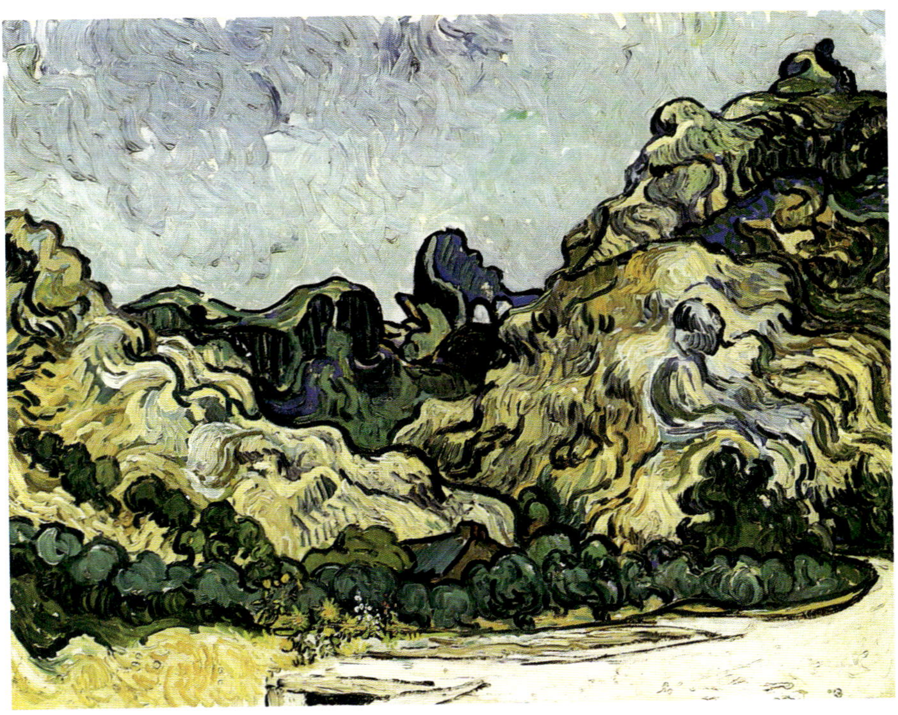

Mountains at Saint-Rémy Oil on canvas, 71.8 × 90.8 cm
Solomon R. Guggeheim Museum, New York (collection of Justin K. Thannhauser)

some homespun wisdom: 'My dear man, don't let us ever forget that small emotions are the great commanders of our lives and that they are the ones we obey without even knowing it.' The comment offers an insight into how Vincent saw himself as a victim of emotions that regularly got out of hand and took him over, like being a puppet on a string.

On the same day, July 15th, Vincent sent Theo the promised batch of eleven canvases, the first he had sent from Saint-Rémy, including those he had brought back from Arles a week earlier. At about the same time Theo decided to rent a small room in the shop of his friend Père Tanguy, a leading supplier of art materials and whose portrait

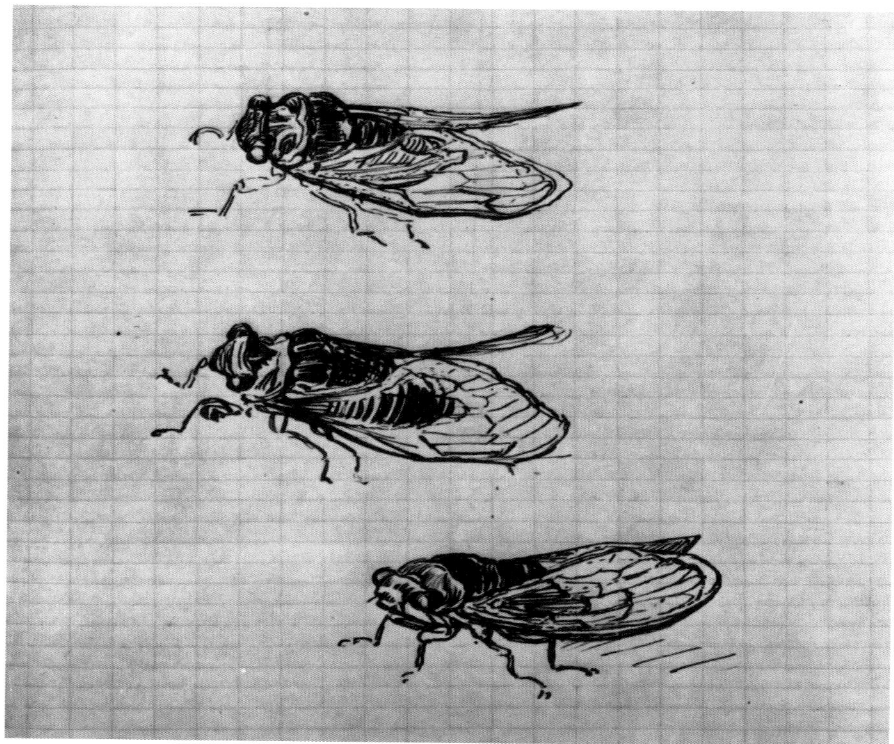

Sketch of Cicadas Pen and ink on paper, 20.1 x 17.8 cm
Van Gogh Museum, Amsterdam

Van Gogh had painted during his time in Paris. With the imminent arrival of a child, Theo's Paris flat no longer had space to display Vincent's regular consignments of canvases, all of which had to be framed and stored so that they could be shown to anyone interested. Since there were to be no fewer than six further consignments of paintings from Saint-Rémy, the space in Tanguy's shop was to prove invaluable, and become virtually Theo's private gallery for showing off his brother's work to the very few clients and art critics who were beginning to take note of Van Gogh.

Theo explained his decision to rent Tanguy's room to display Vincent's paintings in a letter written on July 16th. This was his first communication with his brother for a month and Theo was delighted to tell him how magnificent his *Sunflowers* looked on his wall at home and how several visitors had expressed their pleasure at seeing the paintings Vincent had sent some months ago from Arles, among them the painter Camille Pissarro. Another enthusiastic visitor had been a Belgian, Octave Maus, the secretary of an organisation in Brussels called Les XX which mounted regular exhibitions of contemporary art. Maus had been keen to know if Vincent would like to show some of his paintings in their next exhibition early the following year. Theo was greatly looking forward to the new canvases: at present he had only seen the drawings of them. Of these he preferred, predictably, those that were closest to nature, but he felt sure he would enjoy the others as well when he saw them in the flesh. Furthermore, with Tanguy's room 'it will be very easy to let him go on having new things to show people.'

The letter was encouraging and up-beat. Theo evidently felt confident that at last Vincent's work was beginning to win the appreciation it deserved, from critics and fellow-painters alike, and that it was only a matter of time before it began to sell, provided that is, his brother could be encouraged to stick to 'nature' rather than work 'in a fury'.

The fates had quite other plans. Even as Theo was despatching his letter, the 'fury' he referred to was taking hold of Vincent. Several weeks were to pass before Theo heard directly from his brother what had happened in Provence on that day and Dr Peyron was reluctant to raise the alarm. 'This new attack, my dear brother, came upon me in the fields as I was painting on a windy day,' Vincent eventually told Theo, early the following month. The subject he was painting, probably on July 16ᵗʰ, was one of the ancient quarries not far from the asylum, long deserted but dating back to the building of the Graeco-Roman city of Glanum. In Van Gogh's day it still lay buried beneath the open fields between the asylum and the Alpilles mountains. The painting he was working on, *Entrance to a Quarry*, is another of his wilder landscapes in the same bold, vigorous style as *Mountains at Saint-Rémy* painted only a few days earlier. Dark swirling brushstrokes describe this sunless place with its one splash of ochre in the centre below the pale tones of the rock itself. At the very top of the painting a line of trees is described in contorted shapes, suggesting the violent force of the wind Vincent was experiencing while he was working. There are scratch-marks noticeable in the same area, possibly caused inadvertently by his brush handle as he grappled with the gale. The wind was the celebrated Provençal mistral which hurtles down the Rhône valley and across the southern plains regularly and for days on end. Van Gogh was all too familiar with the ferocious mistral after his year in Arles and during his visit to the Camargue marshes, both areas bearing the full force of the gales.

We have to wait for Vincent's letters, sent in August and September, to learn what actually happened on that day in the mistral. He explained that he managed to complete the painting in spite of the wind and the 'attack' that was brought on by it. The fact that he succeeded in completing the painting 'in spite of' the mistral suggests that he did so on site and not later back in his studio as has sometimes been claimed. This casts doubt on the romanticised accounts offered by some biographers and film directors who would have Van Gogh howling like a banshee as the wind scatters his easel, canvas and paints. We do not know if he was accompanied by an attendant who then helped him back to the asylum; only that the completed painting survived (and today hangs in the Van Gogh Museum in Amsterdam). What is impossible to avoid is that the turbulence which Van Gogh

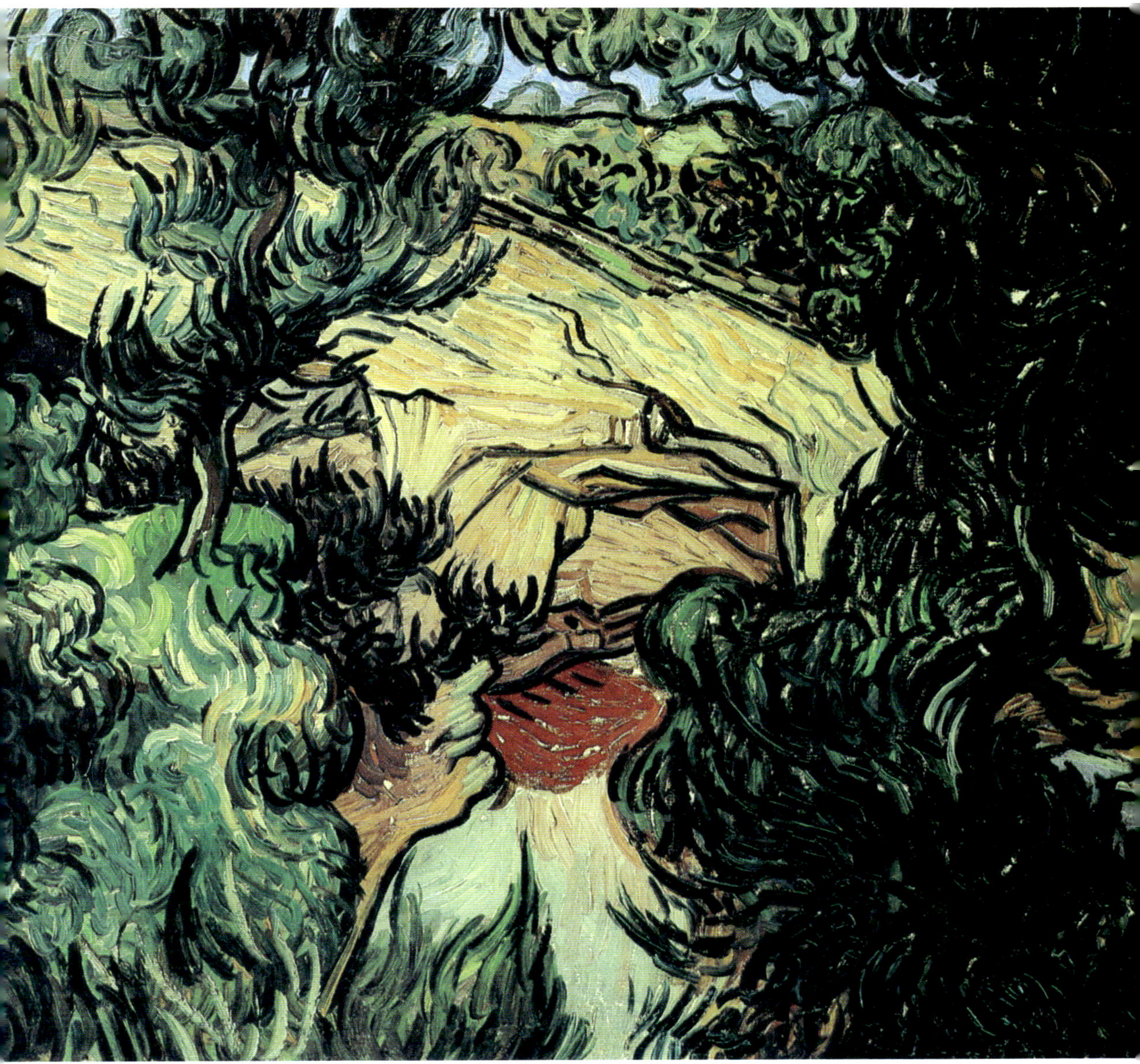

Entrance to a Quarry Oil on canvas, 60 x 73.5 cm
Van Gogh Museum, Amsterdam

had been projecting on to his landscapes ever since being permitted to paint outside the asylum walls, had finally become a reality in the form of the mistral and struck back at him. The elements themselves became his demon.

This was the second major attack Van Gogh had suffered and his first at Saint-Rémy. The mental distress he endured was agonising enough in itself, as well as humiliating; yet perhaps the worst of it was the realisation that he could no longer live in a state of denial. His mental illness was not, as he had often hoped, a unique occurrence caused by special circumstances and which would sort itself out with due calm and rest. It was not some kind of disease he had caught in Arles. It was not something brought on by a hostile environment and the antipathy of ignorant neighbours towards an artist and a foreigner, nor was it the collapse of a dream of a creative partnership between painters of the South culminating in an explosive row with Gauguin. No, the illness was part of what he was; it was a flaw in his brain and it would always recur. It was a condition he was required to live with, adapting as best he could, taking advantage of whatever interludes it would allow him to use, blessed interludes in which every hour, every day, every month if possible, must be employed to the full so that he could pursue the profession he felt driven to practice. It was that drive, on the edge of despair, which may help explain why the Asylum Year became the most fiercely productive period of his life.

The gaps in Vincent's customary flow of letter-writing are invariably indications that all was far from well. Theo was accustomed to an immediate response to any letter he wrote to his brother. But to his lengthy letter of July 16th there came no reply. In all probability it had been written on the very day of Vincent's breakdown. Theo knew nothing of what had occurred on that day in the mistral and for the time being Dr Peyron chose to say nothing. After almost two weeks Theo grew anxious and wrote to his brother again on July 29th. 'I'm a little concerned that you may not have received my letter, which included a money order for ten francs.'

He went on to confirm that he had received the latest batch of paintings Vincent had sent earlier in the month following his visit to Arles. The canvases arrived in perfect condition and he found them 'extremely beautiful'. He itemised several which he particularly liked, including some of the asylum garden in spring. What was more, 'Tanguy himself likes them a lot too…And what a quantity of fine paintings you have produced.' And he continues, ironically, 'how very fortunate that your health is good…Let's hope that it goes from strength to strength.' He thanks his brother effusively once again for the beautiful consignment and with a final stroke of irony he ends 'Tell me how things are going and don't work too hard. A good handshake from Jo as well, Yours, Theo.'

By this time Van Gogh was in the second week of his mental breakdown, under constant supervision lest he commit further acts of self-destruction, or else confined to his room where he suffered horrific nightmares, intense headaches and attacks of vertigo, and passed every day in a state of helpless anguish, all of which the asylum possessed neither the knowledge nor the medicines to relieve.

It was an attack that was to last between five and six weeks.

AUGUST

Van Gogh's attacks came in waves – tidal waves that swamped him and swept him away until he scarcely knew who he was or what he was doing.

Once again confined to the asylum, for a while he was allowed to work in his studio. But very shortly his mental condition deteriorated and he became seriously deranged. He was caught by a warder drinking kerosene from his oil-lamp and attempting to eat paint from the tubes he had been using. Dr Peyron recorded in the asylum register that it had been a suicide attempt and Vincent was henceforth locked out of his studio and his paints and brushes taken from him. Now under constant supervision he was seen trying to swallow dirt from the asylum garden. Day after day he barely ate a meal, developed a painful throat (perhaps from the paint he had tried to eat) and he spoke to no one apart from accusing a member of the asylum staff of being a spy for the secret police. As the situation worsened he was confined first to a dormitory, then to his own room and finally to his bed – where he remained unable to rouse himself for weeks on end.

As with other crises in Van Gogh's life, the little we know about this horrendous period of nearly six weeks is mostly second hand. Vincent himself lived in a state of more-or-less permanent amnesia, in no state to write letters even had he been allowed the materials to do so. Not until August 22nd, when the worst of the mental attack had lifted, did he feel able to 'take advantage of an interval' and tell his brother something of what it had been like – as far as he had any clear recollection of what had taken place. The letter, in pencil (all he was allowed) describes how he now feels 'absolutely distraught' that the attack had been as bad as in Arles and 'even worse'. He now has to assume, he explains, that these attacks will recur in the future. 'It is ABOMINABLE,' he adds furiously.

August was a month of silence. Accurate information of any kind relating to Van Gogh's mental state was all but non-existent, as though a sound-proof screen had been erected round him. Those, like Dr Peyron, who had some idea of what was happening, said as little as possible so as not to raise the alarm and cause friends and relatives to come scurrying off the train from Paris. Meanwhile, for much of that month Vincent himself was lying in his bed unable to stir, enduring horrific nightmares and frequently in a state of delirium and intense anguish, none of which the asylum staff were capable of treating. The best the staff could do was to try to prevent Vincent from harming himself, as he was known to have done in Arles seven months earlier, and from venting his unpredictable fury on his fellow patients and the asylum's employees. It is hard to imagine that he could have been worse off if he had managed to fulfil his earlier ambition to join the French Foreign Legion.

The long silence had begun in the previous month. Theo had written to Vincent on July 29th, not having received the customary reply from his brother for two weeks. But still there was no reply. This time Theo anxiously telegraphed Dr Peyron. The doctor responded straightaway with palliative words explaining that his patient had indeed been ill but was now recovering, which seems unlikely at that time. The letter is lost, but it appears that Peyron offered no alarming details of Van Gogh's condition or behaviour beyond mentioning that he suffered from nightmares. The doctor's reply prompted Theo to write a rapid note to Vincent expressing his concern, even though possessing no idea of the seriousness of Van Gogh's illness. 'Don't lose heart,' he wrote, 'and remember that I need you so much.' Perhaps the intimacy of the appeal caused him to write in Dutch rather than the usual French so that Dr Peyron would not be able to read it.

As the weeks of high summer passed the blanket of silence remained undisturbed. There was still no reply from Vincent and Dr Peyron said nothing further. Theo believed his brother to be well on the road to recovery. Meanwhile Van Gogh spent days lying in bed in a state of mental torment plagued by nightmares and hallucinations, unable to work, write, eat or talk. The silence was temporarily broken on August 16th, exactly one month after Vincent's attack, by a gentle letter from Theo's pregnant wife Jo, also in Dutch. She hoped he would very soon feel better again and begged Vincent to write to her husband 'even if it's just a little word. You can have no idea how often you are in our thoughts and how much we talk about you.' In the reams of correspondence between Van Gogh and his family nothing demonstrates more eloquently the dependence Theo felt for his brilliant and damaged brother. The two of them enjoyed an intense symbiotic relationship in which they identified with each other as if they formed a creative partnership, to such an extent that any lapse in immediately responding to a letter on either side was felt to be an abandonment, even a betrayal.

A further break in the silence occurred with a letter to Vincent written on August 19th from his loyal friend from Arles, Joseph Roulin the postman. He was now living temporarily in Marseille but clearly aware of Van Gogh's situation. Vincent had painted Joseph's portrait, as well as that of his wife and two children, and Roulin wanted to say how deeply flattered he was that these canvases had been sent to Paris and been much admired by Vincent's brother the art dealer and his important clients. Roulin had been Van Gogh's closest friend in Arles and understood the artist's needs better than almost anyone. He now urged him 'to work in the beautiful fields and take advantage of the models nature offers you. With work health will return.'

It took a local postman, rather than the medical authorities, to grasp the importance of work as essential therapy for Vincent and he signed the letter 'Your entirely devoted Roulin.'

Van Gogh's gift for friendship is often overlooked amid the traumas and tragedies of his life. But besides Roulin, and of course Theo and other members of his family, there were a number of others who liked and admired him – even if, through necessity, at a distance. That his friendship with Gauguin should have survived the explosive events in Arles the previous winter is a remarkable tribute to both men. However incompatible their personalities, as fellow-painters they felt a bond that was more powerful than their differences. Another artist, Paul Signac, clearly warmed to Vincent; while Camille Pissarro and Emile Bernard both held him in high personal regard.

In Arles the neighbouring café-owners, the Ginoux, greatly valued his company and remained oblivious to the public protest that had led to the petition being drawn up against him. The Rev. Salles' attentions went far beyond the duties of a local pastor, as Dr Rey's professional help at the hospital far exceeded those of a resident hospital physician. Even at Saint-Rémy, where Vincent's behaviour might have been expected to alienate the entire staff, he managed to develop relationships that were more than cordial. Dr Peyron, for all his shortcomings as a doctor, was invariably kind to Vincent, talked to him at length and even undertook to visit Theo in Paris on his behalf. Then there was the head attendant at the asylum, Trabuc, who accompanied him on his ill-fated visit to Arles as well as shadowing him on numerous occasions when the artist was painting outside the grounds. He felt close enough to his charge to sit for him in the month to come and be the subject of one of Van Gogh's most striking portraits. The fierce-looking attendant (see the September chapter) is nonetheless presented as a man for whom Vincent felt both respect and affection and which were reciprocated. It was a gift for endowing a portrait with a sense of a human relationship between sitter and painter which is as true of Van Gogh's portraits as it is of Rembrandt's.

Roulin's letter urging his friend to go out and 'work in the beautiful fields' would have reached Vincent at a timely moment when he at last felt able to rouse himself from his bed and contemplate being able to resume his life as an artist. Within a day or so of receiving it on August 22nd, he wrote his first letter to Theo since mid-July. In it he described very briefly the circumstances of the attack that came on him while he was painting in the mistral more than five weeks earlier. He found it hard to write, he explained, 'so disturbed is my mind'. It was a short letter by his standards, remorseful and bewildered, at times on the verge of despair, and written in pencil since he was not allowed ink in case he should drink it, or colours of any kind in case he should eat them.

The worst blow, he explained, was no longer having any hope to cling to. The new attack had struck him 'just as I was beginning to imagine it might never return'. His words, scrawled in pencil, carry much pain. Even his studio has been banned to him, a deprivation he finds 'almost intolerable'. Work was his lifeline and he begged Theo to write to Dr Peyron imploring him to permit him access to the studio on the grounds that being allowed to paint was essential to his recovery. What his friend Roulin had understood perfectly well, Dr Peyron apparently could not. On the other hand Peyron's predicament was real enough. How could he take the risk of allowing his patient to work in the interest of therapy, when Vincent might respond by deliberately injuring himself as he had done before and he, the asylum's director, might have a suicide on his hands?

Vincent's letter meanders as his thoughts wander. He has heard from Roulin and is pleased to have received 'a kind letter' from Gauguin in Brittany. Then his thoughts return again to his illness. 'It appears that I pick up filthy things and eat them,' he tells Theo, though he is hardly aware of doing such a thing. He is more aware of not having been able to eat anything for four whole days. Finally he writes in more detail about the canvas he was painting on that 'windy day', *Entrance to a Quarry*. He will send the painting to Theo 'as soon as I can'. He goes on to describe it – how the colours are deliberately sombre, 'broken greens, reds and rusty ochre yellow'. It is a palette, he explains, like the one he used to employ when he was a young man in Holland. The letter ends on a nostalgic note which was to become increasingly dominant in Van Gogh's letters as his thoughts focussed more strongly on his longing to return to the north and familiar territory.

Whether Theo wrote to Dr Peyron with Vincent's urgent request, or whether Van Gogh managed to persuade the doctor that he was now responsible enough to be trusted is not known, but in the last days of August he was finally allowed access to his studio again. He immediately began work with his customary intensity as if there had been no six-week interruption. His next letter to Theo was a lengthy one, written possibly over a period of several days and spelt out, to his brother's huge relief, this new revival in his spirit and his working life.

'Yesterday I started work again, just a little,' he announced. It is clear that he was still being confined to the asylum grounds because the first subject he mentioned in the letter was of the familiar walled field which he could observe from his bedroom window and which he had already painted many times in different seasons. Now, in late summer, he sees it as 'a field of yellow stubble which is being ploughed up'. He emphasises the contrast between the 'purplish colour of the ploughed earth' and the 'strips of yellow stubble and the background of hills'. The painting, *Enclosed Field with Ploughman*, is rich in the sombre colours 'of the north' which he had advocated in his previous letter to his brother. The field itself is an almost abstract pattern of varied browns and yellows, all applied in vigorous strokes of the brush giving the impression that the ploughed earth was on the move and flowing like a dark river across the canvas. In the middle-distance the diminutive figures of the horse and ploughman form a dark silhouette as they make their way along the edge of the golden-yellow strip of stubble that bisects the field from left to right.

Following his careful description of this canvas, Vincent returned inevitably to the theme of his illness and the problems of trying to convince the authorities of his need to work. 'I feel utterly stupid having to ask doctors for permission to paint my pictures,' he declared. Then he reiterated to Theo that if eventually he was cured, it would be due to the work he has done rather than the attentions of the asylum staff, adding, 'If I could throw myself into it with all my strength that might

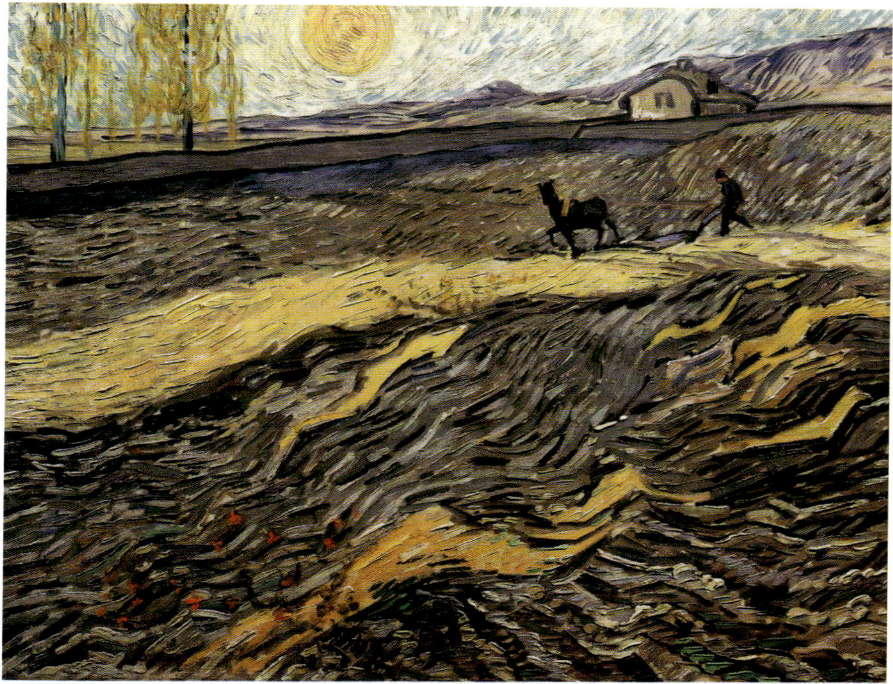

Enclosed Field with Ploughman Oil on canvas, 49 x 62 cm
Private collection, USA

very well be the very best remedy.' He referred, as so often in his letters, to his work as the best possible 'distraction' from dwelling on his illness, which only fills him 'with a kind of fear'.

This was no idle boast: his determination to focus all his energies on creative work as a distraction from self-pity was something he put into practice throughout his time at Saint-Rémy. To a large extent it accounts for the manic productivity Van Gogh managed to achieve during his Asylum Year, in spite of the inactive months when he was too ill to paint.

Among the 'distractions' he told Theo he had in mind, were the prospect of so many 'really beautiful things to do, such as the vineyards and the fields of olive trees'. Throughout the letter, optimism keeps breaking through his fears and frustrations. 'I have a deep desire to go up into the mountains to paint for whole days. I hope they will allow me to in the days to come.' Vincent was anticipating what was to become another of the major series which were to occupy his mind during the following months. After the olive orchards and the cypress trees, the third series would be the mountains, whose dramatic shapes had risen before his eyes ever since his arrival here, but which he was yet to be trusted to explore.

The scene of a ploughman in the field of stubble was not the only subject Van Gogh undertook as soon as he was allowed to paint again and felt well enough to do so. He also turned to a subject he had hitherto ignored since arriving at Saint-Rémy – himself. According to another letter he wrote to his brother just a few days later, he was now working on two self-portraits. 'One of them I began on the first day I got up. I was thin and pale as a devil. It's dark violet, the head white, with yellow hair.'

Whether the first of the two self-portraits was done before or after the canvas of the ploughed field is uncertain. Van Gogh appears to contradict himself, unless he worked on the two canvases simultaneously. What seems clear from the explosive vigour of the brushstrokes is that the self-portrait was done at speed, white-hot, almost certainly in a single session. Van Gogh claimed that he only chose to paint himself 'for lack of another model'. But a new mood of introspection may also have played its part. There is a confrontational atmosphere in this painting. It is the only one of his self-portraits which shows him in his working clothes. He is wearing his painter's smock and holds his palette and brushes prominently, even defiantly, in front of him as if to say: 'This is what I am.' Having been banned from his studio and denied the use of paints for so many weeks, he is telling the world and Dr Peyron in particular, that he is back in the land of the sane and able to practice his profession. It may be no accident that the purple brushstrokes which form the background behind and around the head are like a dark halo.

Yet the defiant pose also has a troubled air. The ghostly pallor of his face and neck is a demonstration of the suffering he has endured, emphasised by the unhealthy greenish shadows lingering on the skin. It is not an image of himself that radiates self-assurance: rather it is a portrait of a man plagued by doubts and fears. He may be proud to present himself as a painter; yet the world he has devoted his life to painting, the wide world outside the asylum walls, is now too frightening a place for him to enter. If there is a message in this self-portrait it is one of hope overshadowed by self-doubt, rather than self-confidence.

(The painting also carries an echo of an earlier Dutch artist Rembrandt van Rijn, who like Van Gogh fell on hard times. Also like Van Gogh, Rembrandt defined himself clearly as a painter, that was what he was and proud of it! Among his many self-portraits is one of the artist, similarly holding his palette and brushes before him. The painting, since the 1920s part of the Iveagh Bequest at Kenwood House in London, was in England at the time of Van Gogh's extended stay in London as a young man and he would certainly have known of it, at least in reproduction. Among the Old Masters, Rembrandt was the artist Van Gogh admired most. One of the qualities they shared was for turning their gaze inwards upon themselves and in doing so creating self-portraits which possess a hypnotic quality of introspection and self-inquiry, portraits that seem to ask the questions 'Who am I?' and 'What makes me what I am?')

In the same long letter to Theo, Van Gogh made an observation which describes what it is in his mind that lifts the greatest portrait paintings above the level of a mere likeness. He wrote of 'a special category (of painting) in which a portrait of a human being is transformed into something luminous and consoling.' For an artist obsessed as Van Gogh was with everything in flux – the passage of seasons and the fickleness of nature – perhaps the consolation in a great portrait lay in the utter certainty of the human presence.

Vincent expressed a strong admiration for a number of artists whose work he knew well. Mostly these were from a generation only a little before his time, chief among them being Delacroix, Millet, Daumier and the Barbizon painters Rousseau and Diaz. Rembrandt was in a

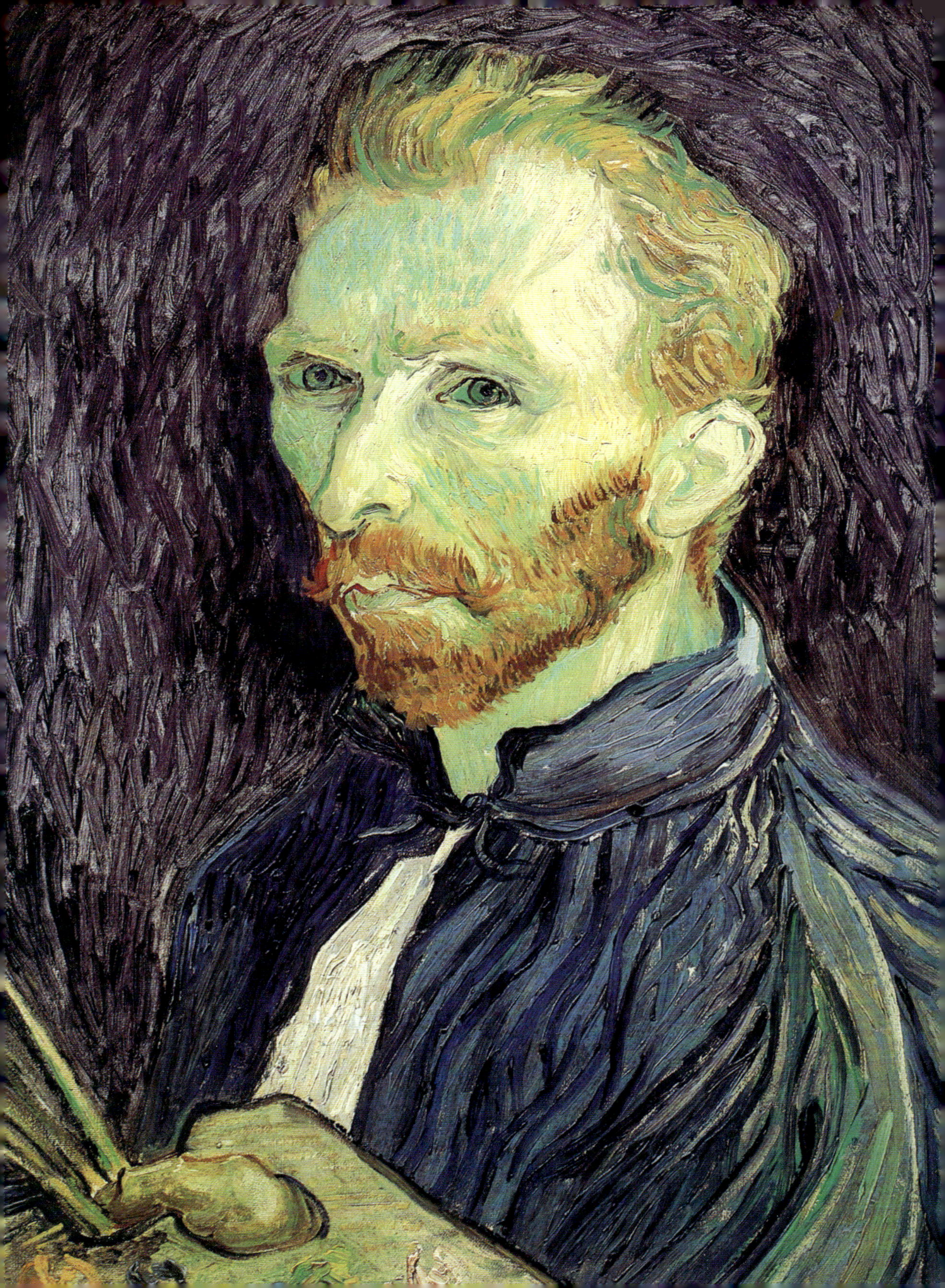

different category: he was two centuries earlier and he was a fellow-countryman. Vincent's admiration for Rembrandt, even identification with him, is a repeated theme running through his letters from Saint-Rémy. On August 22nd, in his first message to Theo since his breakdown he wrote thanking his brother 'most of all for the etching after Rembrandt', of *The Archangel Raphael*, which he admired so much that he urged Theo to send a print of it to Gauguin in Brittany. He repeated his thanks for the 'beautiful etching' in his next letter, adding how much he wished he could see the original painting.

The second self-portrait which Van Gogh mentioned in his letter must have been painted straight after the first. But already the presentation of himself was markedly different. Gone are the dark tones, the halo effect and the heavy strokes of paint. Gone too are the palette and brushes. This is not a demonstration piece to show Dr Peyron he is no longer a sick patient but a man capable of practising his chosen profession. Now the face is still haggard and the expression strained, but he has tried to make himself look composed and self-assured, almost dandyish in the cut of his clothing and the soft blue tones in which the whole painting is executed. There are the customary swirls of colour in the background, but there is no air of turbulence about them: they merely add an elegant, decorative touch to the portrait.

Here is the figure Van Gogh would have liked himself to be at that moment, a man who has finally risen from his sick-bed, put on his best clothes, and is now eager to make up for lost time, free of his demons and free once more to spread his wings. Yet, as he had written to Theo at much the same time: 'People say it's hard to know oneself, but it's not easy to paint oneself either.' The questioning look in both these self-portraits may be the recognition that his demons had not gone very far.

Self-portrait Oil on canvas, 65 x 54.5 cm
Musée d'Orsay, Paris

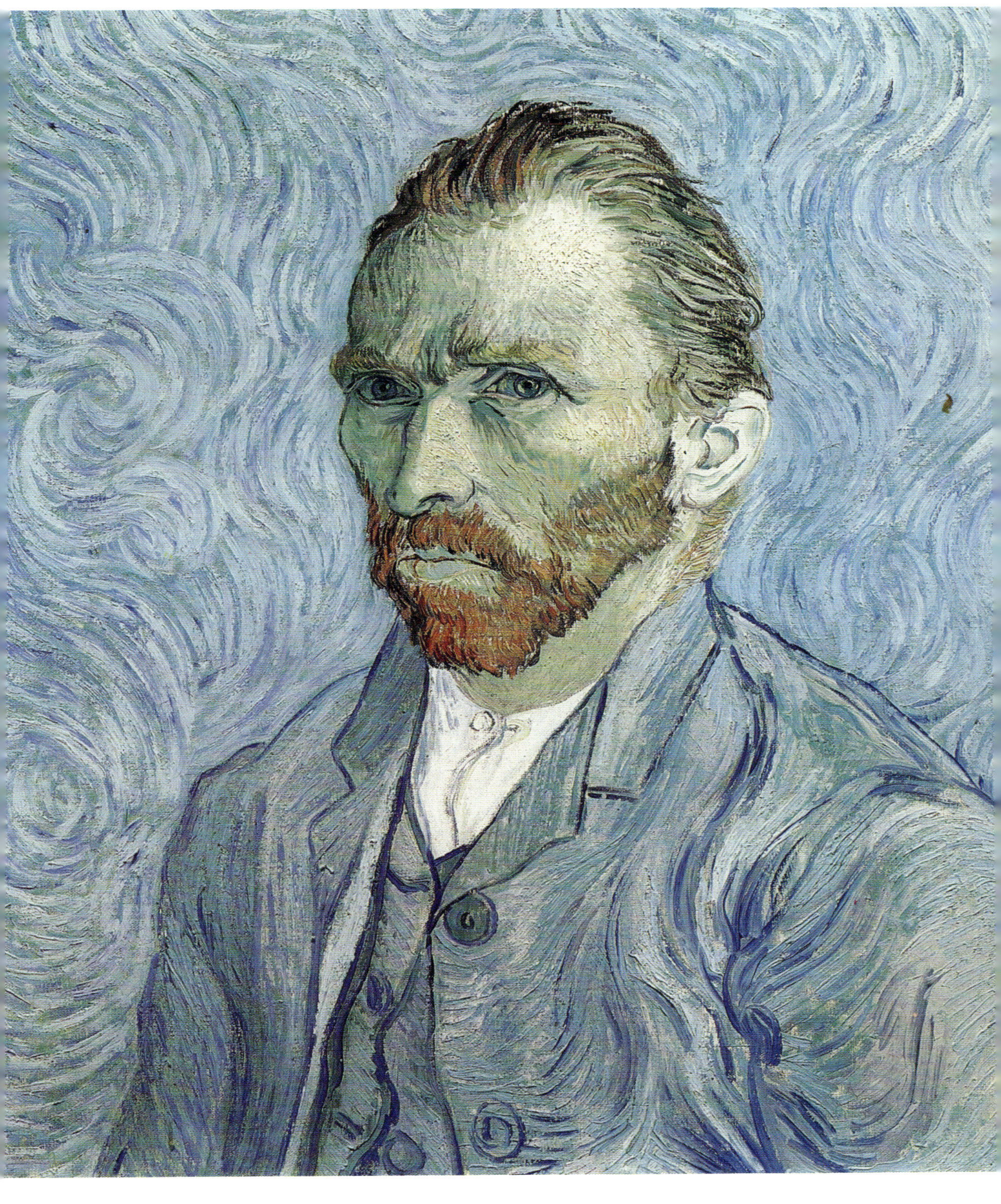

In Paris the fifth annual exhibition of the Salon des Indépendants opened on September 3rd with two of Van Gogh's canvases included, submitted by Theo with Vincent's agreement. One of the paintings was *Starry Night over the Rhône*, which Van Gogh had painted in Arles the previous year. The second was *Irises*, the very first canvas he completed after his arrival at Saint-Rémy in May, painted in the asylum garden.

The opening was a prestigious occasion, especially for younger artists of the avant-garde keen to make an impression on critics and collectors. The Salon des Indépendants had been established five years earlier as a challenging alternative to the government-sponsored official Salon in which selection was on the basis of rigidly traditional principles of what 'fine art' was supposed to be. Any work submitted which contravened those hallowed principles tended to be rejected. Among the most celebrated rejects had been Manet's masterpiece *Le Déjeuner sur l'herbe* which insulted the jury by portraying a naked woman in the company of fully-dressed men at a country picnic. The new Salon deliberately had no selection committee, no jury and no awards were handed out. Strictly speaking it was a free-for-all, an open forum for new ideas. The founders and other leading figures, were mostly prominent younger artists united in their contempt for the conservative art establishment. As a prominent dealer in contemporary art, Theo would have known personally most of the key artists who ran it or exhibited here, including the young Paul Signac, one of the founders of the Indépendants and also a friend of Van Gogh, who had gone out of his way to visit Vincent in the Arles hospital only a few months before.

Van Gogh's two paintings seem to have been hung conspicuously and to have won favourable comments from fellow-artists and a few critics, as Theo was pleased to report. The *Irises*, he noted, 'strikes the eye from afar'. Slowly a tide was beginning to turn in Vincent's favour. He was still not selling anything, yet his work was at least being noticed and talked about. In Parisian art circles interest was beginning to be generated in these boldly-painted images of the south which to Parisian eyes carried an intriguing touch of the exotic.

Van Gogh himself had no contact with the Paris art scene except through his brother. In fact he enjoyed virtually no contact with anything beyond the asylum walls. His sole concern was his health and what it enabled him to do. In September Van Gogh's letters to his brother grew longer and longer as he began to feel confident that his strength and composure were returning and many thoughts and ideas that had been hibernating during the weeks of illness needed to be expressed. At the end of one letter at the beginning of the month Dr Peyron added a reassuring footnote to Theo assuring him that 'Vincent has quite recovered from his crisis…and has completely regained his lucidity of mind. He has resumed painting just as he used to. His thoughts of suicide have disappeared, only disturbing dreams remain, though these are lessening too…His appetite has returned and he has resumed his normal way of life.' Vincent himself was equally convinced that everything had taken a turn for the better. He assured his brother that his energy was returning day by day and that he was now working 'non-stop from morning to night…I could almost believe I have a new period of clarity ahead of me…Anyway, here I am again, recovered for the time being and I'm so very grateful for it.'

The note of euphoria in his comment to Theo was straightaway muted by the admission that 'it is six weeks since I set foot outside, even to go into the garden,' adding, 'but next week however, once I've finished the canvases I'm working on, I'm going to try.' The sequence of contradictions in the letter sum up Van Gogh's predicament at this moment: he had recovered sufficiently to understand the many things he felt compelled to do, but remained totally incapable of taking the necessary action. He was paralysed by his own fears.

In fact it was not 'next week' but several more weeks before Van Gogh could steel himself to venture beyond the protective walls of the asylum. His letters throughout September make little more than passing references to his terror of the outside world; yet it was a fear that dominated his life. What he perceived was a world in which people were hostile and threatening, conspiring against him like the citizens of Arles who had drawn up a petition against him. Adding to this paranoia was the sense that nature itself was a malevolent force, his most recent experience of it being that of a howling mistral tearing at his canvas and inducing his recent attack. The very word 'attack' was appropriate: nature had indeed 'attacked' him on that day when he was painting in the old quarry.

Terror at the prospect of having to face the outside world preoccupied Van Gogh for much of the month of September. Although filled with a 'pent-up fury for work', as he related to Theo on September 5th, he was nonetheless severely restricted in the choice of subjects he felt able to paint. As he was predominantly a landscape painter, he could only paint what was visible from his bedroom window, which amounted to the much-repeated theme of the enclosed wheat field. His friend Roulin's suggestion that what he most needed was to 'work in the beautiful fields' was advice he could not follow.

This limitation of scope did bring one outstanding benefit: it compelled him to concentrate on the theme of the human figure, which he had neglected since arriving at Saint-Rémy. 'Yesterday I began a portrait of the head attendant,' Vincent wrote in the same letter to his brother. The sitter was Charles Trabuc, who lived in a small farmhouse nearby and had been the artist's escort on numerous excursions outside the asylum walls, including the ill-starred visit to

Portrait of Trabuc Oil on canvas, 61 x 46 cm
Kunstmuseum Solothurn, Switzerland

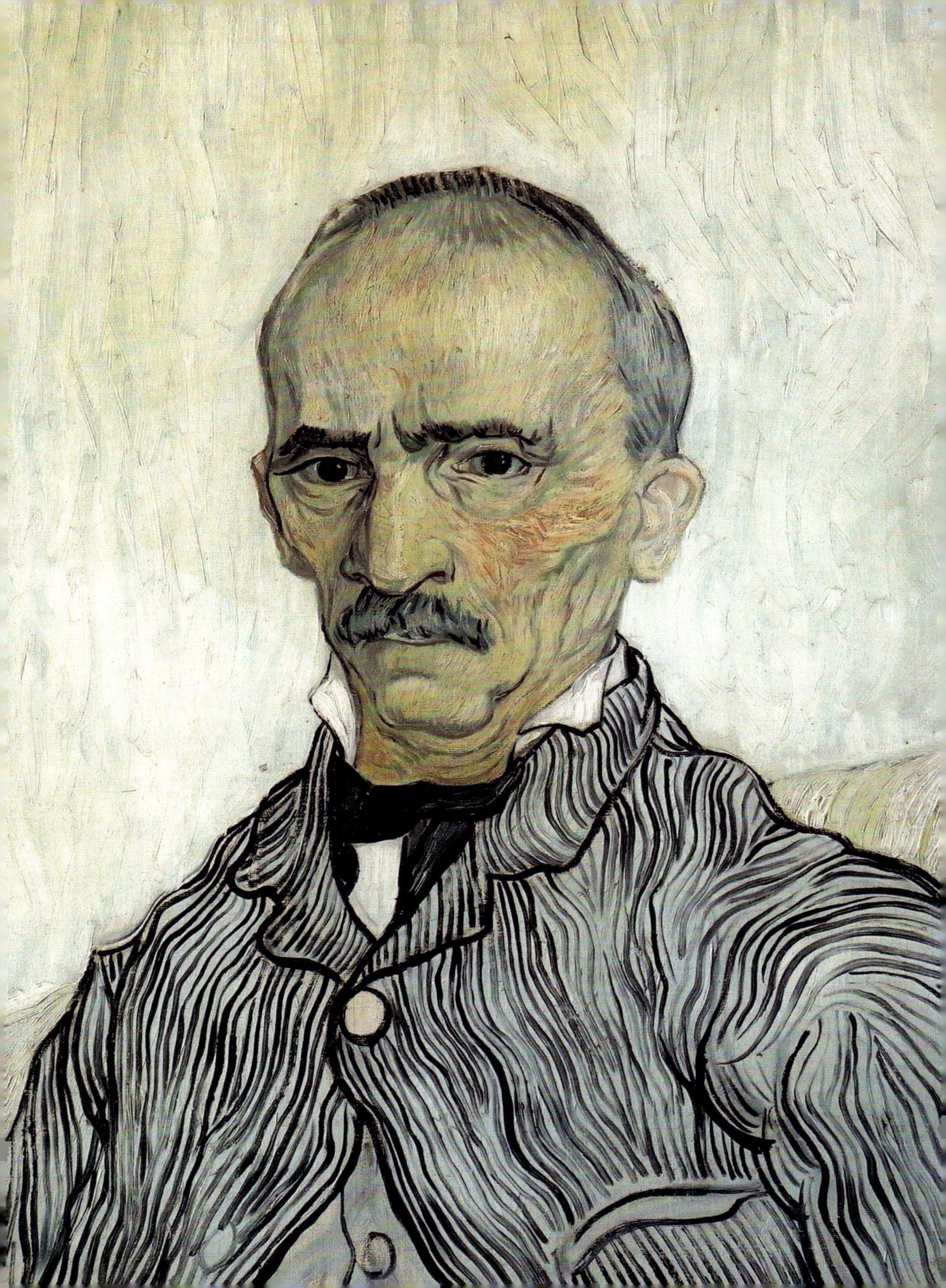

Arles in July. He found Trabuc a fascinating subject to paint and the resulting canvas demonstrates how inquiring and shrewd Van Gogh could be as a portrait painter. Far from being just a model conveniently at hand, it was the personality and striking appearance of Trabuc which particularly captivated Van Gogh and which he was determined to bring out in his portrait. He found his sitter someone 'with a very interesting face', with a look of 'indefinable contemplation about it,' he explained to Theo. He discovered that Trabuc had previously worked at a hospital in Marseille at the time of two cholera outbreaks and so, 'altogether he is a man who has witnessed a great deal of suffering and death and there is a sort of contemplative calm in that face,' Vincent went on.

The *Trabuc* portrait is an almost brutally frank study of the asylum's head attendant. The craggy face looks as though it has been carved out of limestone, while the buttoned jacket he wears is painted in violent dark stripes that make the garment look as though it had been thrown together in a storm. Vincent's own account could hardly be more apt: 'If it were not a good deal softened by an intelligent look and an expression of kindliness it would be a veritable bird of prey.' The juxtaposition of ferocity and gentleness, of hard and soft, creates a most surprising harmony, making this among Van Gogh's most striking portraits. Even with a somewhat heavy-handed technique, the painting manages to convey with sensitivity the affection and friendship Vincent clearly felt for this fierce-looking man.

One day after telling Theo he had begun the portrait he wrote again announcing that he had finished it, adding that he had detected 'something of mystery' in his subject's 'small, quick black eyes'. In fact Van Gogh painted the portrait twice in the space of five days. The original he presented to Trabuc himself (now lost), while the second version (surviving) he sent to Theo, though he delayed doing so, perhaps sensing that his more conventional brother might not respond favourably to its forceful style.

This disparity between them in matters of taste and style was a recurring dilemma for Vincent. He knew his brother preferred him to paint as naturalistically as possible, as this would be the best chance of selling his paintings. Vincent's own inclination was often to paint more expressively, exaggerating aspects of a subject for dramatic effect, or because they engaged his own turbulent spirits. At the same time he was far from oblivious to the need for sales, especially since Theo was paying all the bills. He told Theo he was 'frightened' by never selling anything and was delighted that his brother was renting a room in Père Tanguy's shop in order to show his work, except that here was yet another expense for Theo to bear. By the same count he was flattered to have been asked to exhibit two paintings at the next exhibition of Les XX in Brussels, while claiming that he would feel inferior alongside so many Belgians 'who possess such an enormous amount of talent'. (One wonders who on earth he had in mind).

Each of these protracted letters to Theo stressed repeatedly how hard he was working and how important this was as a distraction. He had repainted the canvas of his bedroom in Arles, which he would send to Theo. He had reworked areas of *The Reaper*, which he had more or less completed in the summer before his breakdown. He had also retouched several other earlier paintings. Among these was a smaller version of a favourite subject viewed from his bedroom window, *Wheat Field with Cypresses*, which he had first painted early in the summer (now in the National Gallery, London). This new version he seems to have deliberately refreshed by applying thick impasto and scumbled effect to the clouds and to the foliage below. One purpose in repainting these early subjects, as he explained to Theo, was to have 'four or five studies which I would like to give to my mother and sister', to show them what he had been doing during his months in Saint-Rémy. A batch of these 'studies', as he called them, went off to Theo at the end of the month.

Making these various new versions kept Vincent busy at full stretch. Yet it was all retrospective. There was nothing new. He still could not bring himself to venture outside to find new subjects, even as far as the asylum garden. 'It's almost two months since I've been in the open air,' he wrote to his brother on September 10th. 'I've tried to make

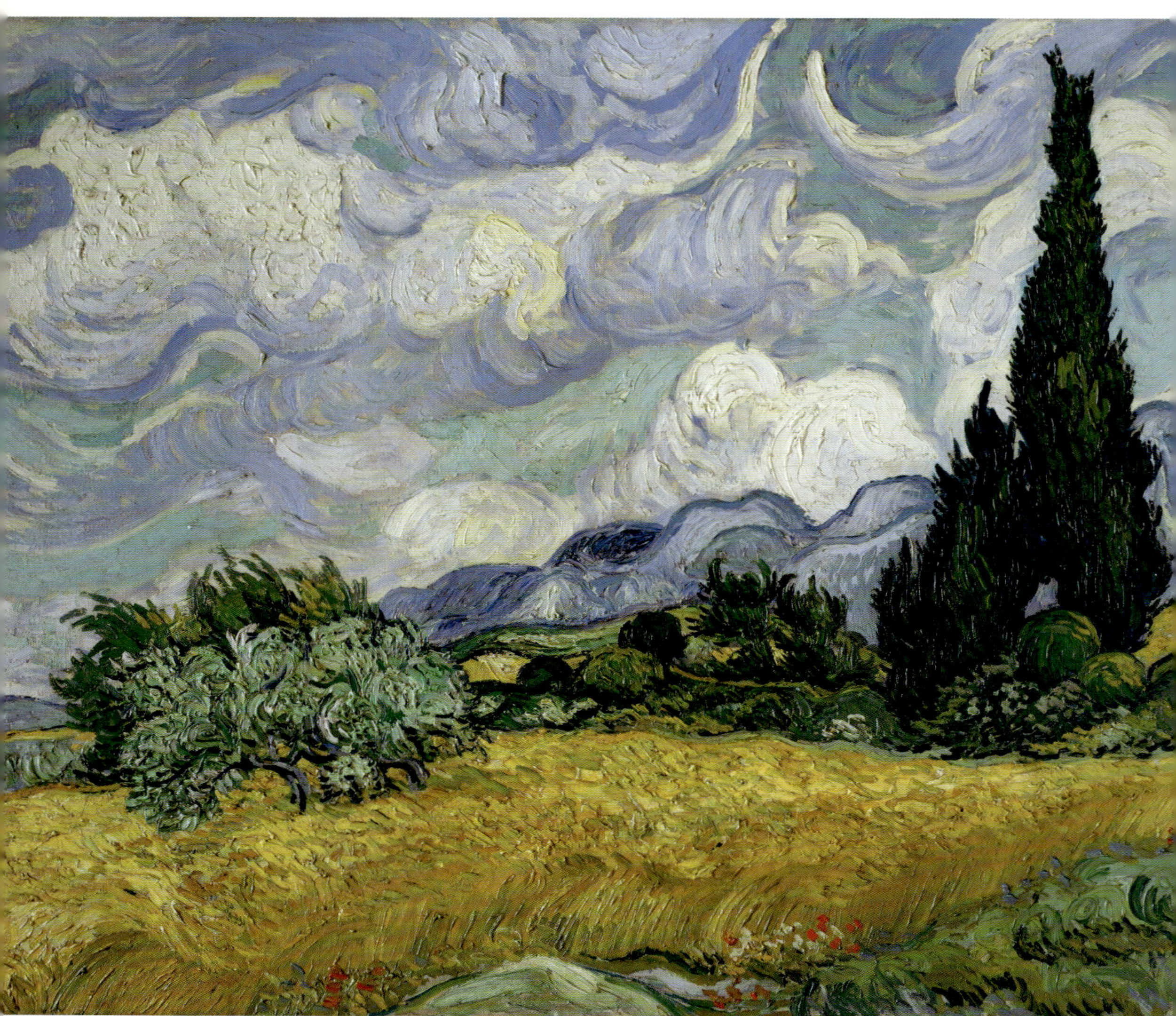

Wheat Field with Cypresses Oil on canvas, 73 x 93.4 cm
Metropolitan Museum of Art, New York

myself go downstairs, but in vain.' He was now living and working in a hermetically-sealed world out of sheer terror of what lay beyond these monastic walls and of what it might do to his brain. He felt a constant dread of suffering a new attack. Increasingly he was becoming convinced this would occur before long, probably around Christmas he thought, to the point of almost willing it to be so. It was this sense of impending disaster which drove him to work at fever pitch because there was so much to be done and such an attack, when it came, 'could destroy my ability to paint for ever'.

Surprisingly, Van Gogh's pessimism brought a certain comfort. Now that he felt he knew what his condition was and had become reconciled to the inevitability of further attacks, he felt 'absolutely normal'. He wrote that he preferred this state of affairs to his time in Paris 'when it was all brewing' and he had no idea what was wrong. Now at least he knew that in all probability these attacks would pass and he would have peaceful 'intervals' in which he could feel calm and carry on painting. He even managed to joke about his state of mind to his brother. 'I'm trying to get better rather like someone who has wanted to kill himself but found the water too cold and so tries to grab on to the bank.'

Another recurrent theme he shared with Theo was whether he might be better off returning to the north. This was partly nostalgia and loneliness, compounded by a feeling of total alienation from fellow patients, amounting almost to disgust – with the inmates themselves, but also with the authorities who did absolutely nothing to help them. He could no longer bear 'living with these weird people here' and it deeply depressed him that they were all left to 'vegetate in idleness'. Vincent also felt there might be more suitable accommodation for himself in the north where he could be closer to family and fellow-artists. He wondered if 'Père Pissarro' (the painter Camille Pissarro, a friend and client of Theo), might be prepared to take him in as a lodger and he asked his brother to make enquiries. This was an early intimation that the genial and generous Pissarro might facilitate Van Gogh's return north, as he eventually did. (It was Pissarro who knew and recommended Dr Gachet in Auvers as someone who might take in Vincent as a lodger and a patient.)

The persistent issue of whether or not he should return to the north became further complicated by Dr Peyron's visit to Paris where he agreed to meet Theo to discuss his brother's predicament. Peyron's view was that Vincent should remain at Saint-Rémy in case of further mental attacks, a view which Van Gogh himself was now inclined to share. By this time Theo was growing exasperated and wrote to Vincent on September 18th asking him to say categorically if he still wanted a place to be found for him in or near Paris; and furthermore 'why do you stay shut away? Why don't you go out and get some fresh air?…Give me an answer.' Vincent's long rambling reply eventually confirmed Dr Peyron's view that he should remain at the asylum for the time being, adding (no doubt confusing Theo even further) that he might suddenly write, 'I want to get out of here'. At much the same time he wrote to his sister Wil, as so often more candid with her than with his brother and paymaster. He described to her the time when he had been painting in the open and had been 'overwhelmed by a feeling of loneliness, so much so that I shy away from going outside'. Then he added: 'But this will change in time. Only when I stand painting in front of my easel do I feel almost alive.'

But standing in front of his easel meant having nothing in front of him to paint, except his own earlier canvases, which he could pass the time touching up. More particularly there were the works of other artists he admired which he could copy. In the claustrophobic cell which was his studio, it was these 'interpretations' as he described them, from engravings or illustrations in publications sent to him by Theo, that occupied his long working days for much of the month of September. These included two copies of Millet's *The Sower*, another of Delacroix's *Pietà* and seven paintings from woodcuts based on Millet's studies of labourers in the field.

Van Gogh's admiration for both Millet and Delacroix was profound and he regarded them, together with Rembrandt, as his artistic ancestors. However, these academic exercises seem a sterile waste of talent in an artist whose first love was to record his response to the wonders of nature. Vincent acknowledged that he made these copies in the absence of real models to paint: it is ironical that he felt the strong appeal of recording peasants working the fields as represented by Millet, while being too frightened to go outside and observe them in the flesh on his own doorstep. He also went to considerable lengths to justify these copies and to stress the virtues embodied in them. Writing to Theo, he asserted that painters should not always be 'composers' but at times 'interpreters', comparing his own role to that of a musician playing a piece by Beethoven, in doing so adding his personal touch to it: 'So my brush rests between my fingers as if it was the bow of a violin, and absolutely for my pleasure.' There is no record of whether Theo was convinced by his brother's argument, though one suspects from his previous letter that he would greatly prefer Vincent to stop shutting himself away and 'go out and get some fresh air'.

Then, without warning and with no comment or explanation from Van Gogh, the self-incarceration was over. At the end of September in a spirited letter to Theo, Vincent expressed regret that there were no vineyards in the region of Saint-Rémy, but that instead he had taken to exploring the olive orchards which were abundant and which he was 'struggling to capture'. He was now clearly out and about and the demons had seemingly dispersed, we do not know why or how. Characteristically, now his crisis was over it was as though it had never happened. 'At present I feel completely normal and no longer remember those bad days at all.'

Van Gogh's paintings of olive orchards make up one of the major series he created during his time at the asylum. He produced at least fifteen canvases on the theme, the first being the one he painted in June soon after being allowed to work outside the asylum grounds not long after his arrival. The series as a whole is in many respects the supreme achievement of his year at Saint-Rémy. Each canvas is strikingly different from any other in the series in colour and atmosphere and each one is a rich expression of the artist's response to a favourite subject at a given moment. There is no certainty as to which canvas was the

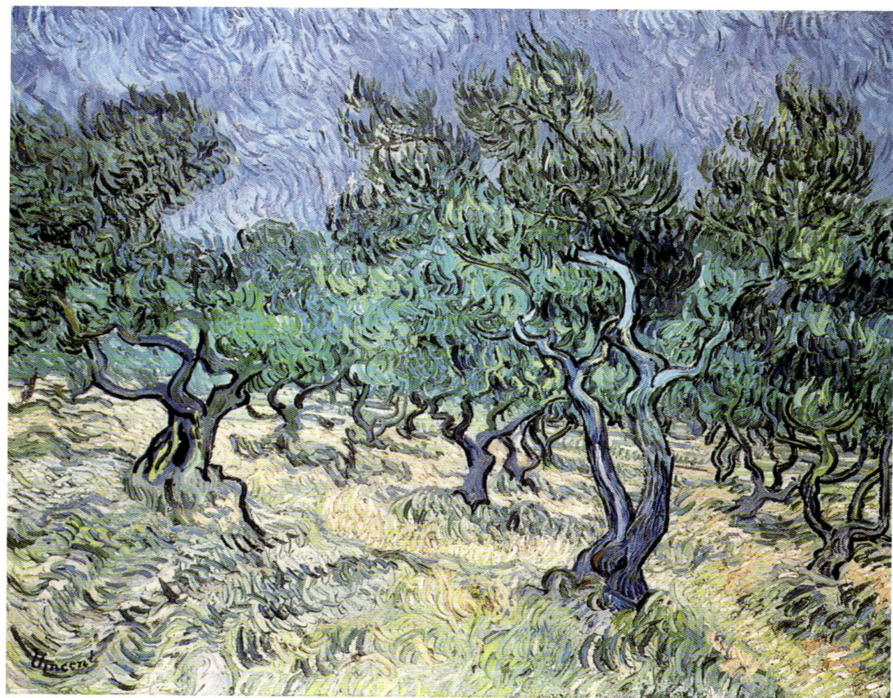

Olive Orchard Oil on canvas, 72 x 92 cm
Kröller-Müller Museum, Otterlo

first of the new group which he painted at the very end of September; nor does Vincent's description to Theo at the time provide a helpful clue. In his letter of September 28th he wrote of the olive orchard: 'it is silver, sometimes more blue, sometimes greenish, bronzed, becoming more white against the ground, which is yellow, pink, purple or orange to dull red ochre…but difficult. Very difficult.'

This colourful description could stand as an all-embracing account of the entire series, which does indeed run the gamut of all the colours he lists. The view that the painting illustrated here is the one mentioned in his letter to Theo is supported by the fragile evidence of the wavy-blue brushstrokes illustrating the sky. These are found in only one other of Van Gogh's paintings from Saint-Rémy, the second of his self-portraits which he had painted just a few weeks earlier.

Establishing the precise order of these fifteen canvases is an academic exercise of limited importance. First in the renewed series or not, *Olive Orchard* is one of the loveliest of Van Gogh's Saint-Rémy paintings. The tangled shapes of the olive branches are described with vigorous curving brushstrokes with none of the hectic turbulence that characterised the June version he painted shortly before his breakdown. There is a serenity and composure about the composition and a rich subtlety in the many tones of green, all of which suggest that the artist had finally emerged from his long seclusion with a refreshed eye for the natural world which for the time being at least was no longer overcast by the dark turbulence of his mind.

A rich vein was opening up and he sensed it. The letter to his brother describing the olive orchards includes a list of colours he needs 'as soon as possible,' he underlines, because 'there are wonderful autumn effects to capture.' He would be making up for lost time.

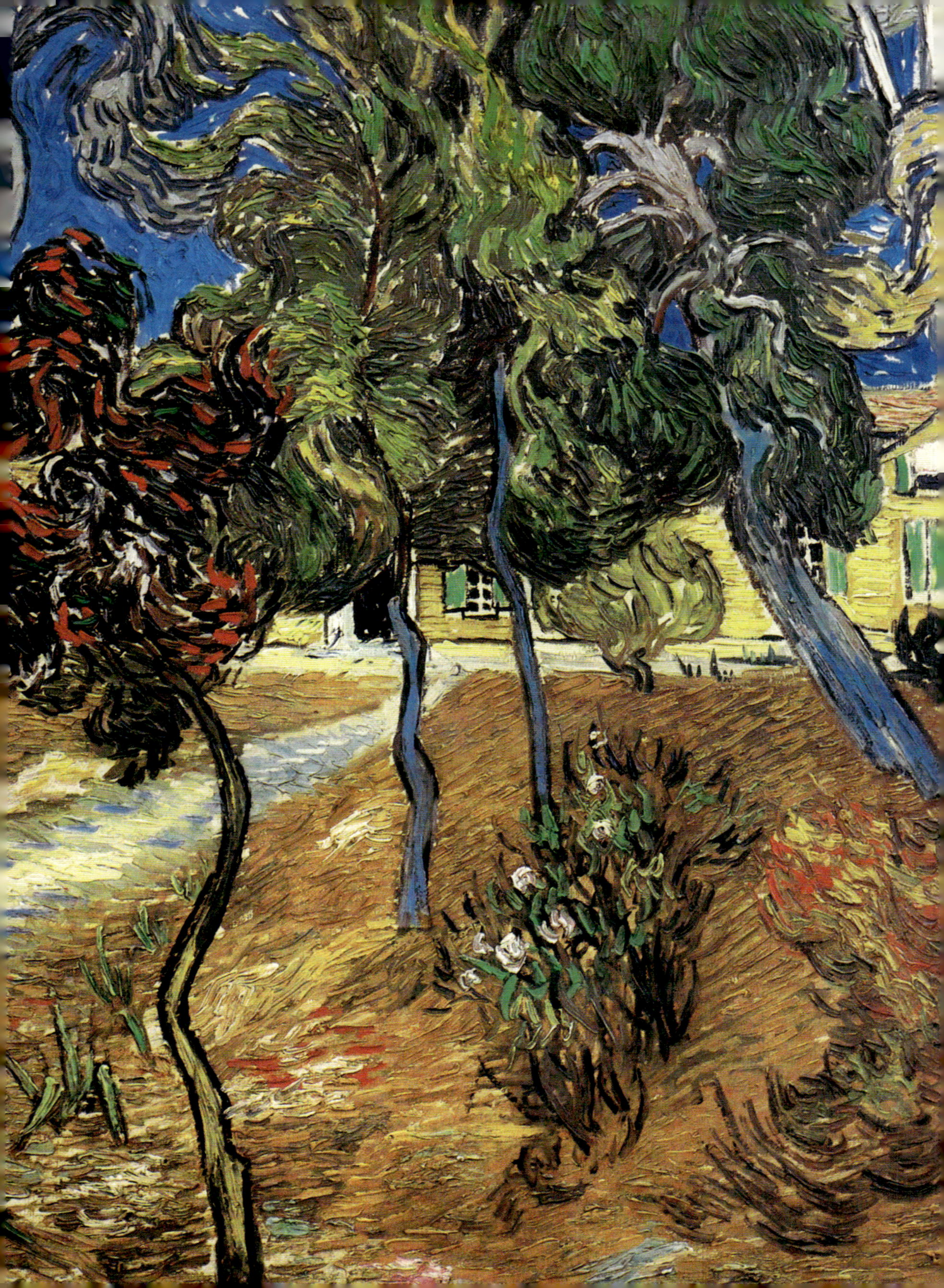

OCTOBER

'We've been enjoying superb autumn days and I'm taking full advantage of them.' Van Gogh's buoyant letter to Theo on October 5th was in response to the letter he had received earlier that day from his brother. The glorious Provençal autumn has spurred him to seek out 'even more beautiful subjects for tomorrow, in the mountains'.

The urge to explore the mountains was one of Vincent's more restless ambitions at Saint-Rémy, though the absence of drawings or paintings of the Alpilles except as a backdrop suggest that it was more often a dream than a reality. It seems unlikely that Dr Peyron welcomed the idea of his erratic patient wandering among the rugged peaks of the Alpilles, even with an attendant. However, the note of adventure in his reply to Theo was a response to several items of good news in his brother's letter. The first of these was the report Theo gave him of his meeting in Paris with Dr Peyron, who had assured him that 'he does not think you are mad at all, only epileptic and that the last crisis he believed to have been brought on by Vincent's visit to Arles in early July. Peyron was also of the view that, while his patient was of course free to go, Vincent should remain at the asylum at least until the winter was over, in case there might be a another breakdown.

Vincent seemed both relieved and in agreement with Dr Peyron's view, though he doubted if Arles had anything to do with his illness

Trees in the Garden of the Asylum Oil on canvas, 73 x 60 cm
Private collection, Switzerland

and in fact had every intention of returning there to see old friends like the Ginoux. Yet almost at the same time as agreeing that he should remain at Saint-Rémy for the foreseeable future, he was responding favourably to another piece of news from his brother. This was something that opened up the possibility of Van Gogh leaving the asylum and finding a place where he might live and be cared for in the north. Theo had talked to the artist Camille Pissarro about Vincent and his needs and Pissarro had suggested a sympathetic doctor in the village of Auvers, a short distance from Pissarro's own village of Eragny. Dr Gachet was extremely well-disposed towards artists, was a friend of a number of the Impressionists' circle, among them Sisley, Renoir and Cézanne, and was an amateur painter himself. Pissarro had volunteered to go over and talk to Gachet on Van Gogh's behalf.

Vincent responded to this suggestion with cautious enthusiasm: 'What you say about Auvers offers an agreeable prospect and sooner

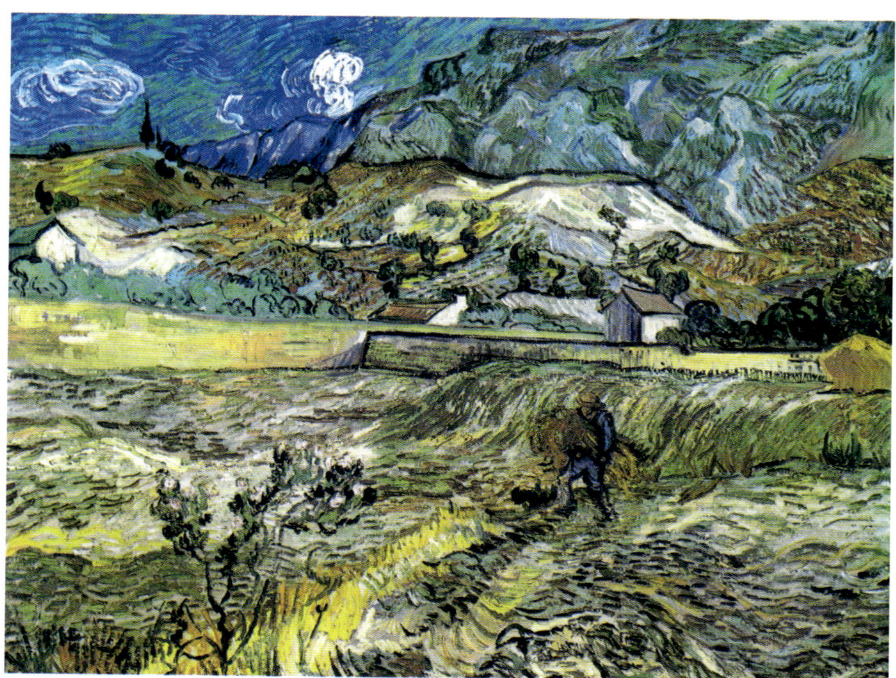

Enclosed Field with Peasant Oil on canvas, 73.5 x 92 cm
Indianapolis Museum of Art, USA

or later it ought to be arranged without needing to search any further.'
As so often with Van Gogh's letters, what we read is not so much a
statement of intent as an airing of his thoughts, as if he was actually
talking to the recipient aloud, sometimes repeating a point several
times, often changing his mind in mid-flow, forever casting fresh
light on an idea or plunging it into sudden darkness. His letters were
like a canvas on which he was continually working. By the end of
his October 5th reply to Theo he had decided definitely to spend the
winter in Saint-Rémy and he now looked forward to the spring and
no doubt the blossom he had missed through being in hospital. But he
liked the idea of Auvers, he reassured his brother, 'and I can assure you
that the north will appeal to me like a new land.'

The third item of news in Theo's letter created an even greater
conflict in Van Gogh's mind. This was the announcement that a Dutch
journalist and critic, J.J.Isaacson, had seen Vincent's latest batch of
canvases, presumably at Père Tanguy's shop or in Theo's flat, and
had been so impressed that he wanted to write an article about the
artist. He had asked if he might take a few paintings home with him,
particularly those of the mountains and the wheat field. Vincent was
clearly taken aback: that a critic should actually wish to write about
his work was an experience so unfamiliar it was alarming; and his first
response to Theo was self-defensive to the point of panic. Isaacson
must be dissuaded from writing any such article. Later in the same
letter he began to have more positive thoughts: he would like to write
to Isaacson and tell him to wait a while longer until he had 'better
stuff' to show him. 'It's not worth writing about my work at present,'
he declared; but soon he hoped to get more 'character' into his work
and then he would be able to show him his 'Impressions of Provence'.
He went on to list some of his favourite themes: fig-trees, vineyards,
cypresses, the Alpilles mountains, 'all characteristic things'.

Van Gogh wrote the promised letter to Isaacson via Theo. It was
clearly not the 'hands-off' message he had first proposed to his brother.
In fact Isaacson had already written and published his thoughts on
Vincent in a Dutch magazine, which Theo forwarded to his brother

later in the month. Meanwhile, perhaps spurred on by the knowledge that someone was at last writing about him, he was determined to take advantage of the 'superb autumn days' and threw his energies into painting a variety of subjects both in the asylum garden and outside the walls. He was discovering 'new landscapes', he told his brother towards the middle of October.

The list he gave Theo of five new landscapes completed since he last wrote also included an old favourite. This was the latest view of the enclosed wheat field seen from his bedroom window, which he had already painted so often and which had become his favourite image of the changing seasons. It was Vincent's first autumn in the Asylum. He had watched the wheat ripen and had seen the harvest. Now the field had become just 'clods of earth against a parched landscape and the rocks of the Alpilles' with a solitary peasant dragging a bundle of straw across it. He felt the canvas would compliment *The Reaper*, which he had repainted the previous month and he urged Theo seriously 'to show them together'. The need to work in series was once again uppermost in his mind. He hoped to demonstrate to Theo and to his new admirer, Isaacson, that creating a sequence of paintings on a single theme was his way of portraying the true character of Provence. *Enclosed Field with Peasant* has a lightness of touch and a windblown freshness about it that suggests it was painted in a single session in a concentrated burst of energy. Short stubby brushstrokes portray the clods of ploughed soil in the foreground as well as the jagged folds of naked rock in the distant Alpilles.

Van Gogh was becoming ever more attracted to these enfolding mountains that were the backdrop to almost everything he painted. To Theo he explained that he would love to 'make an entire series on the Alpilles' and that he was 'going off on long hikes in the mountains to look for new subjects to paint'. He also longed to paint the Alpilles in the sunset, but he was never allowed outside the Asylum at that late hour. He was particularly attracted to a ravine with a rushing stream running through it (today the 'holy spring' at the heart of the Graeco-Roman city of Glanum, not yet excavated in Van Gogh's day).

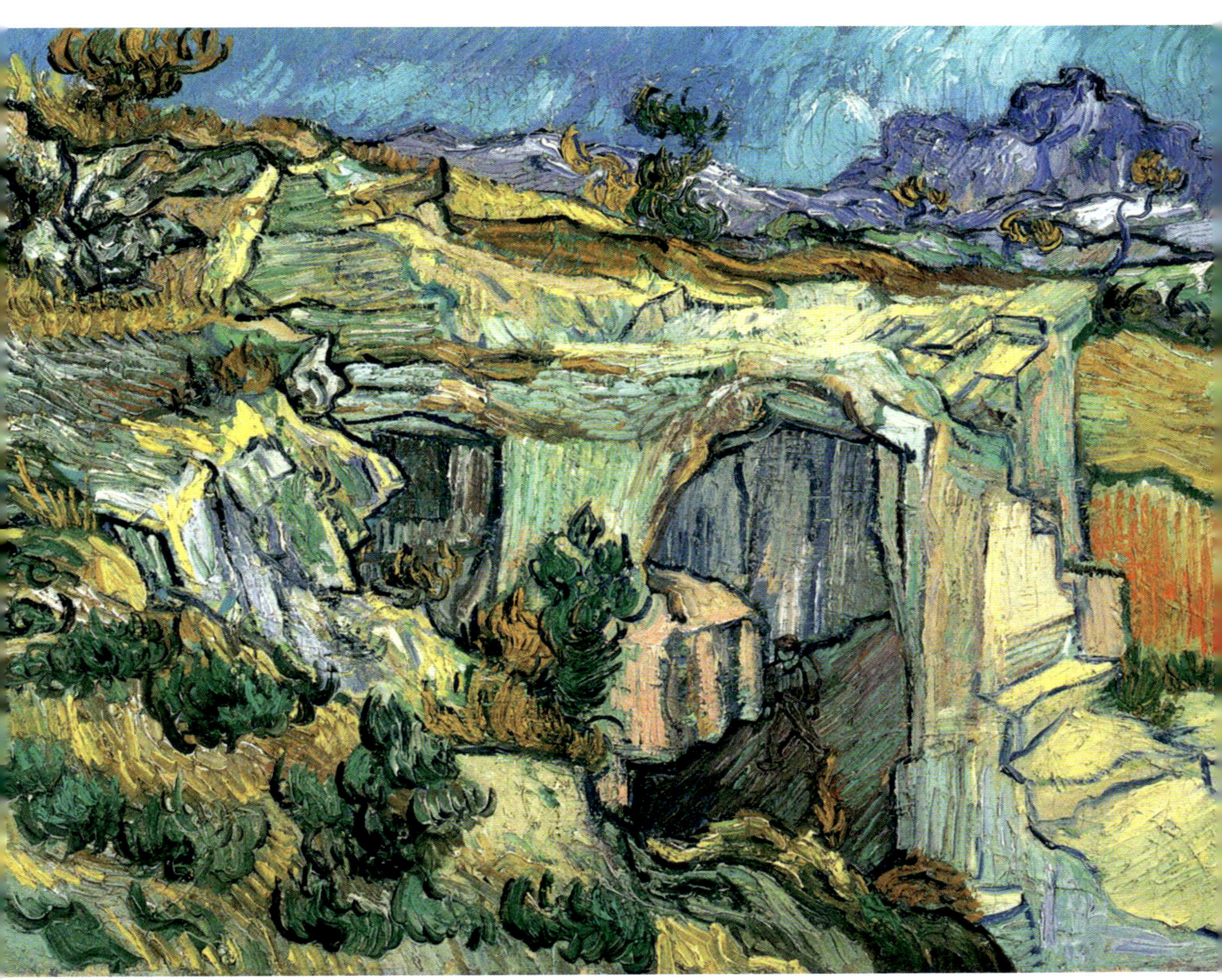

Entrance to a Quarry Oil on canvas, 64 x 52 cm
Private Collection

One of the new landscapes 'recently completed', as he told Theo, was a courageous return to a theme which had been the instrument of his mental breakdown three months earlier. The subject was one of the ancient quarries dating back to Roman times which were striking features of the local area. They fascinated Vincent for the unexpected shapes and colours he found in the weathered fork formations partly overgrown with scrub and trees. *Entrance to a Quarry* is Van Gogh at his most craggy. It is a painting that anticipates Cubism in its concentration on the geometry of landscape described in the subtlest variations of grey and buff, all applied with vigorous strokes of paint in heavy impasto as if he was carving out the landscape with his brush. Vincent described the painting to his brother on October 8th as being very like 'Japanese drawings of rocks where grasses and little trees grow here and there'. He made the same comparison to Japanese drawings in a letter to Emile Bernard, who was then painting in Brittany with Gauguin. To Bernard he added the observation 'Dear God, everything is hard to do here.' In order to describe 'the true soil of Provence you have to work extremely hard and so it naturally becomes a little abstract' – a further anticipation of Cubism.

From the thick impasto of the quarry painting it is easy to understand why Van Gogh frequently ran out of paint. There were sometimes lengthy gaps between Theo's consignments. The chief disappointment lay in Vincent's inability to capture the autumn colours he cherished; and this deprivation accounted for ever-longer 'hikes' into the mountains in search of motifs which, to his distress, he was unable to paint and as the source of paint and canvases dried up, so did the letters. He was naturally unwilling to upbraid his brother who supplied and paid for everything. Instead he seems to have found some perverse comfort, he later told his sister Wil, from reading Dostoevsky's novel *The House of the Dead*.

Supplies of canvas and paint eventually arrived about the third week in October and on the 21st Vincent was able to write to both his mother and sister that the countryside was 'very beautiful' at this moment and he had been able to go out and paint the autumn colours he loved, his only regret being the absence of vineyards in the area, though 'I did go out and paint one a few hours away,' he informed his mother. He concluded the letter by telling her he had been painting a portrait of a fellow-patient. What intrigued him was that 'when one is with people for a long time and becomes used to them, one ceases to think about them as being mad.'

Two days later Van Gogh received his first letter from Theo for nearly three weeks, containing welcome news from Paris. Although Vincent's two paintings in the Salon des Indépendants had been returned unsold there had been a visit by a group of Dutch and Belgian artists, including Theo van Rijsselberghe who was a prominent member of Les XX in Brussels, where Van Gogh was exhibiting two paintings later that winter. The group had been to Theo's apartment and to Tanguy's shop to see the latest consignment of paintings from Saint-Rémy, and 'your work seemed to impress them a lot.' Theo added that the Belgians were much more inclined to appreciate bright colours than the stuffy Parisians. Theo also stressed, characteristically, that his own preference in the recent batch was for the *Irises* rather than *The Starry Night*. 'I consider you are much stronger when you are doing real things rather than those where the search for some style becomes prejudicial to the true feel of things.' The same was true, he felt, of the recent paintings he had received from Gauguin in Brittany. He wished Gauguin's peasants would be made to look like Bretons, not like Japanese. Reading between the lines it seems he suspected that the influence of Gauguin and his friend Emile Bernard was distracting Vincent from his natural bent.

Together with 150 francs, Theo's letter also enclosed Isaacson's published article, or several articles, about Van Gogh. His writing may be seen as an exercise in fanciful rhetoric, yet Isaacson genuinely saw something in Vincent's painting which no one else had perceived: that his vision was one that future generations would understand. The key passage runs: 'Who interprets for us in shapes and colours the great matters of life in this nineteenth century? One I know, a solitary pioneer, he stands alone struggling in the depths of night: his name, Vincent, is for posterity.'

It is hard to imagine the impact such a ringing pronouncement must have had on Van Gogh, solitary within his protective asylum walls, and about whom no one had ever written a word in praise, let alone claim him for posterity. Presented with this totally unexpected accolade Vincent reacted with a dismissive shrug: 'I find what he says about me extremely exaggerated, one more reason why I'd prefer him not to have written anything about me.' The defensive armour soon fell away and in the same reply of October 25th, he suggested to Theo that Isaacson should wait a year until he had better work to show him, but that he would like to meet Isaacson. Then he continued, 'I'm planning to write to him about his article and I'll give him a portrait of myself as a souvenir.' Finally he concludes, bizarrely, that Isaacson might make a suitable husband for his sister Wil, which would be a better role for him than being a journalist.

In the same letter he informed Theo that Dr Peyron had assured him that his health had 'considerably improved', so much so that the doctor had no objection to Vincent making another visit to Arles, which he intended to do 'in a few days time'. It is not clear what prompted the desire to revisit Arles, which had so many unhappy associations for him, unless he was driven by bouts of loneliness. 'Melancholy very often overtakes me with great force,' he confessed to Theo. His life in Saint-Rémy was largely friendless. Apart from fellow-patients to whom he hardly spoke, there was only Dr Peyron, whom he saw rarely and the asylum attendants, including Trabuc, who shadowed him on his excursions outside the walls. They in any case spoke Provençal, or at least in a heavy Provençal accent if they spoke to him at all. In Arles he had a few friends, notably the Ginoux who owned the local café and of course Dr Rey and the Rev. Salles. Vincent may further have been prompted by having just received a letter from his faithful friend and admirer Joseph Roulin, the Arles postman, now temporarily in Marseille. Vincent had told Roulin of his plan to move north, to which came the reply, 'I shall have a very heavy heart to see you go away from us.'

Although he proclaimed his determination to explore the mountains and capture the beautiful colours of autumn, Van Gogh's daily life seemed to have remained for the most part enclosed and secluded. Since recovering from his mental breakdown in August there are surprisingly few landscapes that were actually painted outside the walls of the asylum. In his letters to Theo late in October, Vincent's most fulsome were for a collection of monochrome reproductions of works by Millet, an artist for whom Van Gogh felt an unbounded admiration. The prints were mostly scenes of labourers toiling in the fields, gently romanticised and with strong spiritual overtones emphasising the 'noble peasant'. Vincent's response to Theo was that he intended to 'make a very special collection of copies' of these Millet reproductions, adding later, 'I'm working on them zealously…It seems to me that doing paintings of these Millet drawings is to transform them into another language.' The Millet subjects included *The Two Diggers*, which Van Gogh painted first, a candlelit domestic interior and a group of weary labourers celebrating the end of the working day, both of which Vincent painted soon after; and finally *The Sower*, of which he was especially proud, even making a second copy so that he might send one to his family.

Van Gogh made no fewer than twenty-one copies of Millet paintings and drawings during his year at Saint-Rémy. He had a particular admiration for *The Angelus*, Millet's most celebrated painting which had recently been sold in Paris for more than half a million francs. The price had astonished Van Gogh, as well as causing him to reflect gloomily that only the works of dead artists sold well (a truly prophetic thought in Van Gogh's case).

Vincent's admiration for Millet is entirely consistent with his attraction to the mystique of physical labour which had characterised his work since his early days in Holland. What may seem surprising is that, here in rural Provence where Van Gogh repeatedly expressed a desire to capture the 'true character' of the region, he should prefer to copy the work of another artist from another region and another era rather than go out and paint local peasants working in the nearby fields and olive orchards. It says much about his mental illness that, even at this time of lucidity and high productivity, he should prefer to paint subjects close to his heart second-hand rather than from life. Maybe the memory lingered of his panic-stricken encounter with the working world when he ventured with Trabuc into the village of Saint-Rémy. In the event the peasant world of physical labour he idealised became tangible only through the imagery of other artists or else observed from the lofty distance of his bedroom window. Peasant life had acquired a mythic quality largely divorced from reality. For an artist possessed with a strong gift for personal friendship and a penetrating eye for portraiture, here is yet another anomaly in the tormented psychology of Vincent van Gogh.

Almost as an afterthought, the letter extolling the virtues of copying Millet ends: 'Apart from that I have a rain effect on the go and an evening effect with tall pines.'

'Now that the leaves have mostly fallen, the landscape here looks more like the north.' The note of nostalgia in Van Gogh's comment to his brother at the beginning of the month was symptomatic of Vincent's discontent at being isolated in Saint-Rémy and of his growing urge to leave the place and return to friends and family in old familiar territory. He was feeling more robust and self-confident than at any time since arriving at the asylum back in May and was suffering from 'no more abominable nightmares' he told Theo.

This new sense of purpose was reflected in his view of his own work and of the direction he wanted it to take. He was determined to adopt 'a more virile style', by which he seemed to mean a more vigorous and muscular response to nature. He suspected this might not please Theo. 'I don't quite know if you'd like what I'm doing now,' he wrote in the same letter, 'but I find myself driven to seek style.' Theo disliked what he called 'exaggerations'. Vincent's response was restrained, urging his brother: 'Don't be too hasty to adopt a prejudice against it.' He was well aware that Theo would have much preferred his brother to be a gentle Impressionist, content to record his straightforward pleasure at the beauty of nature in the manner of Monet or Renoir.

At the same time Vincent's 'virile' approach to nature was quite opposed to the imaginary 'abstractions' now being practised by Paul

Gauguin and Emile Bernard. As a result he was beginning to feel caught between two opposing camps, while remaining determined to follow his own path. Hence November was becoming a combative and self-assertive month and from the correspondence flowing to and fro among all parties Vincent sometimes sounded like a prize-fighter taking on three opponents at once.

It was also a month during which he seemed to have banished many of his fears of the outside world. He had re-established himself as a

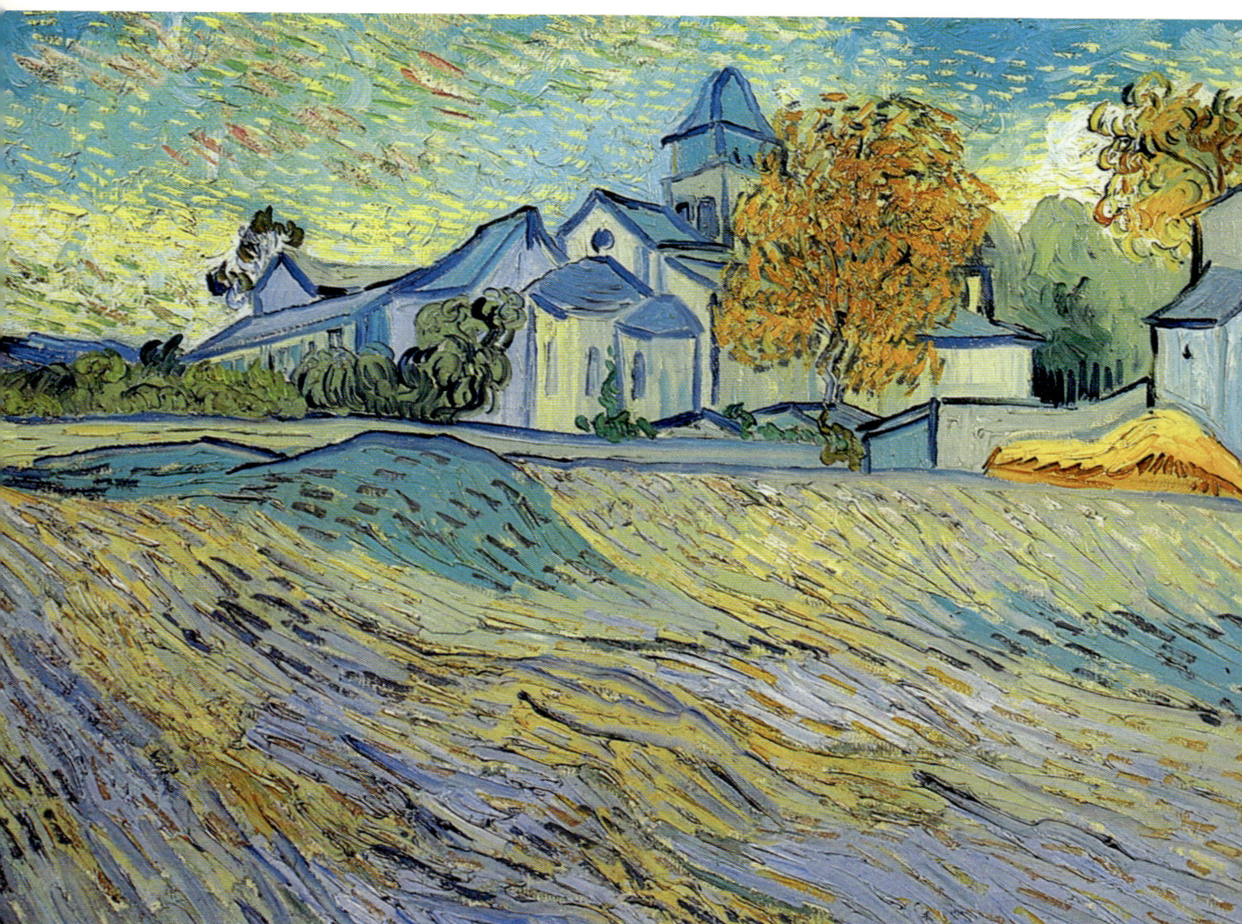

View of the Church of Saint-Paul-de-Mausoleo Oil on canvas, 44.5 x 60 cm
Private collection of Elizabeth Taylor, USA

painter who once more felt able to go out to explore the countryside and record the impact of landscape. There were even thoughts of his being cured, or at least capable of confronting the wider world without being reduced to a mental wreck.

His landscape paintings at this time possess a freshness and a direct response to the subject with no hint of the turbulence or exaggerated effects which characterised much of his work during the summer. *View of the Church of Saint-Paul-de-Mausoleo*, dashed off in bright pale colours in celebration of autumn colours and autumn light, is also his only known representation of the 12th century monastery church with its handsome Romanesque tower. With Calvinist blood in his veins Van Gogh was otherwise scrupulous in avoiding any pictorial reference to the asylum's monastic origins.

A further indication of a new self-confidence was his successful two-day return to Arles, where he saw the Rev. Salles and called on the Ginoux, paying the café-owners for continuing to store his furniture. He encountered no antagonism in the town, he explained to Theo. Far from it, everyone was most friendly; and he had taken himself off to buy a supply of paints just as he used to when he lived here. He had even contemplated taking the train to Paris, he later confessed to Theo on November 19th, and would have done so, he said, had he realised the ticket only cost twenty-five francs. However, commonsense had prevailed and it had seemed sensible to remain in Provence at least until the spring, by which time his health might be so improved that 'we may not have need of the doctor in Auvers or the Pissarros.' Meanwhile, he added cautiously, it remained to be seen if the visit might provoke another attack. He had high hopes that it would not.

Theo's letter of November 16th had included the welcome news that Vincent was formally being invited to send paintings for the next annual exhibition of contemporary art in Brussels mounted by the association Les XX. Theo had previously told his brother that this might be forthcoming; but now he enclosed the official letter from the Secretary, Octave Maus. 'The association requests you, Sir, kindly to inform us as soon as possible if you accept.' M. Maus announced himself as a Barrister at the Court of Appeal in Brussels; certainly this was not the kind of language Van Gogh was accustomed to hearing from art bodies. The invitation also included the names of other artists invited, principally Renoir, Lucien Pissarro (son of Camille), Sisley, Signac and Toulouse-Lautrec. Van Gogh was in distinguished company and had no hesitation in replying immediately, 'I accept with pleasure.' The space available, he was informed, was limited to four metres. Vincent was undeterred. 'Here is the list of paintings I am intending for you,' he told Maus in his reply. Then he listed six canvases, followed by the hopeful comment: 'I am perhaps exceeding the permitted four metres, yet as I believe that the six I have chosen would make a richly varied colour effect, maybe you could find a way of hanging them together.'

Four of the six canvases dated from his time in Arles the previous year and included two of the sunflowers series. Of the two paintings from Saint-Rémy, one was a modest study of ivy in the asylum garden, while the other he described as *Wheat Field with Rising Sun*. As we know from letters to Theo and others later in the month, this was a canvas Vincent was actually working on at the time he wrote to Maus and in all probability was intended to be a show-piece for the Brussels exhibition. It was also the last painting he did in the extended series on the enclosed field seen from his bedroom window. The previous canvas in the series, three weeks earlier, had been of the field in the rain, streaked, pale and sunless. Now the wheat sown just those few weeks before had sprouted in the bright winter sunlight and a richly-varied carpet of green is laid across the field which suddenly appears twice as large as before, stretching to the far boundary wall towards a golden sun rising above the purple Alpilles and enclosed within a vast halo.

It is a majestic finale to the series. Whether or not Van Gogh always intended it to be the last, it was a painting of which he was especially proud, judging by the lengthy descriptions he gave of it in several letters. It was also an eloquent demonstration of the new style which he had outlined to Theo early in the month – 'I feel myself greatly driven to seek a style (that is) more virile and more deliberate.' Instead of the heavy impasto he had been employing in many of the

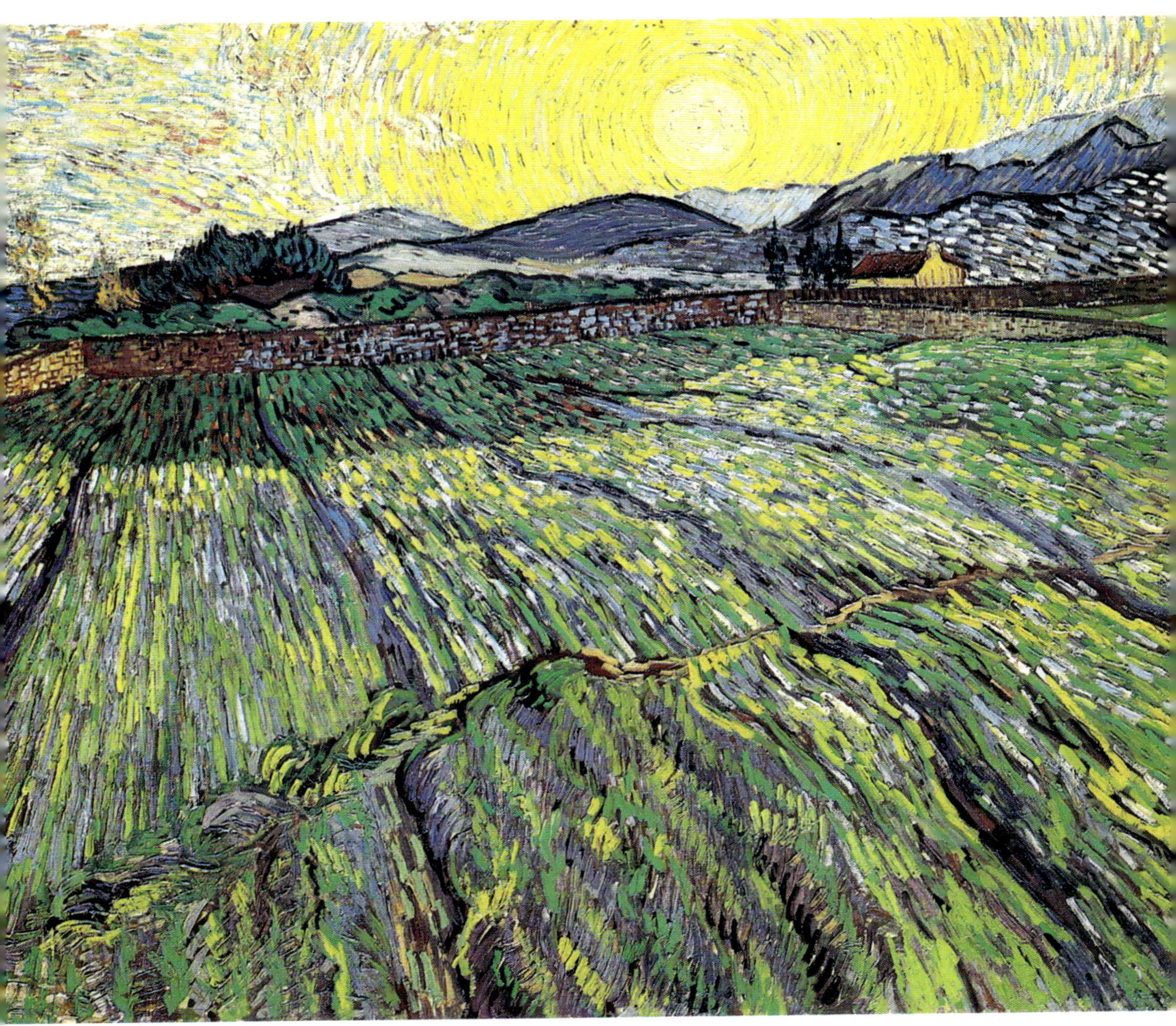

Wheat Field with Rising Sun Oil on canvas, 28 x 38.9 cm
Private collection

recent landscapes, the field of young wheat is described in thin parallel strokes of yellow and green, all tightly packed together and directed like a flowing tide towards the mountains and the rising sun. It is a painting combining vigour and a sense of movement with an air of tranquillity. It reflected the state of inner calm which Vincent had been searching for all these months and now, for the time being at least, may have achieved.

Van Gogh's love of working in series became uppermost during his time at Saint-Rémy. They become a pictorial calendar of the changing seasons as he worked his way through the year, recording his fascination for the cycle of nature. Perhaps the appeal to him of that cycle was its assuring predictability and coherence, qualities patently and painfully absent in Van Gogh's own life.

Theo's letter of November 16th enclosed a long letter for Van Gogh from Paul Gauguin in Brittany. This was in response to Vincent's earlier enquiry, asking for news of what Gauguin was doing and saying he would very much like to know. The reply took Vincent at his word, describing at some length his recent work, adding two coloured sketches to give him some idea of what he was writing about. The letter seems deliberately provocative, though politely so, as though Gauguin was continuing the kind of debate he used to have with Van Gogh in Arles which had finally driven Vincent towards his first breakdown. 'I have an unfortunate nature which is always hungry for things new,' he wrote. 'In the matter of abstract ideas I am drawn to seek symbolic form and colour…And here I have something that I think would suit you.' The painting he was referring to and which he illustrated in his letter with a sketch, was *Christ in the Garden of Olives*.

To Van Gogh this was like a red rag to a bull. Whether Gauguin's provocation was deliberate or merely a product of his 'unfortunate nature' is impossible to say. What is entirely clear is that nothing Gauguin could have offered Van Gogh to 'please' him could have displeased him more. Vincent's reply has not survived, but the substance of it was included in his letter to Theo written within twenty-four hours after hearing from Gauguin. He may not have wished to unload the full weight of his feelings on his brother, who was after all a friend of Gauguin besides being his dealer; and his comments to Theo were brief and curt. 'It is perhaps best to attack a subject with simplicity rather than seek abstractions,' he wrote, adding coolly, 'I am not an admirer of Gauguin's *Christ in the Garden of Olives*.'

Van Gogh's words point to the wide gulf that lay between his own and Gauguin's view of what it was appropriate for an artist to paint in the modern age and what constituted 'reality'. 'Personally,' he told his brother, 'I wouldn't try to paint *Christ in the Garden of Olives* except in relation to the olive-picking as it is still practised today.' If he employed the same argument to Gauguin the latter may well have felt that his friend had entirely missed the point of what religious painting was about and that olive-picking in Provence had nothing whatever to do with it. Gauguin's concern had been to present in a modern idiom the poignant moment of Christ's betrayal and imminent arrest on the evening before his crucifixion. Van Gogh's more pragmatic concern was with the unreality of Gauguin's olive trees. As he insisted to Theo, the realities of our own day should be the basis of art today.

But actually the principal target of Van Gogh's disapproval was not Gauguin, but Emile Bernard, an altogether lesser figure in Van Gogh's estimation, but one who had written to Vincent at the same time as Gauguin and sent six photographs of his recent work. Both the letter and the photographs are lost, but the paintings he wanted to show Van Gogh included a number of biblical subjects and probably Bernard's own version of *Christ in the Garden of Olives*. The photographs were quite enough to provoke a diatribe from Van Gogh. His lengthy reply of November 26th begins gently enough: 'My dear friend Bernard' but thereafter friendship is set aside in favour of an exercise in demolition amounting to a manifesto. Poor Bernard got it in the neck. The first victim was Bernard's *Adoration of the Shepherds*, prompting Vincent to wonder why the infant Jesus should be depicted lying in the middle of a road (a not unreasonable comment). 'Is that a sincere canvas?' he went on. 'No, you can do better…Please become more yourself again.' He then switched to Gauguin's *Christ in the Garden of Olives*, describing it as 'a nightmare'. It would be better, he suggested, to paint an actual olive orchard 'or a real garden'. (He had earlier remarked to Theo that he suspected Bernard had never even seen an olive tree.)

Van Gogh's judgments can sound simplistic and inappropriate, even hypocritical given that he had recently painted biblical subjects himself based on works by Rembrandt and Delacroix. But in his less virulent passages to both Bernard and his brother, Vincent made it evident that his deeper objection to Gauguin's and Bernard's biblical paintings was not so much their unreality as the absence of an appropriate historical sense – in costume, in setting or in mood. The paintings did not belong to their time, or to any time at all. To Bernard he singled out Corot as a modern artist who had also painted a *Garden of Olives*, which he had found 'sublime': 'in his work you feel the presence of Homer, Aeschylus and Sophocles.' The association feels pertinent. Corot's painting bore the authority of history; it was anchored in time and place (even if it was the wrong place). Van Gogh's own life being so often adrift it seems natural that he should have valued such an anchor and projected it on to works of art: hence his suspicion of abstractions which were free-falling, out of time and place and therefore disturbing.

At length Vincent's diatribe to Bernard softens into an account of his own plans and ambitions. He is now entirely against exaggerations, he explains, even rejecting *The Starry Night* with its abstraction of stars that are far too big – 'I've had enough of all that.' The rejection of 'exaggerations' represented an important change in Van Gogh's style. He had already advocated in his letter to Theo earlier in November a more direct and 'virile' approach to a subject, manifested in his *Wheat Field with Rising Sun*. What brought about this change of heart was never explained in his letters. It seems impossible not to associate his earlier turbulent paintings of the summer and their heavy impasto with the mental turbulence that brought about the attack which laid him low for much of July and August. By the same count his rejection of that style, now in late autumn, seems to relate directly to a new self-confidence and sense of purpose. Gone now are the days when he pronounced his intention to take long hikes in the mountains in search of fresh subjects, only to shut himself away in his studio making copy after copy of Millet prints. Now he was out and about once more, confident enough to take on Gauguin, Bernard and even Theo in argument, and starting to work on one of the themes closest to his heart. This was the series on the olive orchards around Saint-Rémy which is among the finest achievements of Van Gogh's Asylum Year.

Vincent's dislike of his friends' choice of the *Garden of Olives* as a theme is likely to have been intensified by the fact that he was now devoting his energies to painting real olive groves – 'seeking the different effects of a grey sky against the yellow soil,' he explained to Bernard. 'This interests me much more than so-called abstractions,' and he pressed home his conviction that art should be about the real and humble things of modern life – 'My ambition is now truly restricted to a few clods of soil, sprouting wheat, an olive orchard and cypress trees.' So much for biblical fantasies!

'I've been working in the olive groves from morning to evening during these bright cold days, but in very beautiful sunshine and the result is five canvases.' This was Vincent's announcement to Theo on November 26th and in the same letter he offers effusive thanks for the latest consignment of paints and for 'the excellent woollen waistcoat' which he had already found essential now he was working out of doors all day.

One reason the olive orchards exercised so powerful an appeal to him, he said, was because the olives, like the cypresses, 'have rarely been painted before'. Painting them was part of his desire to put Provence on the map for art-lovers in Paris and elsewhere. As he explained to Theo they also gave him a humble sense of being an honest craftsman rather than a spinner of fanciful tales (perhaps a dig at Emile Bernard). He preferred to work 'assiduously from nature…as if I was making shoes…Slow lengthy work is the only road to take.' The analogy with being a cobbler is far-fetched, yet it emphasises his requirement for paintings to be circumscribed by their subject. He needed to recognise the limits of what an artist can do, just as a shoemaker may enjoy a certain freedom in his work, but in the end it has to be a shoe. Hence, in this new mood of purism Vincent's disapproval of his own *The Starry Night* for painting stars 'too big'. Van Gogh's Calvinist inheritance seemed to be re-emerging.

'I've come to the very end of my supply of canvas,' he wrote to Theo on November 26th, 'and please send me ten metres more as soon as you can.' Then, he assured his brother, he intended to follow the olive orchard series with an 'attack on the cypresses and the mountains'.

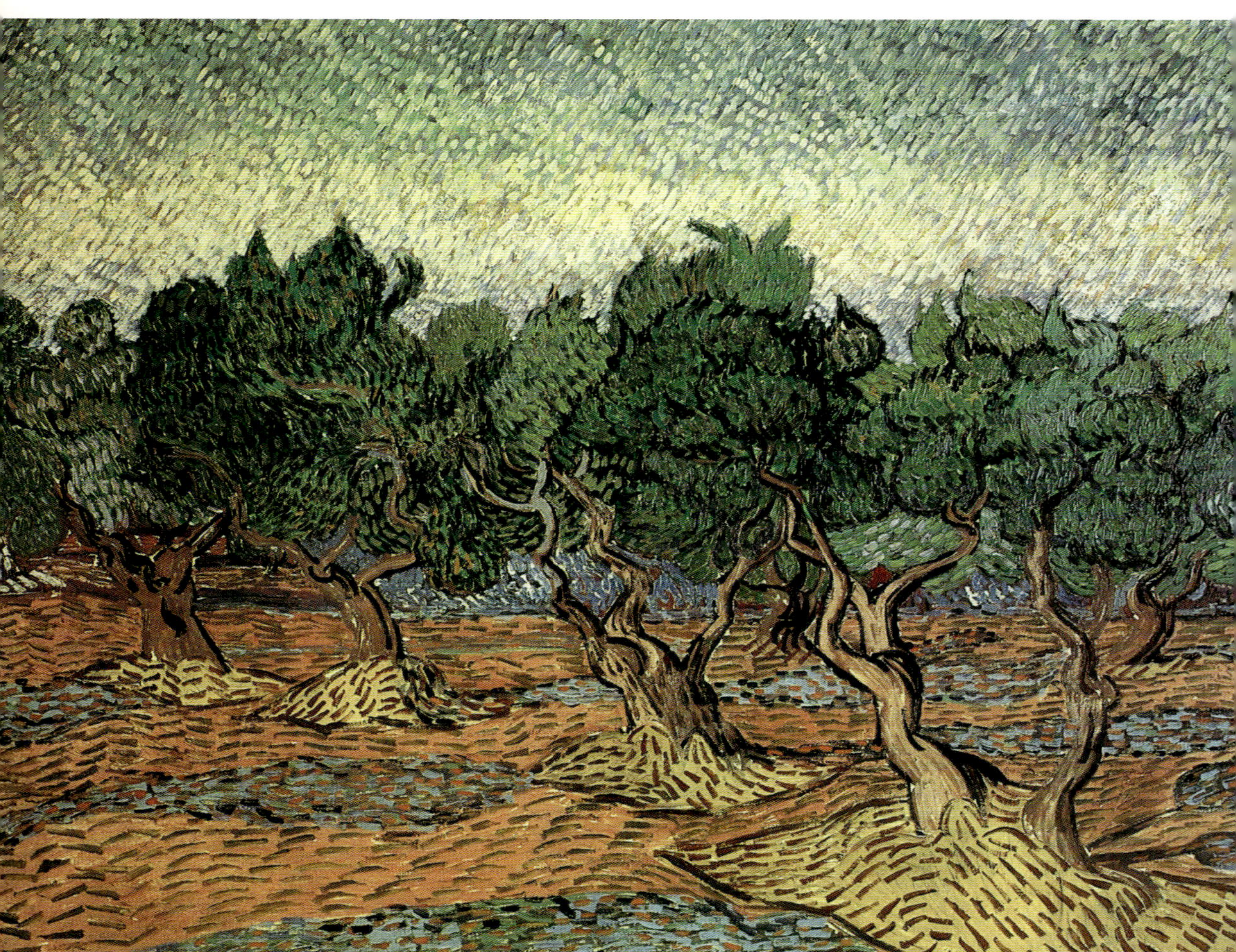

Olive Grove Oil on canvas, 73 x 92 cm
Van Gogh Museum, Amsterdam

This, he maintained, would bring his stay in Provence to a satisfactory end. Then, if he came to Paris his burning ambition would be to paint a bookshop 'such an essentially modern subject (which) would look very good between the olive grove and the wheat field.' What sounds a surprising ambition – to paint a bookshop – was perhaps nostalgia for the intellectual and social life of the Paris boulevards so far distant from the empty corridors of the asylum. Perhaps by hanging such a painting sandwiched between the olive orchards and the wheat field two recent strands of his vagrant life could be pulled together.

The olive orchard series consisted finally of at least ten canvases of which we know eight were sent to Theo. Three of these Van Gogh had painted during the summer months, including the turbulent one which he did in June, soon after being allowed outside the asylum for the first time and a few weeks before his mental breakdown. The more recent five which he announced to Theo were painted in succession from the end of October through November. Together they are a majestic achievement, each canvas in the sequence leading naturally to the next. All five were painted from more or less the same spot: as a result they form a continuous cycle of changing effects as if we are standing there watching the days pass one after the other and the light and colours alter miraculously before our eyes. In the first canvas a winter sun bathes the orchard in warm tones of ochre and turquoise. Next, the sun disappears and a dark veil has been drawn across the orchard. Then it is morning and now the villagers are out picking the olives from the trees. But by afternoon the labourers have departed and the trees are stripped of fruit. Finally the orchard stands bare as the sky darkens and dusk approaches.

Van Gogh's olive orchard series, like his wheat field paintings, was a product of his preoccupation with the changing seasons and how nature reflects the passage of time. It was a passion he shared with his older contemporary, Claude Monet, whom Vincent much admired. In this respect his olive tree paintings are natural companions to Monet's great series on Rouen Cathedral and on the haystacks. They also demonstrate Van Gogh's return to a more Impressionist style, being content to reflect the colours of nature without overlaying it with exaggerated effects as he often had during the summer. Now the olive trees are his 'very beautiful things to do…They are silver, then more blue, then greenish, bronze, becoming white against the soil,' as he described them to Theo. Nowhere in his entire body of work is such a repertoire of colour and atmosphere expressed in his treatment of a single subject.

Of the five paintings in the series, *Olive Trees with Yellow Sky and Sun* was probably the first and is the most distinctive. It is the only one with a clearly-defined setting against a background of the Alpilles; while above the mountains the translucent disc of the winter sun has turned the sky golden and burnished the soil bronze around the ancient trees. One piece of artistic license suggests that Vincent may actually have added the sun late, back in his studio: the long shadows cast by the olive trees across the ground fall in quite the wrong direction.

The question of artistic license raises itself again in the painting entitled *Olive Pickers*. This is the third canvas in the series and it shows two figures, a man and a woman, reaching up among the branches to gather the fruit and drop them in the wicker basket at the woman's feet. Little more than a week earlier Van Gogh had described to his brother 'Recently I saw women picking and gathering the olives, but as I had no chance of obtaining a model, I did nothing about it.' So, where did these two figures suddenly come from? The painting *Olive Pickers* turns out to be an almost exact replica of its predecessor in the series entitled simply *Olive Orchard*, except that hot colours have now been replaced by cool: otherwise even the brushstrokes and undefined shapes in the background are identical. Vincent later described this second canvas to Theo as 'a variant with figures'. Either he made this version back in his studio, adding the figures from memory, or, more likely, at some time after his statement to Theo he went out to observe and sketch the two figures as they were picking the olives and deliberately made his second version as a vehicle in which to place them.

What appears to be true is that one outcome of Vincent's new self-confidence was his ability to overcome his terror of confronting the

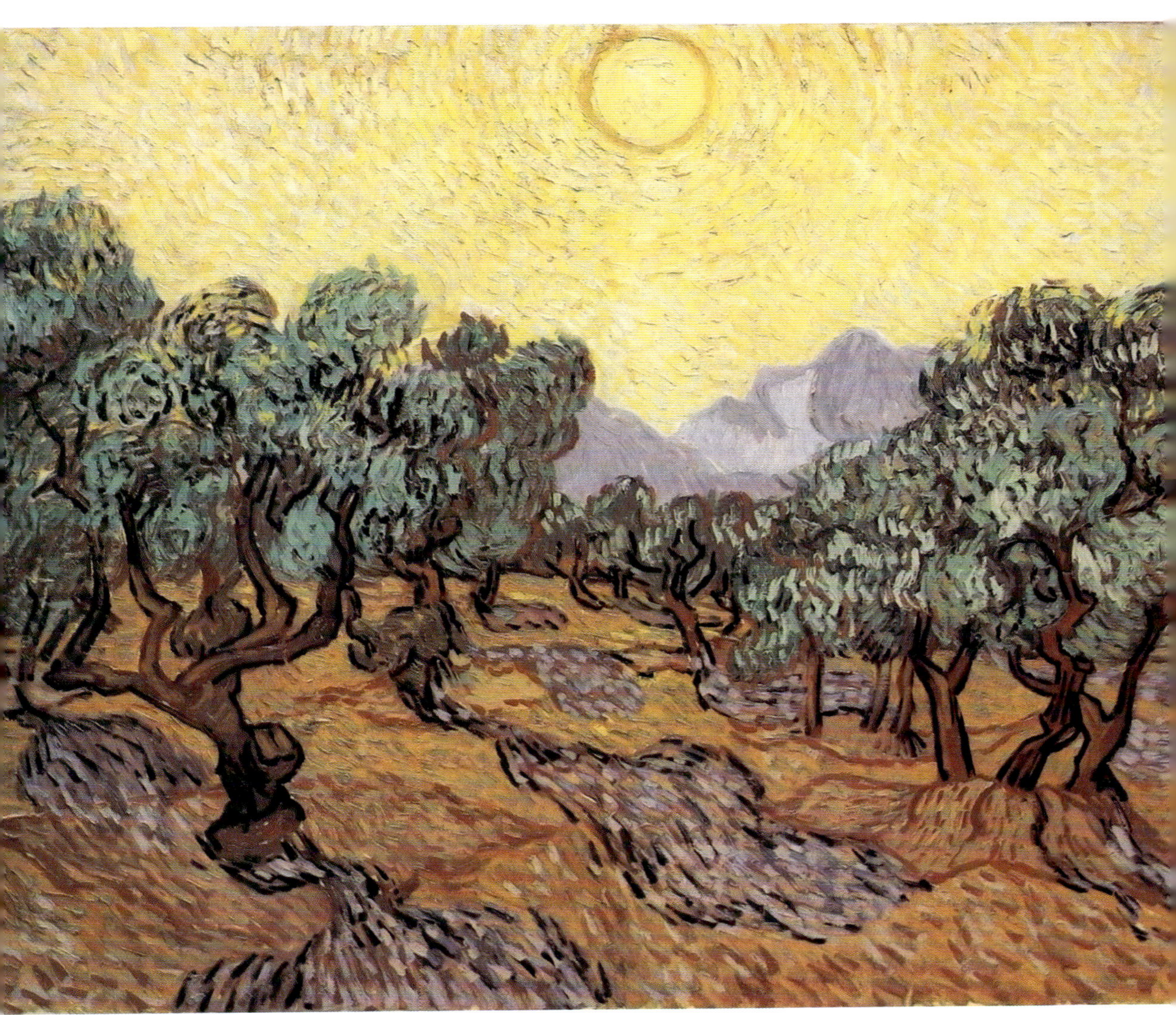

Olive Trees with Yellow Sky and Sun Oil on canvas, 73.6 x 92.7 cm
Minneapolis Institute of Arts

day-to-day working world, which for months had made him virtually a hermit. Earlier in the month he had found it possible, enjoyable even, to return to Arles, mixing with ordinary people and making purchases in shops. Now, instead of shutting himself away to make second-hand versions of Millet's peasants tilling the land, he had been keen to observe and draw labourers harvesting the olive crop. Very soon he would be casting aside memories of his disastrous visit to the village of Saint-Rémy early in the summer and be able to set up his easel beside the public highway to paint the road-menders laying blocks of stone along the busy main street.

Van Gogh, it seemed, had come back to earth.

A further ten metres of canvas arrived from Theo at the beginning of the month. In turn Van Gogh posted his brother three packages of recent paintings. These represented merely a proportion of his prolific output in November. Only small paintings were included as the larger canvases were still pinned up around his studio showing little sign of drying out in the damp winter weather in an unheated room. Vincent listed the ones he had posted. They included several of the olive orchard series, a self-portrait and his recent version of the artist's bedroom in Arles. Several of these, he did not specify which, were intended as gifts for his mother and sister Wil in Holland. He wrote long letters to both of them a few days later.

The cold weather had not deterred him. Whereas for much of the summer his fears and anxieties had kept him indoors, in December he felt able to venture out and brave the elements. Remarkably he even took himself off to Saint-Rémy itself, the village a short distance from the asylum; whether alone or accompanied by an attendant is unclear. No doubt mindful of his disastrous visit in the spring he described the occasion proudly to Theo: 'The most recent study I've done is a view of the village street with people working under enormous plane trees repairing the pavements.' The day-to-day working world which six months earlier had reduced him to a state of panic now drew him to set up his easel by the roadside and record what he saw: 'there are piles of stones and colossal tree trunks – their foliage yellow, and here and there the glimpse of a house and little figures.'

During his entire year in Saint-Rémy this was his only study of the village itself and, as was his practice, he made two versions, the first done in some haste on the site, the second painted in the studio at his leisure, 'more finished' as he explained to Theo. Unique though it is

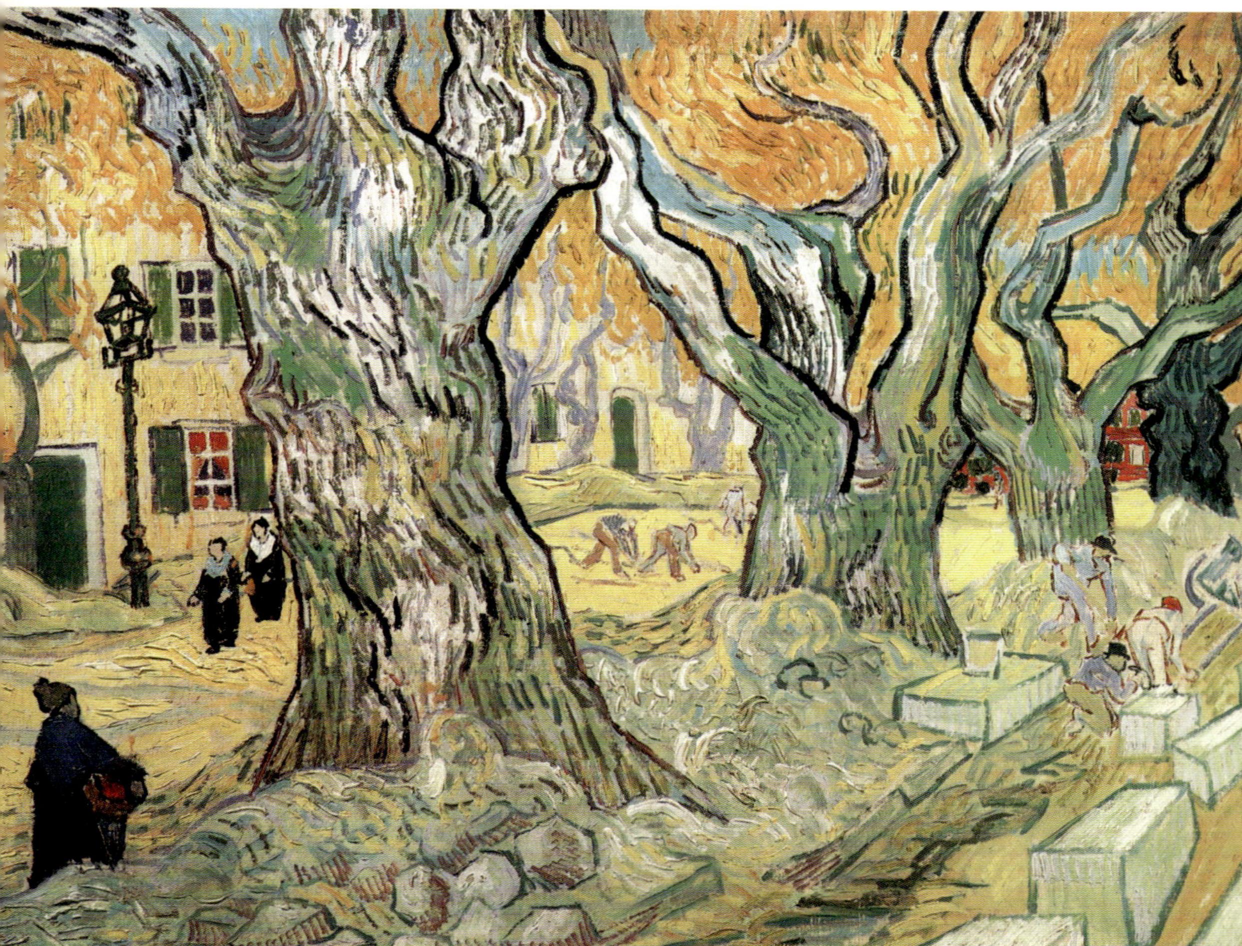

The Road Menders Oil on canvas, 71 x 93 cm
Phillips Collection, Washington D.C.

as a subject it is easy to see what attracted him about the theme: the massive knotted trunks of the plane trees echo the gnarled shapes of the olive trees he was painting at this time, while the roughly-hewn stones piled up beneath them are reminiscent of the rock shapes that fascinated him in the ancient quarries close to the asylum and in the jagged peaks of the Alpilles. Besides, with its canopy of yellow foliage, the painting of the road-menders echoes another of his preoccupations – his love of 'autumnal effects'. Following his description of the painting Vincent pointed out that he had abandoned the use of heavy impasto, adding (no doubt to his brother's relief) that he was now using less paint as a result.

Theo's reply on December 8th was his first letter to Vincent for three weeks and as usual Theo was keen to bring his isolated brother up to date with recent events in the Paris art world. The latest batch of his paintings had arrived safely. Theo's enthusiasm was somewhat muted – many of them had 'less dazzling tones than usual,' he commented, adding cryptically that they possessed 'a lot of atmosphere'. It had become a feature of their relationship that in spite of Theo's unwavering support and good will Vincent rarely produced work that his brother enjoyed unreservedly. His judgment must inevitably have been influenced by hard commercial reality. As a junior employee of the art dealers Goupil et Cie he was spending part of each month's salary on supporting his brother in a mental asylum, but his work had yet to bring him a single sale. He may be excused for wishing Vincent would just once in a while paint something the well-to-do clients of Goupil et Cie might actually want. He must have grown sick of watching customers who were accustomed to acquiring the titillating nudes of Bouguereau and the exotic fantasies of Gérome at the Paris Salon gazing with distaste at Van Gogh's *Sunflowers*.

After his cool reception of Van Gogh's latest batch of paintings Theo struck a more enthusiastic note. 'Recently Tanguy has been showing a lot of your paintings and tells me he has hopes of selling the one of the stone bench with ivy.' Silence tells us that nothing came of the sale but the hint of optimism was an indication that among his

Parisian clients a few were beginning to look more than once at what this unconventional Dutchman was producing in the depths of rustic Provence. There was also another young critic by the name of Aurier who had come to the gallery 'and he's very interested in what you are doing.' Altogether there were thin rays of hope that something would soon be happening and that the tide might be turning. Theo's letter continued with an assurance to his brother that 'one day there will indeed be better times for you and we'll see one another more often.' Meanwhile he was writing to Dr Peyron requesting a fire be made available for Vincent in his studio, for which he offered to pay.

Van Gogh responded immediately to the new mood of optimism. He straightaway wrote to his mother and sister in Holland to bring them up-to-date with developments. He assured his mother that he felt 'stronger', 'healthier' and 'calmer' than before, but that he imagined he would spend most of next year here in Saint-Rémy. This would not be for health reasons but because his work would benefit. 'The region has hardly been painted at all,' he explained, most artists preferring to travel on down to the Riviera. Vincent's recurring theme of wanting to open Parisian eyes to the beauty of Provence was once again dominating his thoughts about his immediate future, overriding for the moment his nostalgia for the north and a determination to move there as soon as the winter was over.

To his sister Van Gogh was more confidential, as he invariably was with Wil. 'I have twelve large canvasses on the go', he explained. These included no fewer than six of the olive orchards, which suggests he had continued with his favourite series well after the original five he had announced to Theo in November. He also confessed to his sister that 'some of my paintings, when I compare them to others, do definitely bear the look of a sick man having painted them. But I assure you I didn't do it that way on purpose.' Vincent failed to specify which paintings he now judged to have been painted by 'a sick man', though from comments he made elsewhere it seems likely that he had in mind those wilder landscapes with exaggerated images, *The Starry Night* among them.

Vincent then described to her the canvas he was working on at the moment, a study of 'tall weather-beaten pines against a red evening sky'. *Pine Trees with Setting Sun* is the very last of Van Gogh's studies of pine trees in autumn and the most dramatic of them, the dark skeletal trees set against an orange sunset. There follows a rare moment when, acting on a momentary impulse, he gives us a snapshot of himself at work. There is a break in the letter to Wil, then he continues: 'while writing to you I don't know what came into my head.' But as he looked at the picture he was describing to his sister he knew he was not satisfied with it. 'So I took a colour that was there on my palette, a dull dirty white which you get by mixing white, green and a little carmine – and I then spread this greenish colour right across the sky; and hey presto, from a distance it softens the colours and yet you'd think you would have ruined the painting.' Instead the effect was magical. Later, recounting this working process to Theo, he described these ghostlike trees which he had achieved, silver and dark against the sunset, as producing a look of 'beautiful black lace', which indeed it has.

In mid-December Paul Gauguin, in Brittany, eventually responded to Van Gogh's diatribe against religious painting in a modern style. Vincent confessed to his brother that he found Gauguin's argument muddled and unconvincing. The gist of it was that in a work of the imagination a religious painting could be 'mannered' and 'natural' at the same time, Gauguin maintained; and the two could not be separated. The tone of Gauguin's letter was altogether more gentle and open-minded that Vincent's outburst, but it would have been a reminder to Van Gogh of the ferocious arguments that had broken out between them in Arles, bringing about Vincent's first breakdown. It was just as well the two artists were now separated by several hundred miles, although Van Gogh in his naïvete and loneliness would continue to suggest to Theo that he and Gauguin might once again work together, even if only to be able to share expenses.

Van Gogh's *Wheat Field with Rising Sun* was finally dry enough to be sent to Theo to be framed by Tanguy and forwarded to Brussels

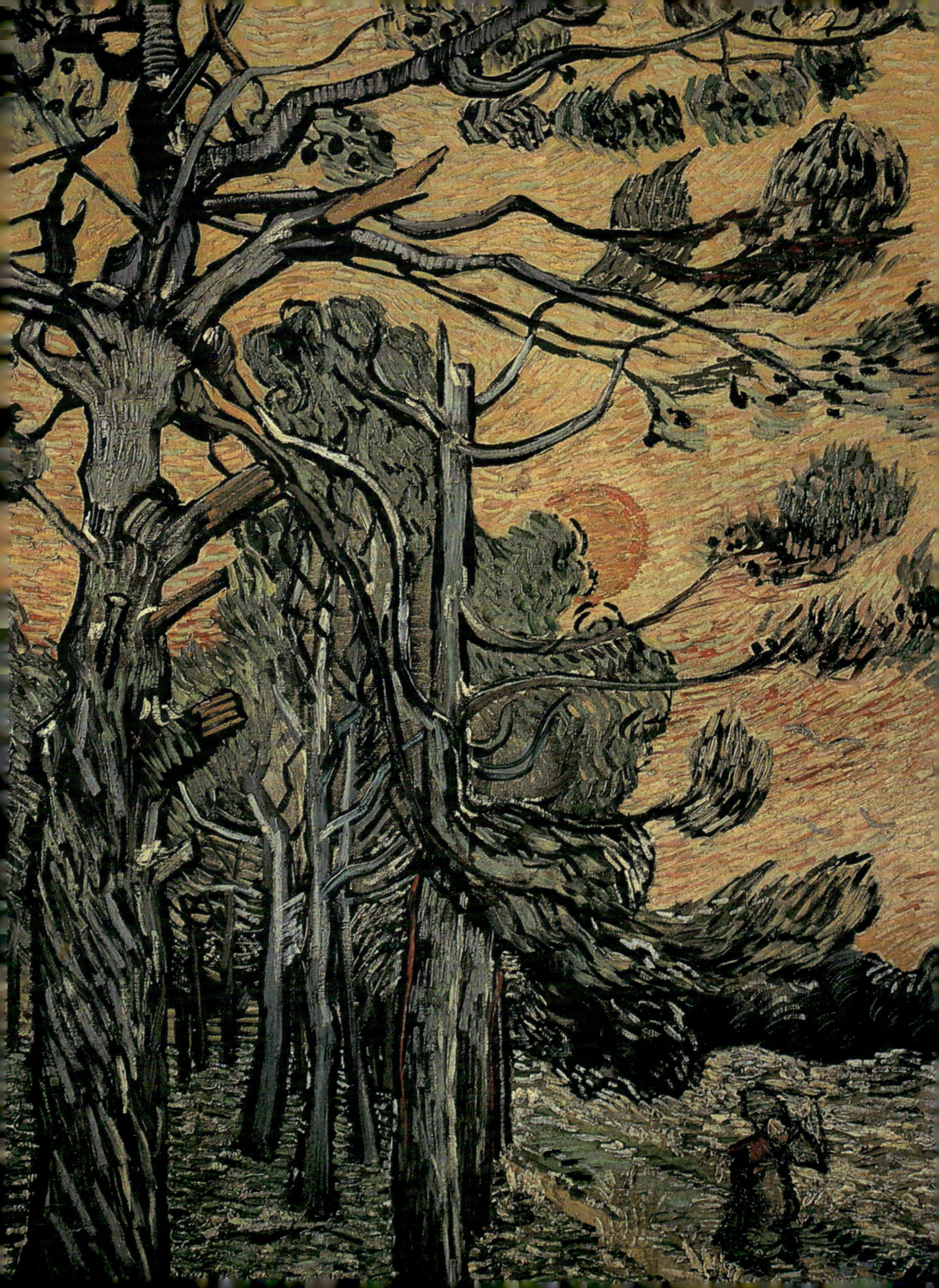

for inclusion in next month's exhibition of Les XX. It was a canvas Vincent had painted specially as his showpiece. A few days later, on December 19th, he wrote to Theo in an ebullient mood, picking up on his brother's prognosis that one day better times would come for him. On the contrary, he assured Theo, 'I'd say that these better days have already begun for me.' And he offered as proof 'when I glimpse the possibility of completing my work so that I have a series of Provençal studies which are done with real feeling and will stand the test of time – that is what I most sincerely hope for.' He went on to express much the same view of his present position as he had given to his sister Wil, insisting that it was in the best interests of his work that he should remain at Saint-Rémy for much of next year. He stated his immediate ambition: 'I have a strong desire to do more on the cypresses and on the Alpilles', which would entail 'going for very long walks in different directions. I've already noticed many subjects and good places for when the fine days return.'

He even suggested to Theo that he would like to paint again in Arles in springtime, just as nearly two years ago he had arrived in the south for the first time at the very moment when he was able to capture the almond blossom.

Vincent also explained at some length to his brother why he no longer applied paint thickly in impasto. It was a decision he had made 'as a result of leading a calm life of seclusion which suits me well and makes me feel better. Basically,' he added, 'I'm not as violent as that and I feel more myself in a state of calm.' It is a revealing statement. The search for calm is a recurring cry throughout Van Gogh's correspondence. It was more often a mirage than a reality. He longed to feel calm when he painted, rather than violent and here he acknowledged the direct connection between his style of painting and his state of mind. Temperament and style were inseparable. It is often claimed by scholars that Van Gogh's 'exaggerations' and deviations from a straightforward response to nature were due to a desire to emulate Gauguin's free-wheeling treatment of the subjects he painted. Yet Van Gogh's admiration for Gauguin was invariably for the latter's work that

Pine Trees with Setting Sun Oil on canvas, 44.5 x 60 cm
Kröller-Muller Museum, Otterlo

was closest to nature, not his 'abstractions' and certainly not for his free interpretations of biblical themes, which Vincent abhorred. Van Gogh's own style during his year in Saint-Rémy varied widely between the dramatically turbulent (as in *The Starry Night* and *Entrance to a Quarry*) and the lyrical naturalism of his wheat field studies and the olive orchard series. There can be no doubt which, in retrospect, he preferred.

Theo continued to brief his brother on events in Paris, assuring him that Tanguy was now framing all Vincent's paintings for Les XX and they would be despatched to Brussels by the beginning of January. Meanwhile Père Tanguy had been exhibiting two of Vincent's sunflower paintings in his shop. They certainly cheered the place up, Theo added: 'Tanguy himself loves them a great deal, but he can't sell any.' It is the same old story. Meanwhile Jo's baby, he reminded Vincent, was due early next month and their sister Wil was arriving to help out on January 2nd. 'I hope you'll paint the little one's portrait in the spring,' Theo added.

The subject of Gauguin came up again in the letter. Theo, as his dealer, was becoming exasperated with him: 'he seems incapable of working in the same style from one day to the next.' As a result Theo had been 'unable to sell a single thing of his…He is even less saleable than he was last year.' In the middle of the long letter Theo also expressed his concern for Gauguin. One of his children by his estranged Danish wife had fallen from a window in their Copenhagen home and been picked up 'almost dead', though it was now believed the child might recover.

On December 23rd Van Gogh wrote to both his mother and his sister with the same thought uppermost in his mind: today was the anniversary of his first mental attack on that gruesome evening in Arles exactly a year ago when he cut off part of his left ear after a furious argument with Paul Gauguin.

'When I was first taken ill,' he told his mother, 'I couldn't possibly accept that I needed to go into an asylum. Now I admit that I should have been treated earlier.' Then he slipped into his customary refrain:

'So now I go on with relative calm and do my best.' To his sister he was more candid, assuring her that although he did feel calm, 'from time to time I feel frightened that it may return.'

To both of them he was keen to describe what he had been painting recently. To his sister he explained he had sent her as a gift a new study of women picking olives, which he hoped she will enjoy. To his mother he described what he was painting right now: 'At present I am working on a painting of a path that runs through the mountains, with a narrow stream which forces its way between the boulders.' He particularly loved the variety of colours in the ravine: 'the rocks are solid lilac-grey and pink, with shrubs here and there, box and a kind of broom, which have all sorts of colours in them, green, yellow, red, brown, all the tones of autumn.'

The canvas he was describing, *The Ravine*, could hardly be more different from the gentle scene in *Women Picking Olives* which he had just completed as a gift for his mother and sister. The subject was the narrowing gorge at the head of the valley where the Graeco-Roman city of Glanum once stood (still unexcavated). Vincent had painted the ravine before, with its rushing torrent and dramatic rock-shapes. Stylistically this version belongs to the studies of mountains and rocks which he had painted in July. The swirling brushstrokes and heavy outlines in black are clearly designed to emphasise the turbulence and instability of nature, far removed from the tranquil scene of women working peacefully in the olive groves.

This sudden return to an earlier, turbulent style of landscape painting seems unexpected and would be more puzzling if there was no personal context in which to place it. As it is, the day after describing the painting in some detail to his mother, Van Gogh suffered another mental attack, his second in Saint-Rémy and third in all. As with his last breakdown there followed a silence while he felt unable to communicate, though this time the attack passed quickly and the hiatus lasted barely a week. On the last day of the year Vincent wrote to Theo surprisingly coolly, 'Monsieur Peyron must have written to you that my mind has once more become very disturbed.' Peyron had indeed written to Theo explaining that Van Gogh had again suffered an attack and had tried to poison himself by swallowing his paints, as he had done back in July. Vincent's own explanation to his brother was straightforward and matter-of-fact: 'I'd been working perfectly calmly on my canvases…until quite suddenly confusion took hold of me once more.'

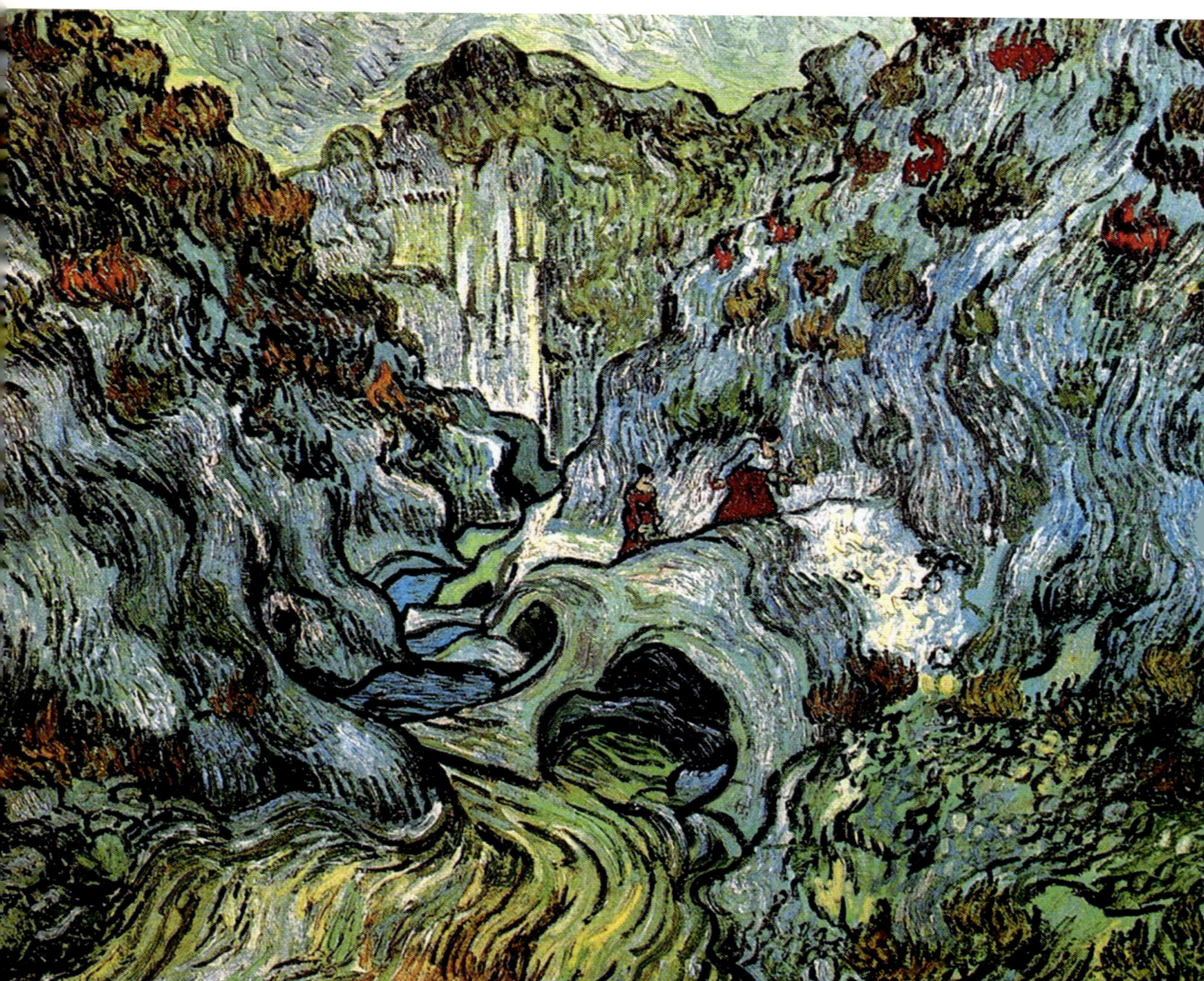

The Ravine of the Peyroulets Oil on canvas, 44.5 x 60 cm
Kröller-Muller Museum, Otterlo

Unlike his previous two attacks this one was not only brief, it seems to have left him remarkably level-headed and with none of the phobias and nightmares that attended his earlier breakdowns, as though the attack had cleared the air like a sudden storm. He had no choice now, he admitted to Theo, but to accept that these attacks would now recur: they were part of his life. Yet he also felt convinced as a result that being cooped up in the asylum with no company except fellow inmates was contributing to his condition and he now planned to 'make a clean break with this place', particularly if Dr Peyron continued not to allow him to paint. His paints had once again been taken from him. All he was permitted to do was to draw and gaze about. He explained to his brother that when he was ill he had got up one night to gaze at the quiet countryside beyond the asylum wall. Snow was falling across the winter fields and the mountains. 'Never, never has nature appeared so touching and sensitive to me,' he assured Theo. Now he felt recovered, he added, and could hardly wait to get back to work. That was what he needed most.

The breakdown just before Christmas had long been anticipated by Van Gogh. He predicted it so often in his letters that he may even have willed it to happen. It can be no coincidence that it occurred on the anniversary of his first attack. This was a landmark foremost in his mind, as he had told both his mother and sister. The new breakdown also repeated the pattern of self-destruction. Having mutilated himself during the first attack in Arles, he then tried to poison himself by swallowing his own paint in July and now he did exactly the same in December. Dr Peyron believed (correctly as it turned out) that Vincent was a prime candidate for suicide.

The landscape Van Gogh was painting just before this latest breakdown bears strong affinities, both of subject-matter and style, to the canvas he was painting just before his July attack. Both were studies of rocks and were described in agitated swirling brushstrokes as though nature was in the grip of an earthquake. In this December painting, *The Ravine of the Peyroulets*, it is made to look as though the mountains on either side are about to crash into the valley below where a torrent is thrusting its way between the rocks as if trying to escape before everything collapses and chaos reigns. There are tiny human figures in the ravine, but they are scarcely more than blobs, barely distinguishable in their red clothing from the red shrubs scattered across the mountainside. Unlike Van Gogh's reaper, his ploughman or his labourers copied from Millet, these figures are mere fragments of the landscape. The painting suggests that when the power of nature takes over, humanity is reduced to shadowy objects without features or substance; a total negation of self and self-empowerment.

Whether *The Ravine* prefigures Van Gogh's state of mind as he approached the anniversary of his first mental breakdown in Arles can only be a matter of speculation. Nonetheless it is tempting to see the insignificance of those little red figures engulfed by the terrible majesty of nature as a parable of the artist's own fearful journey in the world, in which he too was about to be crushed by forces greater than human powers could withstand.

Vincent himself expressed an understanding of the relationship between his painting and his state of mind, just as he had to his sister a short while before. He concludes his long letter to Theo with a reprimand to himself about his attack: 'this may be a lesson for me to work more straightforwardly without so many preoccupations with things that trouble my consciousness.'

And so Van Gogh's momentous year, 1889, ended on note of guarded optimism.

Vincent celebrated the New Year by sending his brother a consignment of eleven large canvases, representing the cream of his autumn output. It was the sixth batch of paintings he had despatched to Theo since his arrival at Saint-Rémy eight months earlier, comprising a total of fifty-nine canvases. It was still only a proportion of his work during this period, the remainder being held back until his final departure, whenever that might be. Altogether it amounted to a formidable cargo for Theo to deal with, all of it virtually unsaleable at that time. It is hardly surprising that he had acquired extra space adjacent to Père Tanguy's shop in order to store it.

Compared to his time at Saint-Rémy, Vincent had spent almost twice as long in Arles, yet had sent only three batches of paintings to Paris during that period: this suggests that a powerful sense of urgency had gripped Van Gogh as a result of his first breakdown in December 1888. At Saint-Rémy, isolation, loneliness and frustration no doubt played their part, contributing to a pent-up state of fury which governed much of the artist's life at the asylum and which burst out from time to time, entirely overtaking him. This was in sharp contrast to the state of 'calm' which he repeatedly claimed to have achieved in correspondence to Theo, his mother and sister. It seems that letter-writing was what calmed him; daily life did not.

The New Year consignment included a version of *The Ravine*, the landscape Vincent had painted just before his recent breakdown and which he now described to Theo as 'done on a day the mistral was blowing. I had wedged my easel with large rocks.' The finished version, he explained, was not yet dry. 'It's in a more taut style of drawing and contains a great deal of suppressed passion and more colour.' This passage in the letter is particularly revealing. There was no mention of a howling mistral when he first described the painting to his mother ten days earlier. What seems now to have reminded him was that a powerful mistral had also been blowing when he was painting out of doors in July just before his first breakdown. In other words both breakdowns, in July and December, had occurred immediately after he had been working on a landscape in the midst of a roaring gale, the strain of which reveals itself in the turbulent style of both the paintings he was working on, as well as precipitating the breakdowns that followed.

Women Picking Olives, *The Road Menders* and the study of *The Wheat Field in the Rain* were among the other canvases in the New Year consignment. Van Gogh felt particularly proud of them, instructing Theo not to look at them properly until Tanguy had stretched them and framed them all in white, which he insisted would set off the colours most effectively.

Vincent's proud announcement that the best of his autumn canvases were now on their way to Paris unfortunately crossed with Theo's response to the news from Dr Peyron of his brother's breakdown on Christmas Eve. Theo was not aware that Vincent had recovered a great deal more rapidly than the last time, only that his brother had tried to poison himself by eating his paints. He responded anxiously with the suggestion that it would be best if Vincent put his paints aside for a while and concentrated on making drawings. Van Gogh replied instantly and with some indignation: 'I've never worked more calmly than in my latest canvases.' He repeated his familiar prescription for recovery, that he should continue working as if nothing at all had happened. In fact, he went on, far from putting his paints aside he would soon have the opportunity to 'work outside once the weather improved'. It was his burning ambition before he left the south, he insisted, 'to give a true impression of Provence,' and in order to do this 'it is essential to do more paintings of cypresses and the mountains.' Then he added: 'Work makes me retain a little presence of mind.'

In the same New Year's spirit, Van Gogh sent two canvases to his devoted friend Roulin, the Arles postman now living in Marseille. By way of demonstrating that he could be trusted to work with paints without endangering his health, he undertook to make the portrait of a boy employed at the asylum, which he proudly presented to his mother as a gift. Now recovered from his breakdown, Van Gogh told his brother he was keen to return to Arles 'just once more', partly 'to see friends, which always cheers me up', but also to test whether he would feel capable of undertaking the overnight train journey to Paris, because 'my stay here cannot be prolonged indefinitely.'

As usual the return of buoyancy induced restlessness. Frustrated by the January weather he felt unable to go out and paint the many subjects he had stored in his head from earlier expeditions. There were small compensations: a day of winter sunshine drew him out on a long walk, as he told his sister; and he was delighted to notice wild flowers, even if only dandelions, appearing in the meadows. A further pleasure came in the form of another letter from Theo telling him the large consignment of paintings had arrived safely, 'and it's most remarkable.' He particularly liked *The Road Menders*, noting with pleasure that Vincent has ceased painting in thick impasto. He also singled out 'a superb pen drawing of a fountain in a garden' which Vincent had included in the batch. This was one of a group of drawings he had done of the asylum garden soon after his arrival.

Theo's plea that Vincent should sometimes set aside his painting materials and concentrate on drawing was not only as a precaution against his brother poisoning himself again, it was also out of profound admiration for the drawings Vincent repeatedly sent him. The inclusion of the drawing of the garden fountain from so many months ago may have been Vincent's recognition of this admiration. Being from Holland both men inherited the Dutch tradition, dating from

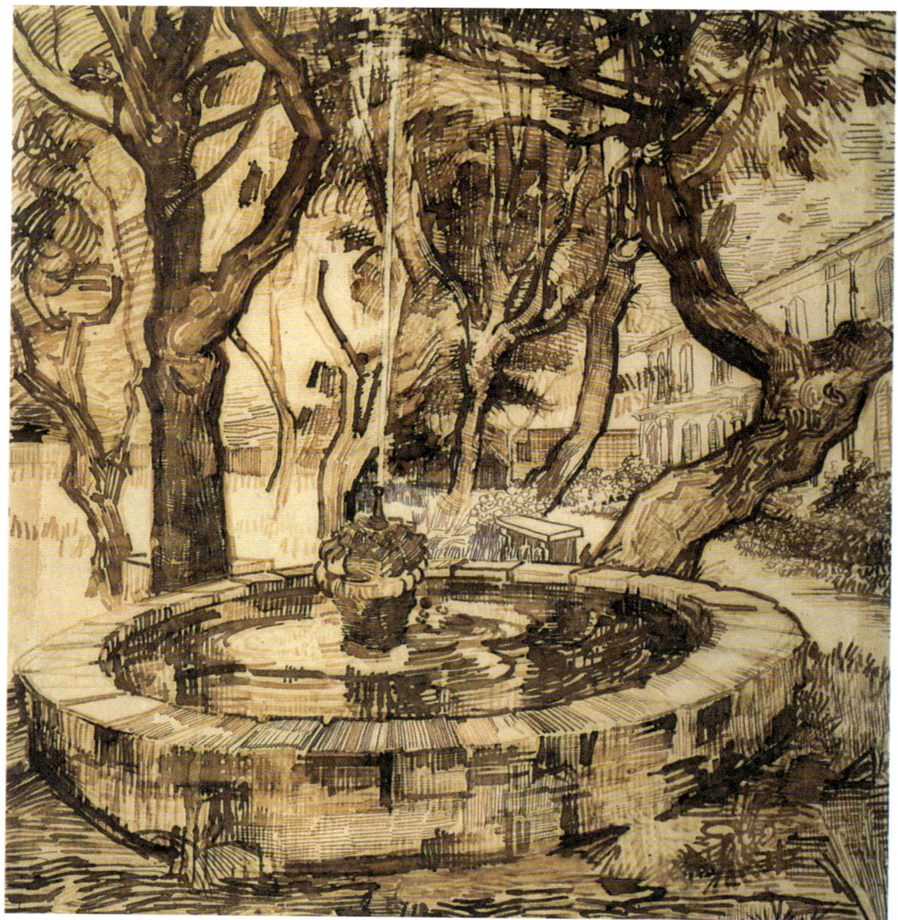

Fountain in the Garden of the Asylum Black chalk, reed pen and brown ink on paper, 49.8 x 46.3 cm, Van Gogh Museum, Amsterdam

before Rembrandt, of treating drawings as complete works of art in themselves and not merely preparatory sketches for a painting. Several of Van Gogh's drawings from his Asylum Year belong in this category, including the fountain drawing which Theo so admired, as well as one of the finest of all the drawings from St-Rémy, the pen-and-ink version of *Wheat fields with Rising Sun*. This is a perfect demonstration of Van Gogh's search for a graphic language capable of describing the feel of a landscape as distinct from being a painstaking attempt to copy every detail in a way that would inevitably lose the essence of it.

In this way he developed a kind of pictorial shorthand – a distinctive vocabulary of dots, strokes and swirls which bear little or no resemblance to anything in nature, yet they manage perfectly to convey the essential form, texture and character of what he is describing. It may

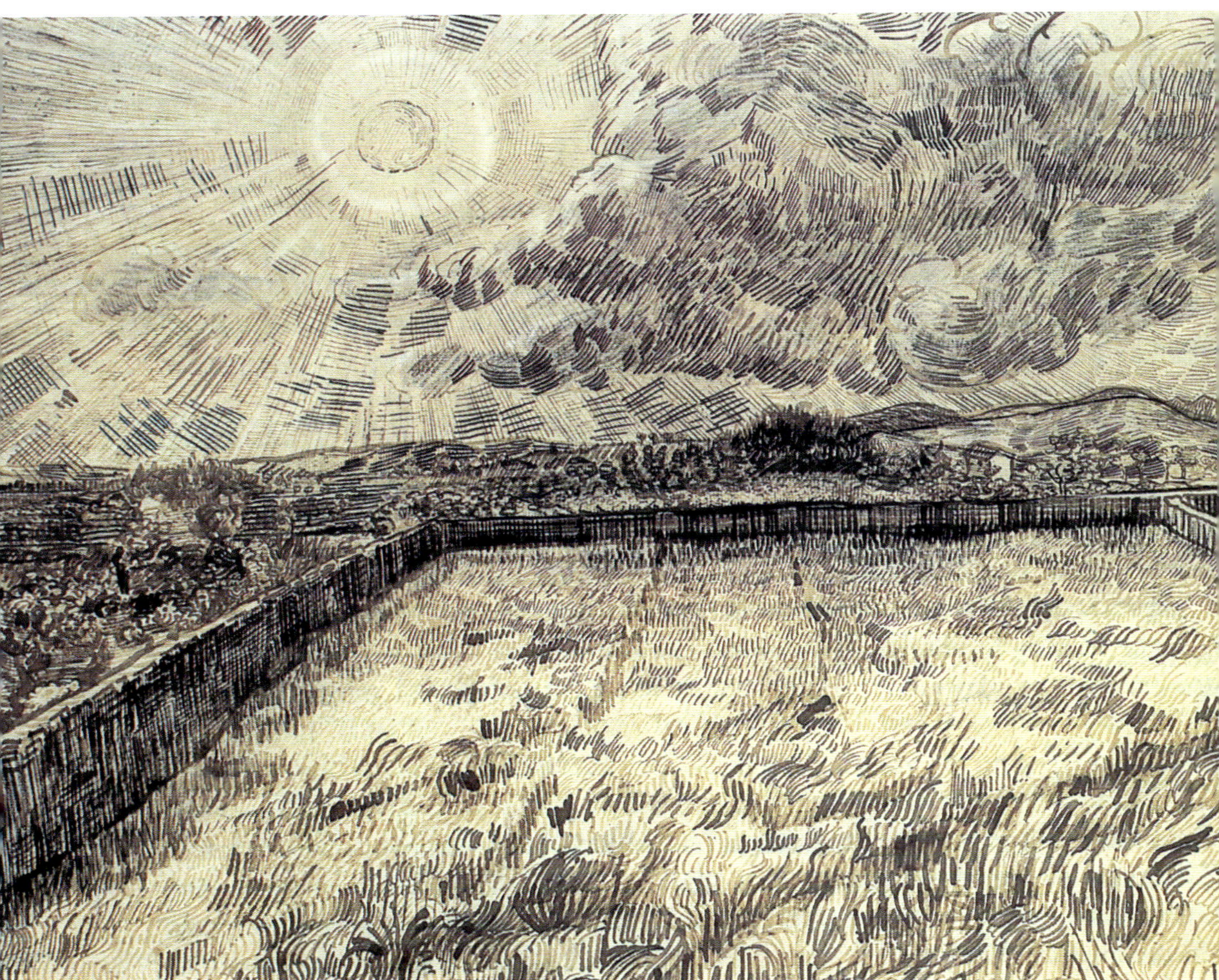

Wheat Field with Sun and Clouds Black chalk, reed pen and brown ink, heightened with white chalk, on Ingres paper, 47.5 x 56 cm, Kröller-Muller Museum, Otterlo

be a cornfield, a stony path, shrubs, grasses, a misty sky, or the mysterious aura of the sun. *Wheat Field with Rising Sun* is like a tapestry woven of little threads each of which is no more than a stroke of his favourite reed-pen. There can be no more eloquent demonstration of Van Gogh's achievement as one of the most imaginative draughtsmen of modern times.

Drawing was the foundation of his art. It was how he recorded his initial response to whatever caught his eye, above all in landscape and nature in general. When it came to expressing that response in paint, frequently his brushstrokes are precisely those of his reed-pen, only in colour. The vocabulary of swirling brushstrokes describing the sky in *The Starry Night*, for example, is more or less faithfully repeated in the dramatic rendering of the sun's aura in the wheat field drawing, though the subject and the mood of the two works are quite different.

Van Gogh's restlessness was further aroused by a discussion with one of the warders about an alternative asylum nearby. 'I need to talk to you once more about what I think we could do to reduce costs,' he wrote to Theo on January 13th. The establishment was near Avignon and it was cheaper than Saint-Rémy largely because the patients were required to work on the asylum's farm, so helping to make the place self-sufficient. There was also a forge and a carpenter's shop. Physical labour provided an occupation for the inmates, in contrast to the soul-destroying boredom endured by patients at Saint-Rémy. Vincent himself fancied the idea of working on a farm. It took him back to memories of his youth in Holland. Besides, he added, the place would provide him with ready subjects to draw and paint, without needing to make so many copies of Millet's labourers.

Underlying frustration had by now become the dominant mood reflected in Van Gogh's letters. It was frustration with the asylum and the prevailing inertia of the place and with the weather which continued to prevent him from working out of doors. There was a deeper frustration too, with his continued inability to sell even a single painting, so imposing a mounting financial burden on his brother who was about to acquire the additional burden of fatherhood any day now. Then there was the perpetual frustration generated by his mental condition. Illness had trapped him. He longed to be free to travel, to enjoy the places and works of art he could only read about or see in reproductions. 'If I had the leisure to travel,' he confided to Theo, 'how I would love to go and copy the works of Giotto.' What he regarded as the 'primitive' in Giotto appealed to him so much more deeply than the sophistication of the High Renaissance.

Then there was the frustration of loneliness, in particular the absence of other artists with whom he could share thoughts and ideas. Letter-writing offered some compensation, but not enough. Van Gogh was a social animal. When he wrote to Gauguin in Brittany, enclosing two recent drawings as a present, he suggested he might even join Gauguin there. Surprisingly, given the disastrous experience of having shared a house with Vincent in Arles, Gauguin did not dismiss the idea out of hand. He had remained deeply fond of Van Gogh in spite of everything. In fact we know from later correspondence that he was thinking on similar lines, although not in Brittany, and to a considerable extent motivated by the prospect of sharing expenses. On January 17th he replied to Vincent, 'Life is very long and very sad.' He had only thirty francs left in his pocket. 'What of us poor artists? What happens to the seed we plant? And where is the harvest?' But he loved the drawings Van Gogh had sent him, 'especially the one of the women picking olives'.

Van Gogh's nostalgia for Arles and his determination to return there 'just once more' met no opposition from Dr Peyron, in spite of the doctor's conviction that his patient's breakdowns were brought about as a result of his visits to the place, associated as it was with so many painful experiences. From Vincent's comments to his brother it seems clear that Peyron had more or less given up on Van Gogh and had become happy to let him get on with his life as best he could and doubtless leave the asylum sooner rather than later. Accordingly on January 20th Vincent wrote to his friends the Ginoux, the café-owners, alerting them to his imminent arrival, explaining that he had been ill but that in his view illness had done him good – 'it has calmed me'.

The prospect of seeing Arles again raised his spirits. Dr Peyron's compliance with Van Gogh's wish to return there a second time may have been because he had come to understand just how much Arles meant to him. The place may have contributed to his breakdown on at least two occasions, but it was also his promised land. Arles was where he had discovered the South; the sun, the intense light, the Mediterranean, the almond blossom bursting out of winter, the vineyards and the thyme-scented olive-groves. Perhaps Arles was where he felt he had discovered himself and it was where he had dreamed of creating a Studio of the South, a magnet for other painters who would flock there to share his great discovery. The fact that disaster had struck and put an end to his dreams could not erase golden memories. They could still be relived, even if at a price. It was irresistible.

On the day he told his brother of the forthcoming visit, Vincent also wrote to his much-loved sister, buoyant with the prospect of very soon being able to work outside again. 'Now, better than at the beginning', he added, 'I can capture the real countryside of Provence.' Even as he was planning to leave, he still felt the urge to discover and describe the elusive character of the region.

Immediately afterwards Vincent made the promised visit to Arles, where he saw a few old friends including Madame Ginoux. Two days later, on January 22nd, Theo wrote to his brother expressing relief that the visit had taken place 'with no bad consequences'. He assumed as much, not having heard anything to the contrary. In fact the consequences had been dire, exactly as Dr Peyron must have feared when he gave permission for the visit to Arles. Shortly after his return to the asylum Van Gogh suffered another attack. It was his second within a month and his third since arriving at Saint-Rémy.

Unaware of this new crisis Theo's letter continued enthusiastically. He brought Vincent the welcome news that the exhibition of Les XX in Brussels had opened and he had read in a newspaper that the paintings arousing the greatest interest were the landscapes of Van Gogh together with those of Cézanne, Sisley and Renoir. Vincent was in good company and Theo was now confident that sales would eventually follow. His optimism had led him to look again at the latest consignment of paintings. 'When I looked at your olive trees again', he wrote, 'I found them more and more beautiful.'

Equally ignorant of Vincent's condition, Gauguin wrote from Brittany on January 23rd responding to Van Gogh's suggestion that they might share a place together again. Gauguin was clearly in two (or more) minds about the proposal. Considerations of money were as ever uppermost in his thoughts and he came up with the idea of a collaboration between the two of them and his friend, the painter De Haan. It should be more convenient and less isolated than Brittany; and he suggested the Belgian city of Antwerp. The fanciful reason he offered for the choice was that they might act as agents for Theo's art business in Paris, selling paintings (their own as well as others) to the well-off citizens of Antwerp. Gauguin admitted that such a partnership might have its problems, as past events had proved, acknowledging (surprisingly) that his own behaviour might well have contributed to Vincent's breakdown in Arles a little over a year ago. It is hard to know what was really going on in Gauguin's mind. Since he was at that moment trying to negotiate a free passage to the Far East, all these thoughts and projects are likely to have been 'pie-in-the-sky'. Gauguin, as ever, was guided by a wandering star, and perhaps it was as well that Vincent was too unwell at the time to offer any response.

A more coherent despatch that reached Vincent while he was still in the grip of his illness was sent to him by Theo. This was a copy of a lengthy article about Van Gogh by the critic Albert Aurier which had recently been published in *Le Mercure de France*. The piece was entitled *Les Isolés: Vincent van Gogh* and it was the very first extensive critique to have been written of the artist's work and of his standing in contemporary art. It was an article designed to put Van Gogh on the map, alerting the metropolitan art establishment to the importance of this unconventional loner who lived and worked in the depths of Provence beyond the boundaries of their polite world of salons and urban studios. Theo's wife Jo and his sister Wil, gathered in the Paris apartment in anticipation of Jo's imminent labour, were deeply excited by the publication. On January 29th, as midnight approached, Jo wrote to Vincent to explain how the three of them, Theo, Wil and herself, had all been talking about him as they sat round a table waiting and wondering 'will the baby be here tomorrow morning?' while the doctor, who had insisted on staying, was fast asleep next door.

The day after Vincent received Jo's letter he felt well enough to reply, briefly: 'It touches me so much that you should write to me on such a difficult night. How I long to hear that you will have come through it all safely.' He then explained that he had been ill again, 'but calm is returning'. As with the previous attack this one had lasted no more than a week; although Van Gogh did not feel able to tell Theo what had occurred and why, until the following month.

On the last day of January Theo wrote Vincent a hurried letter. Dr Peyron had informed him of the latest attack, which had occurred apparently just two days after the recent visit to Arles. Peyron added that Van Gogh had only been capable of responding incoherently to any questions put to him. Theo was shocked: 'My poor brother,' he wrote, 'I'm so deeply sorry things aren't going for you as they should.' He went on to say that this was the only cloud on their horizon. 'Jo has given birth to a fine boy who cries a great deal but seems to be in good health…We are naming him after you and I'm making a wish that he will become as determined and courageous as you are.'

January ended much as December had ended, with Van Gogh incapacitated, unable to work and scarcely capable of communicating even to his brother. For the entire month he had been prevented from working out of doors because of the weather, only taking the occasional long walk to identify places he would like to paint once winter eased its grip. Restricted to the asylum grounds there was nothing for Vincent to paint even when he was allowed to do so. Where another artist (such as Cézanne or Renoir) would have found satisfaction in painting a still-life of a jug on a table or a bowl of fruit, Van Gogh took no interest in mere objects that had no meaning for him. In Arles he

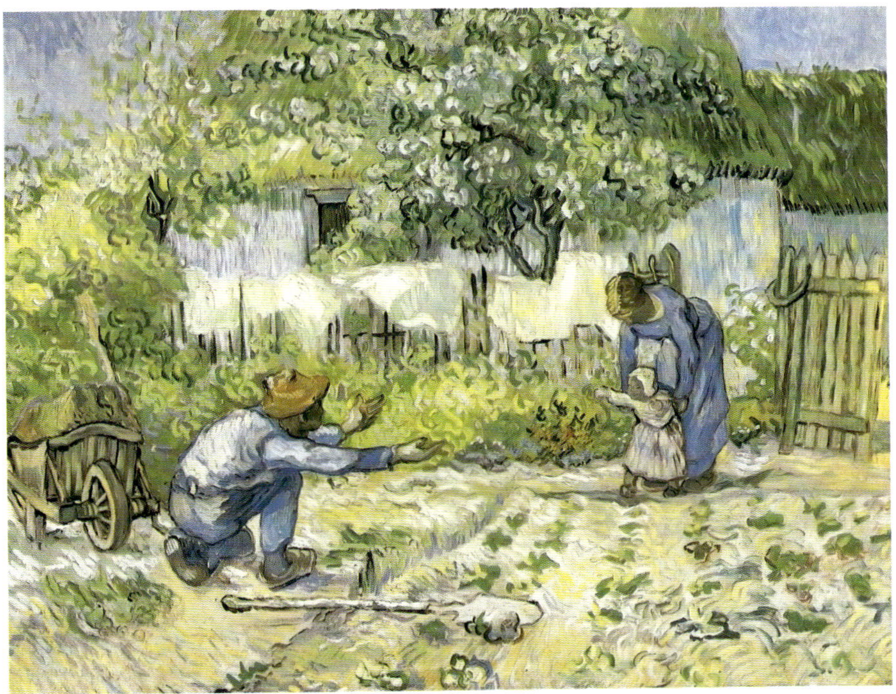

First Steps (after Millet) Oil on canvas, 72.4 x 91.2 cm
Metropolitan Museum of Art, New York

had lovingly painted his own bedroom but in Saint-Rémy, ignoring his own room and studio, he once again channelled his urge to paint into making numerous adaptations of other artists' work, copied from prints faithfully sent to him by Theo.

A few months earlier Theo had given him an extremely misty photograph of a work by Millet of a child taking its first steps between its proud mother and father, who holds out his arms to receive the child. 'How beautiful that Millet is,' Vincent wrote at the time. Now, perhaps with the birth of Theo's child imminent, he took out the photograph and squared it up in preparation for a delightful painting, *First Steps.* The study is so fresh it would be easy to imagine it had been painted from life. There is no better example of Van Gogh's gift for making another artist's vision his own. The pale colour-scheme, in soft greens and yellows, is quite unlike the bold, vibrant colours he had been using in his Provençal landscapes, as if his eyes were already enjoying the more gentle sunlight of the north. Vincent made no further comment about the painting, but sent it to his brother the following spring a few weeks before he himself left Provence for the north.

On the first day of February Van Gogh wrote joyfully to Theo, 'Today I received the wonderful news that you've become a father.' It was a long letter and the first he had written to his brother since his latest breakdown. It had taken something as important as this, he said, to sweep aside dark memories of the last few days when 'I had absolutely no idea where I was and my mind was all at sea.'

The letter was also Vincent's first opportunity to comment on the enthusiastic article about him written by the critic Albert Aurier in Le Mercure de France, which Theo had sent him the week before, not knowing of Vincent's breakdown. Van Gogh had now been able to absorb and reflect on Aurier's article. It had taken him completely off guard and it delighted and disturbed him in equal measure. 'I was extremely surprised by it,' he told Theo. He didn't think he painted that way at all, he added with some indignation, probably referring to Aurier's pronouncement that his work possessed a 'childlike simplicity …characterised by excess', and that he was 'a strong and turbulent artist with the brutal hands of a giant'.

This was hardly the kind of language Van Gogh would have considered appropriate when applied to his own work. Equally unfamiliar and disconcerting, was to find himself referred to as 'a great painter'. At the same time, though reluctant to admit as much, he felt deeply flattered, assuring Theo that he felt 'extremely grateful for the article'.

Aurier's view of Van Gogh would have conflicted strongly with Vincent's own very clear opinion of his place in contemporary art and in particular of where he stood in relation to artists of the past, from Giotto and Rembrandt to Delacroix and Millet. Aurier's flowery accolade offered the romantic view of Van Gogh as the childlike genius isolated from a world which was incapable of understanding him (a view that has widely prevailed ever since). Vincent was torn, even more than he had been by Isaacson's more superficial article several months earlier. Quite unaccustomed to being flattered by critics, or having radical opinions on his work thrown at him, Van Gogh became haunted by Aurier's article. For weeks and months ahead the subject would re-emerge time and again in his correspondence, usually quite out of context. Towards the end of the same long letter to Theo, Vincent returned to the subject once again, acknowledging to his brother that 'partly because of that article I'm now feeling completely well.' Then, in a footnote he added that he was proposing to write a letter to Aurier and hoped also to present him with a painting in gratitude for his article.

The following day he expanded similar thoughts in a letter to Joseph Ginoux, the Arles café-owner he had seen just before his recent attack: 'Work isn't going at all badly, having had an article on my paintings both in Belgium and in Paris where I've exhibited them and people are now saying much more favourable things about them than I personally would wish.' Self-denigration was the invariable accompaniment to Van Gogh's pleasure at being praised. Reading between the lines, Vincent was beginning cautiously to feel that recognition was gradually coming his way.

Winter weather and the aftermath of his recent attack was once again confining Van Gogh to his studio. As usual he whiled away the time making copies of his own work and that of other artists. Theo had sent him a collection of wood-engravings illustrating celebrated work by earlier artists admired by Van Gogh, which he had acquired during his time in Paris. From these he contrived to create two of the most unprepossessing canvases of his entire Asylum Year. One was a painted version of an engraving by Honoré Daumier depicting a group of beer swilling drunks, a crude concept crudely painted. The other was from a grim engraving by Gustave Doré with some forty robotic prisoners trudging round and round the cell-like yard. Unlike Van Gogh's

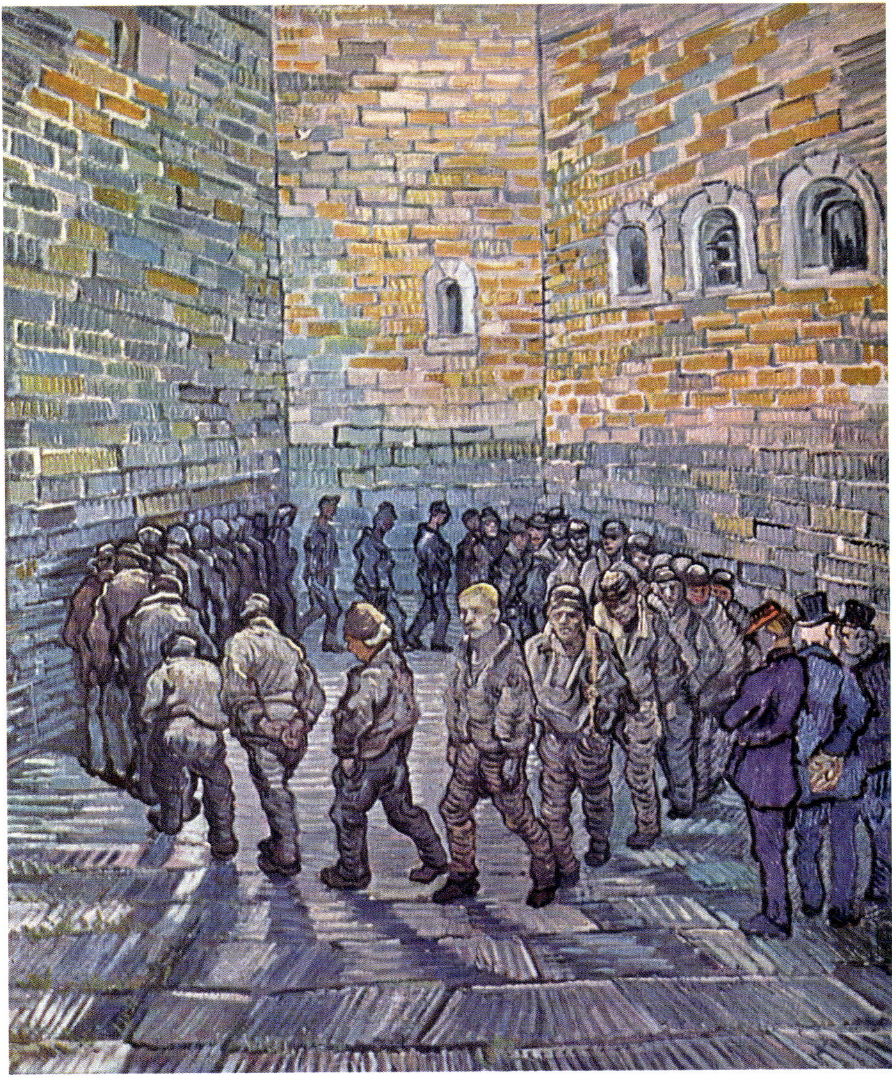

Prisoners' Round (after Doré) Oil on canvas, 80 x 64 cm
Pushkin Museum, Moscow

copies of Millet and Delacroix there is little in either composition that would have been naturally appealing to him, no exuberant strokes of colour or soulful peasants tilling the soil to the sound of a church bell. Daumier's drunkards may have reminded Vincent of traditional Dutch paintings of tavern scenes, or perhaps they touched a chord in him, a reminder of the days in Arles when he would drink the evening away on absinthe. As for the prisoners' exercise yard, was the image of men trapped in a punitive ritual within oppressive walls a recollection of his own illness and the mental prison in which he was so frequently condemned to live?

After the silence that invariably shrouded his days of illness, once Vincent had recovered in early February, there followed the customary flurry of letters to Theo in early-February, catching up on all the accumulated thoughts he needed to communicate to his brother. The subject of Aurier's article continued to be in the forefront of his mind. On February 10th he promised to enclose the letter he had at last written to the critic, though in fact he tore it up and rewrote it. He had grown convinced by now that Aurier should have written about Gauguin rather than himself, Gauguin being so much more deserving of praise. This train of thought led Vincent along a dreamy avenue, maintaining that if only Gauguin could have remained with him in Arles they could have worked together so much more profitably than apart, Gauguin in Brittany and he alone in Saint-Rémy. As so often loneliness had overcome all sense of reality. 'By now,' he daydreamed, 'we'd have a little cottage of our own…and might even be accommodating other artists.'

As the old dream of the Studio of the South still sometimes lingered, so Gauguin remained Van Gogh's mentor, the contemporary he most admired. In spite of the explosiveness of their relationship during those months in Arles, memories of their highly-charged discussions on art remained vividly in Vincent's mind. In St-Rémy he was starved of intellectual debate and locked behind the walls of the asylum where all he could do between bouts of illness was to make copies of other artists' work. His thoughts wandered impotently round and round like

Doré's convicts in the prison yard. Gauguin's view that colour was a language of its own, independent of what it described, continued to intrigue and disturb him. He felt tempted sometimes, he told Theo, to 'create tonal music with colour'. But instantly he rejected the idea because 'the truth is so dear to me'. There follows one of his favourite homilies: 'I prefer to be a shoemaker than a musician.' 'Truth,' he concludes, 'is perhaps what helps me combat my illness.' Then the subject of Aurier returns yet again. The canvas he wanted to paint for him 'must be something good'.

The letter he wrote and rewrote to Aurier became a touching document that laid bare his most private thoughts about art. Although Aurier was a total stranger, Vincent evidently believed that he was someone capable of understanding the workings of an artist's mind. 'I rediscover my own paintings in your article', he wrote. He was anxious to send him a painting in the next consignment to his brother; and this was to be 'a study of cypresses', a subject that specially fascinated him because of the shape and intense blackness of the trees. Aurier had pointed this out in his article, commenting that Van Gogh succeeded in making black a colour. He particularly admired the way the cypresses 'shot upwards in silhouettes of blackened flames'. Vincent explained in his letter that after he had completed his sunflower series in Arles he had looked for a subject that was the very opposite, while at the same time being 'their equivalent' – hence, after the brilliance of the sun, the blackness of night.

The theme of cypresses became one of his major preoccupations in Saint-Rémy. He naturally omitted to tell Aurier that the series had been cut short by his lengthy breakdown in July and August. Now, in late-winter, no doubt spurred on by the critic's words, he had decided this was the moment to resume the series. The canvas he had earmarked to send Aurier was one he had painted during the summer, he explained, but he was now re-working it, adding a human touch by putting in two small figures dressed in typical Provençal clothes, so helping to make the canvas express the character of the region. The painting, he explained, was of 'a group of cypresses in the corner of a cornfield with a mistral blowing', the cypresses 'adding a note of blackness enveloped within the windswept blue of the sky', an effect he compared (somewhat curiously) to a Scottish tartan. He was determined, furthermore, to complete the cypress series before he finally left Provence.

In his long letter to his new-found admirer Vincent took the opportunity to share some private thoughts about painting the local landscape: 'The emotions that take hold of me when I am confronted by nature can sometimes lead me to a state of total collapse, resulting in a period of several weeks in which I am incapable of doing any work.' The bald honesty of this confession to a complete stranger comes as a surprise. It is an intimate statement about himself more open than anything he was in the habit of writing to his brother and the clearest summary we have of what brought about the attacks that repeatedly overwhelmed Van Gogh during his year at Saint-Rémy. If revisiting his old haunts in Arles precipitated these attacks, it was the demands of actually painting the landscape which most often tipped him over. There was a visceral connection between the artist and his subject-matter which may be hard to understand, yet it was capable of creating an emotional stress in Van Gogh which could become too powerful for him to bear; and it broke him. Painting was both his cure and his curse.

Vincent's letters at this time are dotted with personal insights, as though the recurrence of his illness had induced a deeper self-awareness in him, born of a realisation that his condition was now here to stay. It was a part of what he was as a human being and as an artist. The revelations about himself which he offered to Aurier were matched by comments to both his mother and his sister. To his brother he sticks mainly to practical matters, he is delighted that Jo and the baby are well, he curses that he cannot justify the expense of being a painter, but he has bought a suit for 35 francs which will last him for the whole year. But to Wil he is more confidential. He hopes to go to Arles 'one more time' to test if he can bear the prospect of returning to Paris and becoming part of 'ordinary life'. Then he writes about how being fearful and nervous makes him especially sensitive to colour 'and its special language...

Cypresses with Two Female Figures Oil on canvas, 92 x 73 cm
Kröller-Muller Museum, Otterlo

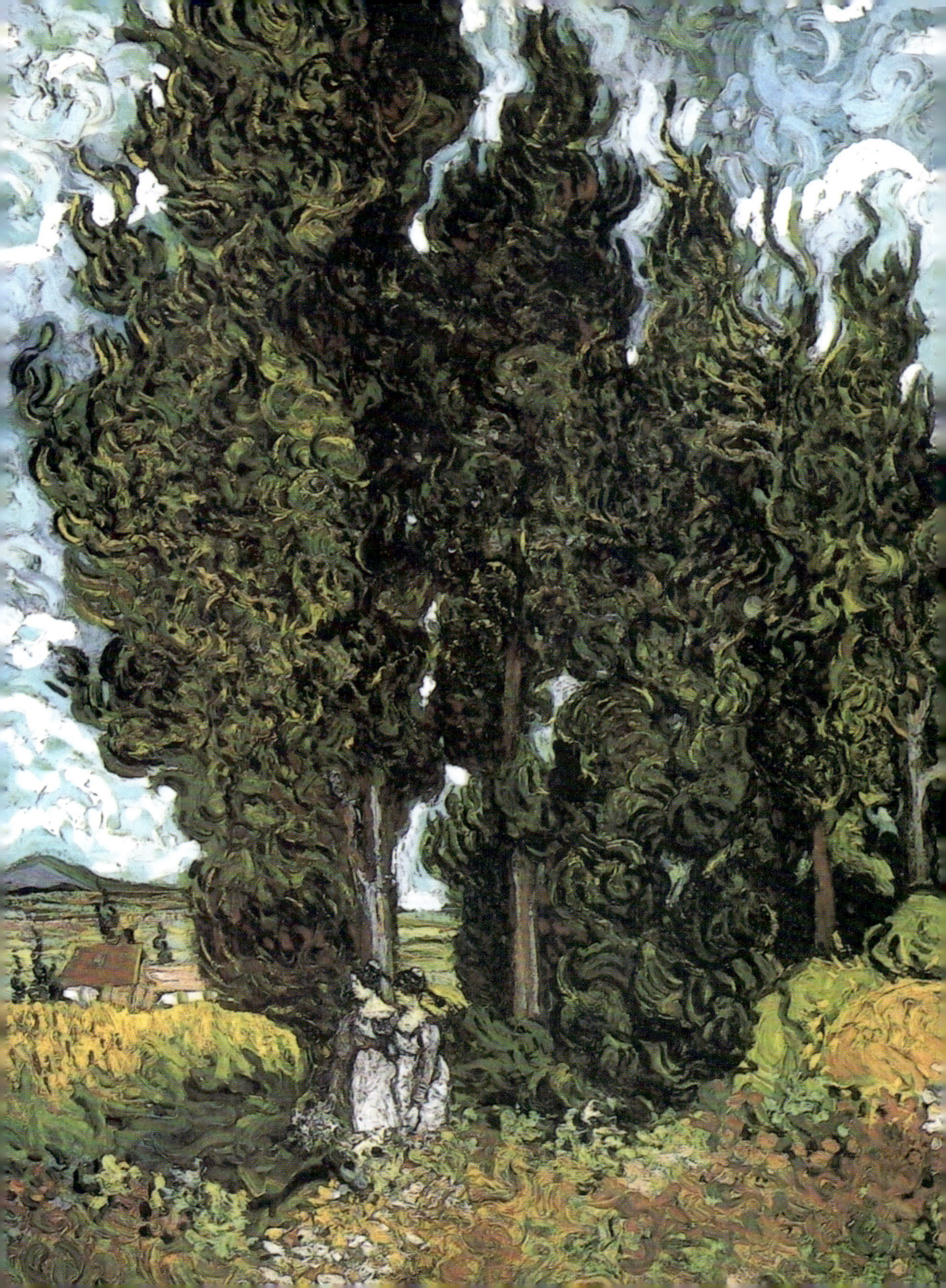

My paintings,' he adds in an echo of his words to Aurier, 'are almost a cry of anguish.'

At about this time, although the letter is lost, Van Gogh heard from Theo that one of his paintings exhibited at the Les XX exhibition in Brussels had been sold for 400 francs. This was a good deal less than was being paid for the works of more established artists; nonetheless it was a beginning. The painting sold was *The Red Vineyard*, which dated from his

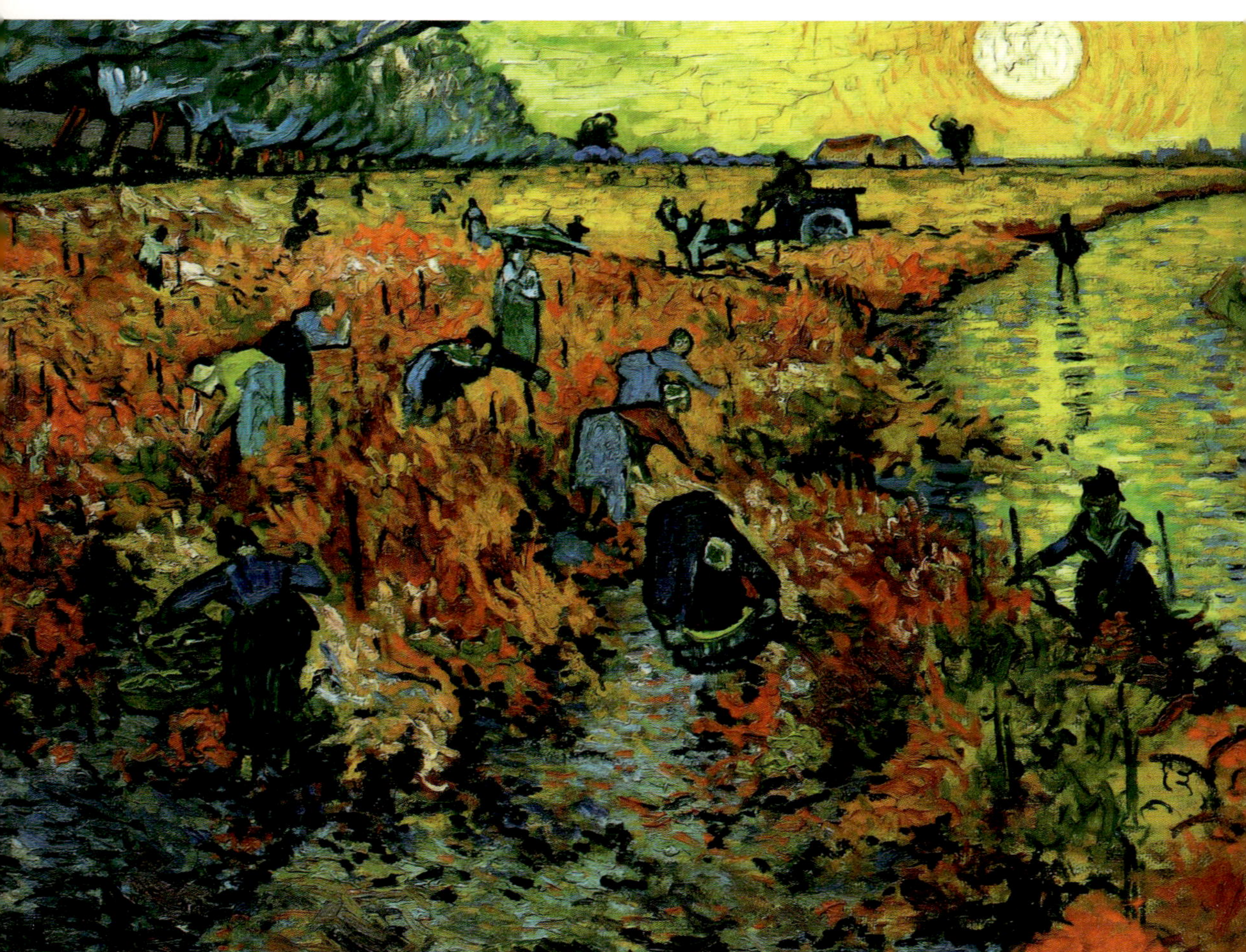

The Red Vineyard Oil on canvas, 75 x 93 cm
Pushkin Museum, Moscow

time in Arles, a month before his first mental breakdown following the argument with Gauguin and the slashing of his ear. The canvas depicts the rich red foliage of vines in the sharp November sunlight and is among the first studies of autumn tints which fascinated Van Gogh a year later at Saint-Rémy. The painting was among the large batch he had sent to his brother in Paris shortly before leaving Arles. Theo had it framed by Tanguy it before sending it with Vincent's other paintings to Brussels.

The Red Vineyard is not one of Van Gogh's best-known canvases, but it carries the distinction of being the only one of his paintings to be sold in his lifetime, (in the light of subsequent history an extraordinary thought). Just how thrilled Van Gogh was by the news of the sale can only be gauged by reading between the lines in his letters. On February 19th, probably the very day he heard of the sale from Theo, Vincent made no more than a casual reference to it in a letter to his mother. He suggested to her that he was considering using the profits from the sale to sponsor 'a week or so in Paris' to see his brother and new nephew. That was all he said. The letter had begun on a cheerful note about the weather: 'Today was a real spring day and the fields of young wheat and the lilac-coloured hills in the distance are beautiful and the almond trees are starting to blossom everywhere.'

He explained almost casually to his mother that he had already begun a study of that almond blossom for a special reason. He expressed his delight to his mother about the birth of his nephew, 'and I started straightaway to make a painting for him to hang in their bedroom.'

Blossoming Almond Tree is one of the gems of Van Gogh's year in Saint-Rémy. There is a simple magic about this single branch of a flowering tree, not stuck in a vase but a selected fragment of a living tree painted from below. Twisted stems and scattered blossom fill the entire canvas and are set against the backcloth of an intensely blue Provençal sky. There are subtleties, meticulously painted, which enrich it. The ceiling of unbroken blue is varied in intensity of colour and in different patterns of brushwork. He has picked out barely noticeable differences in each individual flower in various stages of opening. The gnarled grey twigs which wander across the surface speak of great age, contrasting with the freshness of new flowers. There are meanings that lie beyond the image itself. The symbolism of nature always appealed to Van Gogh, especially the analogy between the seasons of the year and the cycle of human life. There was a special and personal meaning in the picture. The image of the first blossom to emerge out of the harshness of winter was a metaphor and Van Gogh's personal blessing, for Theo's new son, named after Vincent himself.

Disarmingly ordinary, this tender celebration of a new life is as touching as any portrait he painted, as well as the most eloquent demonstration of that deeply emotional relationship to nature which is at the heart of Van Gogh's genius.

Almond blossom had been special to him ever since his arrival in Provence from Paris exactly two years earlier. Then, as now, almond trees brought the first promise of spring. Van Gogh had come to Arles just as the blossom appeared and he made it the subject of his first series of paintings in his new promised land. The following February he was in hospital after his first breakdown and could not continue the theme. This year he decided to create a new series, perhaps with a more detailed approach, as in the painting he intended for his young nephew's bedroom.

Meticulously painted, with close attention to the smallest details of texture and tone, the new study of almond blossom took Van Gogh unusually long by his standards and he was still putting the finishing touches to it on February 21st. The following day he made the promised journey to Arles he had mentioned to his sister. The visit, he had explained, was to be a test of his resolve to resume some kind of ordinary life outside the asylum and therefore be a preparation for his eventual return to Paris and the north.

On February 22nd Vincent travelled to Arles carrying a version he had painted of Gauguin's portrait of Mme Ginoux, which he intended to present to her. But in the event neither Mme Ginoux nor her husband were there when Van Gogh called. There is no record of what Vincent did at that point, or where he went, except that he was apparently found the following morning wandering the streets unable to explain who he was or what he was doing. What happened to the painting, where he had spent the night and whether he had been drowning his sorrows in wine and absinthe, are not known. Nor do we know if Dr Peyron raised the alarm because his patient had failed to return, or whether the police managed to alert him; but two orderlies from the

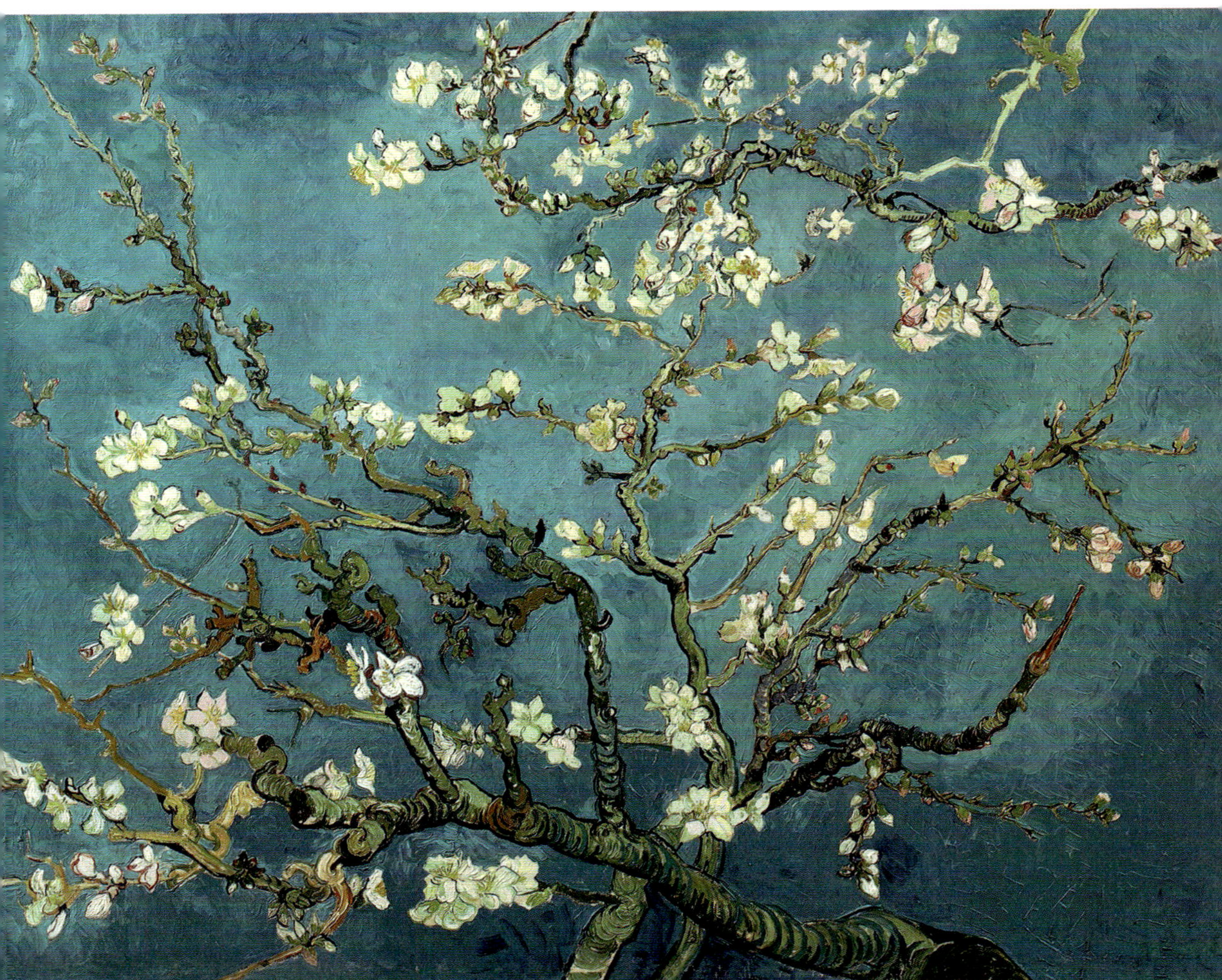

Blossoming Almond Tree Oil on canvas, 73.5 x 92 cm
Van Gogh Museum, Amsterdam

asylum were promptly despatched in a carriage to pick him up.

So began the fourth of Van Gogh's mental breakdowns since his arrival at Saint-Rémy nine months earlier. It was not to be the brief relapse like the previous two, as Dr Peyron optimistically predicted. It persisted through the following month and well into April, not consistently nor apparently as severely as the attack in the summer, yet sufficiently grave to render Van Gogh inert and silent for much of that time. We have little idea of how the weeks passed, as if time was frozen. He seems to have been capable of making drawings occasionally during this long period, but that was all.

The saddest loss artistically was the proposed new series on the almond blossom which he had excitedly planned. The painting intended for his new nephew was to be the first of the series. That single masterpiece, unlike anything else he had painted at Saint-Rémy, remains a tantalising promise that could never be fulfilled, because by the time Van Gogh had regained his mental faculties, the almond blossom was over. As for the painting he made for his newborn nephew, Vincent included it in the seventh and final batch sent to Theo in April shortly before his departure from Saint-Rémy. He saw it on his arrival at Theo's and Jo's apartment in Paris hanging over the piano, since his earlier canvas of an almond tree which Vincent had sent from Arles already hung above the child's bed.

MARCH

March was a silent month. It was a particularly eerie silence. Van Gogh had been in the habit of filling every daylight hour painting and drawing and the lonely evenings writing letters to family and friends. In the letters he described in detail what he had achieved that day and what thoughts and fears had occupied his mind. For much of his time in Saint-Rémy his life had been an open book; his paintings and his letters had formed a continuous autobiography in serial form. Suddenly the covers of the book had closed. Until well into the second half of the month there was no news of his condition and no information about how he passed each day. Even Dr Peyron, usually so conscientious in keeping Theo up to date on his brother's state of health, remained silent. Perhaps understandably so: he had predicted that Vincent's latest attack was likely to be as brief as the previous two; and he was mistaken.

Just how mistaken is hard to tell. There are no reports from the asylum of any of the extreme behaviour that had characterised Van Gogh's earlier attacks: no violent outbursts, no assaults on the staff, no attempts to poison himself by swallowing his paints and turpentine and accordingly no precautionary measures such as banning him from his studio and forbidding him to paint. He was allowed to work, he explained later. What seems likely is that an overpowering malaise prevented him from actually doing so. He was the victim not of an attack of madness but of a prolonged and debilitating depression. Whereas in previous attacks he had insisted that work was the only cure, now it was as though he had lost the will to be cured. He had given up the fight.

A further puzzling feature of the breakdown was that it is reported to have lasted almost two months, considerably longer than any of the previous three attacks. Yet only three weeks after a demented Van Gogh had been brought back from Arles in a special carriage, he was sufficiently recovered to write a low-key letter to Theo, the first to his brother for over a month.

'Today I wanted to read your letters that have reached me,' he began, 'but I wasn't clear-headed enough to understand them…All the same, I'm making an effort to answer you right-away.' They sound like the words of a man confused though slowly recovering rather than in the depths of a mental breakdown, especially since he followed up with the complaint that he felt 'extremely bored…and I'm almost, or completely, in despair of myself.' What depressed him most was not having been able to continue the series he had planned on the almond blossom. The one canvas he had completed, intended for his new nephew, Vincent considered to be 'the most patiently-worked as well as the best thing I've done…painted with absolute sureness of touch.' But now it was too late: the almond blossom was over. He had good reason to feel depressed.

Theo's immediate response, on March 19th, was one of profound relief to have heard from his brother at last, but at the same time 'we both regret from the bottom of our hearts that you couldn't give us better news.' There was a small ray of hope – 'Cold weather has always had a bad effect on you, so we can only hope that the milder days to come may cure you completely.' It was a further regret, he went on, that Vincent couldn't have joined him at the great event of the day. It was evening now, but a few hours earlier he had been with Jo to the private view of this year's Salon des Indépendants. It was held as usual in the Pavillon de la Ville de Paris on the

Champs-Élysées and this year's opening was attended by no less a figure than President Carnot himself.

Theo commented on several impressive works on view, especially those by Seurat and Toulouse-Lautrec. But Vincent's ten paintings were 'well hung and looked extremely good', Theo assured his brother. 'So many people came up to me and asked to send you their compliments.' Gauguin was among the artists present and had told Theo that Van Gogh's paintings were 'the best things in the whole exhibition'. Gauguin then suggested that he and Vincent might swap paintings, one each. He particularly liked the one of the Alpilles mountains. As for the public, Theo went on, they were beginning to come round to the Impressionists and other younger painters, 'and a number of art lovers are beginning to buy them.' Furthermore the critic Albert Aurier was coming round to the apartment the following Sunday with Emile Bernard to see more of Vincent's paintings. There was further good news, he had also received the money from the sale of *The Red Vineyard* in Brussels. The organiser of the exhibition, Octave Maus, had written to Theo 'Please tell your brother I was so happy he participated in Les XX where his work had found much support and created some lively discussions.'

Theo's pride and sense of anticipation coloured the whole letter. He ended it with the suggestion that Vincent approach Dr Peyron to enquire if a journey to Paris might be thought not too dangerous once he had recovered from his present attack. Theo clearly felt confident that the tide was beginning to turn in Vincent's favour and equally confident that he would benefit, in health and in spirit, from a return to Paris and the north where he could be cared for more humanly and be refreshed by the company of those who loved him and understood his work. The combination of winter and rural isolation had contributed heavily to his brother's repeated breakdowns. This was a view shared by Gauguin, who would be writing to him, Theo explained.

It was also in Theo's mind that now would be a propitious moment for Vincent to return to the fold. It was Theo who had been the architect of the Salon success. He had been responsible for putting together

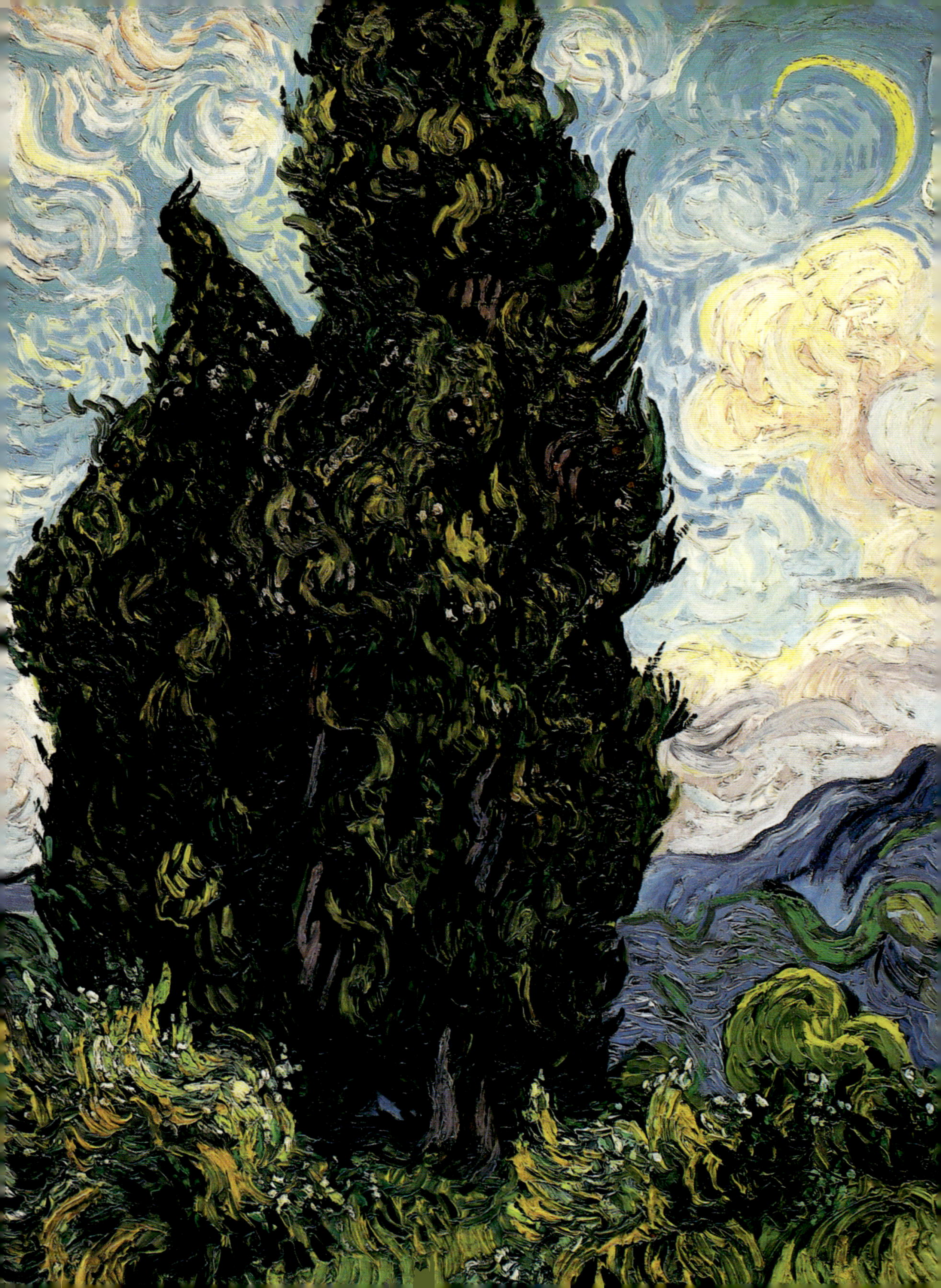

the group of ten of Van Gogh's canvases; and whether he planned it to be so or not, the result had become a miniature retrospective of Vincent's work in Provence over the past two years. Together the canvases presented his vision of this sun-baked land to a Parisian audience that was largely ignorant of the place. Van Gogh was making a statement not only about himself but about the charms of a region he had discovered and was anxious to share.

Two of the paintings exhibited at the Salon were from the sunflower series, his personal emblem of Provence, symbol of the sun itself, and dating from his year in Arles. Then, hanging close to the sunflowers was a later symbol of the south, a canvas of cypress trees under a wild sky, belonging to a series executed at Saint-Rémy. The example shown here was one of the first canvases Vincent had painted the previous June shortly after being permitted to work outside the asylum grounds for the first time. As he described it to Theo at the time, 'the trees are tall and massive; in the background violet hills, a green and rose-coloured sky with a crescent moon.' It was one of two similar canvases he had painted at the same time, the other being the study he later reworked in order to give it to Albert Aurier in gratitude for his article.

A particularly rich series from Saint-Rémy was the view from his bedroom window of the enclosed wheat field, recording the cycle of ploughing, sowing and reaping of the field as the seasons changed. Theo had included two from the series, hanging side by side. One was *Wheat Field after a Storm* which Van Gogh had painted in June at the time when he was preoccupied with the wilder aspects of nature, a preoccupation which also led to the most memorable of all his Saint-Rémy landscapes, *The Starry Night*. The second painting was the majestic *Wheat Field with Rising Sun,* the final canvas in the series which Vincent had created specially to be his showpiece in the Brussels exhibition of Les XX earlier that winter. Now, in the spring, it became one of his showpieces in Paris.

The fourth series represented at the Salon des Indépendants was the study of olive orchards. It is quite likely that most of the Parisian visitors to the Salon exhibition had never set eyes on an olive tree

Cypresses Oil on canvas, 93.4 x 74 cm
Metropolitan Museum of Art, New York

except perhaps in a glasshouse. Paintings such as these, along with his cypress trees, would have contributed to the exotic impression Van Gogh's work would have made at the time, easily overlooked in our well-travelled era. Both in style and subject-matter his paintings still discomforted the conventional Parisian art collector, though there were signs that this was beginning to change, as Theo, being an art dealer, was becoming aware. The painting from the olive orchard series he had included in the Salon exhibition was a particularly powerful one, the gnarled and aged trees spread massively across the baked earth under a heavy sky streaked with red. This was one of the five studies of olive trees Vincent had announced to Emile Bernard in November, intending them to be an antidote to the imaginary olive groves favoured by both Gauguin and Bernard in their paintings of *Christ in the Garden of Olives*. He offered instead 'a hard and coarse reality' and 'a rustic quality with a smell of the earth'.

Another of Van Gogh's ten canvases in the Salon was *Ravine of the Peyroulets* the turbulent study of the Alpilles gorge which had contributed to Vincent's sudden breakdown in December. It was this painting, with its heavy brushstrokes and dramatic exaggerations of style, which particularly appealed to Gauguin.

This miniature retrospective of Van Gogh's Provence which Theo had prepared for the spring Salon in Paris included several further key works. One of these was *The Road Menders*, the sole study he made of the village of Saint-Rémy during his entire year in the asylum. Theo may have included it to suggest an affiliation with similar urban street scenes by the more established Impressionists, in particular Manet and Pissarro. Another urban scene was *Avenue with Chestnut Trees in Blossom*. One of the loveliest of Van Gogh's studies of the public gardens in Arles, it was painted in May, during the artist's final week before leaving for Saint-Rémy. It was the only example on show of Vincent's love of painting spring blossom. It also demonstrated his gift for capturing the effect of light and shadow falling on cobblestones, a skill shown in other paintings of Arles, most famously in the night scene outside the café in the Place du Forum.

The most private of Van Gogh's Provençal themes were the close-up studies he made of plants and undergrowth, all painted with meticulous attention to the smallest detail. They were mostly the fruits of his convalescent days when he was not permitted to leave the asylum grounds and occupied himself drawing and painting in

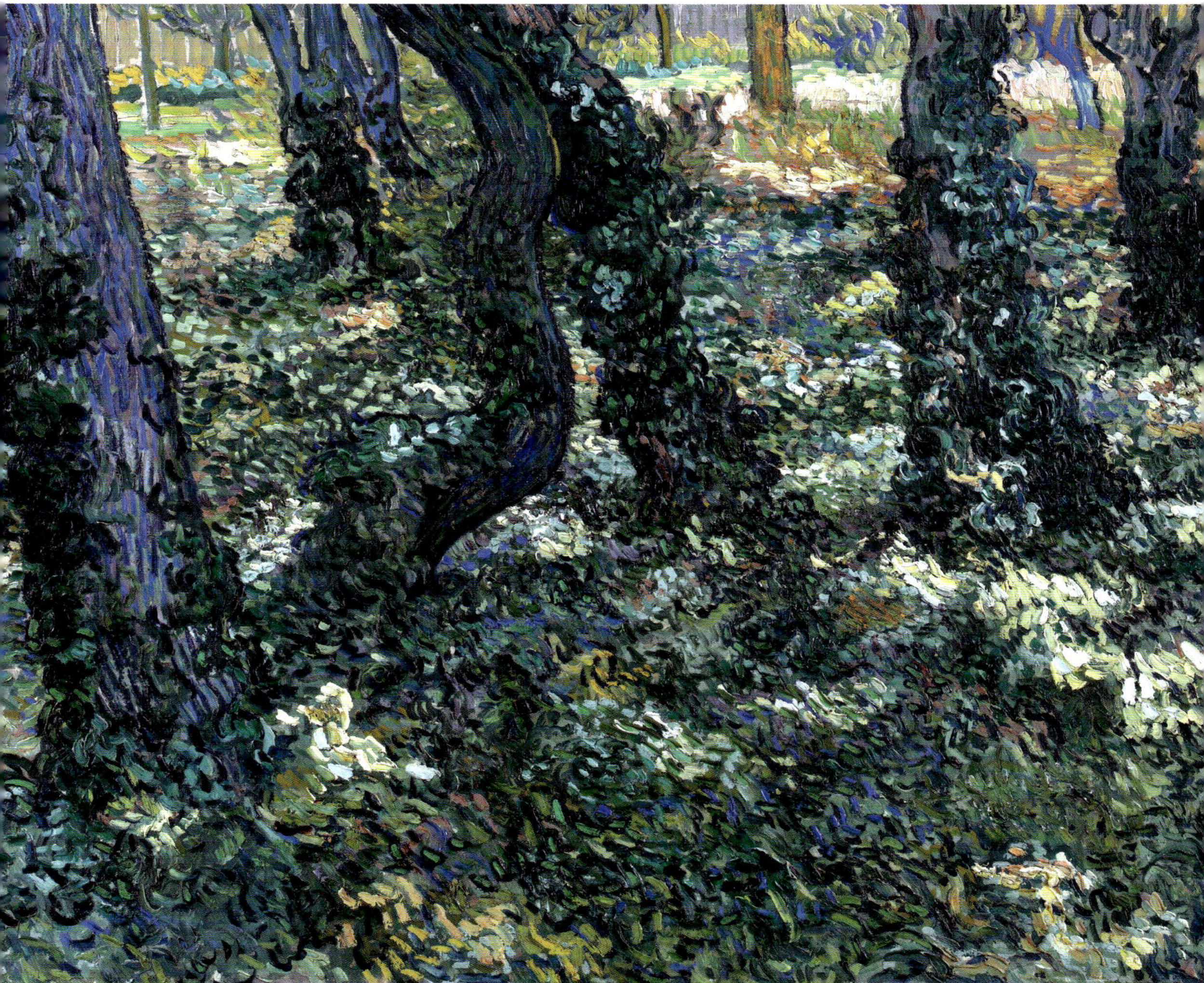

Undergrowth Oil on canvas, 73 x 92.5 cm
Van Gogh Museum, Amsterdam

the overgrown park that had once been the garden of the former Augustinian monastery. The example Theo chose for the Salon was listed simply as *Trees with Ivy*. At the private view the painting found a devoted admirer in his wife Jo. She later wrote to Vincent explaining that while Theo was doing his social round of talking to artists and clients she took herself off and 'spent a quarter of an hour enjoying the wonderful coolness and freshness of the undergrowth. I came to feel I knew that spot intimately and had often been there, I loved it so much', Jo explained touchingly. The painting disappeared some time afterwards, but its companion picture, *Undergrowth*, was acquired by Jo shortly after Van Gogh's death and remained a treasured possession for the rest of her life, finally inherited by young Vincent, her son.

Theo's hopes of a breakthrough in his brother's fortunes soon withered. For all the compliments and expectations aroused by the exhibition not one of the ten paintings in the Salon des Indépendants found a buyer. In Saint-Rémy, Van Gogh himself remained in the grip of depression and despair, incapable of working while the blossom he had longed to paint in the orchards surrounding the asylum faded and fell. Letters continued to reach him. Whether he read or understood them is impossible to know. Certainly he failed to reply to them, which for someone normally so quick to respond was a clear indication of his mental state. Gone were the days when Vincent would bounce back after a breakdown, avid to get back to work as the only 'cure' he knew for his illness.

All that survives from this extended period of silence is the correspondence that continued to flow his way. On March 20th, immediately after the opening of the Salon des Indépendants, Gauguin wrote warmly to Van Gogh, repeating the enthusiasm he had shown to Theo at the private view for the ten paintings on show. His treatment of Vincent, as ever, was one of remarkable gentleness and appreciation, in contrast to Van Gogh's often abrasive comments about Gauguin and his 'abstractions'. Reading between the lines of his letters over the past year it seems clear that he felt some responsibility, even guilt, for the arguments the two artists had in Arles which culminated in Van Gogh's breakdown and self-mutilation: perhaps regret too that he had hurried away from the scene leaving Vincent lying in hospital. The tone of this new letter could hardly have been more consoling and appreciative. He had been keenly following Vincent's work 'most attentively since we parted,' he explained. As for the paintings in the Salon, 'I offer you my most sincere congratulations. For many other artists too you are the most remarkable in the exhibition. When it comes to painting from nature you are the only one who looks good.'

Gauguin went on to write about the painting he would like to exchange for one of his own – Van Gogh's *Ravine of the Peyroulets*. He described it as 'a mountain landscape, with two travellers who seem to be climbing up in search of the unknown. It possesses an emotion worthy of Delacroix, with very evocative colouring.' It was a painting he had discussed at length with Aurier, Bernard and others, he explained and they all of them sent their compliments. Only Guillaumin remained unconvinced, but then 'he only sees material things with his brainless eyes'.

This was high praise. Van Gogh, even in the depths of depression, cannot have failed to be touched and reassured. For all Vincent's harsh criticism of his friend's deviations from reality and his biblical fabrications it was Gauguin's opinion of his work that he valued above all others. When Gauguin praised Vincent's *Ravine of the Peyroulets*, suggesting it possessed touches of Delacroix, Van Gogh must have felt doubly honoured. The painting that had tipped him towards a breakdown was suddenly up there with the gods.

Gauguin's letter included a rough sketch of the painting in question in case Vincent in his present state might have forgotten what it looked like. He concluded with a plea to his friend not to consider replying until he felt strong enough to do so.

Towards the end of the month letters reached Van Gogh from his brother and from Jo, both of them concealing their anxiety over Vincent's continuing silence with messages of good will for his forthcoming birthday. He would be thirty-seven on March 30th. A year earlier, on his birthday, he had been recovering in the Arles hospital: now he was ill once again. Jo wanted to tell him about the child they had named after him and whom she referred to as 'your godson'. She was so much longing to show him the boy, assuring him that the child 'always gazes with great intensity at Uncle Vincent's paintings', in particular the one of almond blossom which hung above their bed. 'It really fascinates him,' she said. The painting was of a sprig of a flowering tree placed in a vase which Van Gogh had painted in Arles the year before. Now he had followed this gift with the new painting of almond blossom done specially for his new nephew and completed just before his breakdown towards the end of February.

Theo wrote to his brother on the same day. 'How thrilled I would be to be able to see you and shake your hand on your birthday.' Might Vincent be able to celebrate the event, he enquired, certainly knowing the answer all too well. 'What do you find to do all day?' he added. Theo would probably have guessed from Vincent's silence and his inability to draw or paint that each day was likely to have been a routine of dark introspection and despair. Theo was pinning his hopes on getting his brother back to Paris as soon as possible. He had now met the doctor recommended by Pissarro, Dr Gachet. The doctor lived outside Paris in the village of Auvers, but kept a practice in the city for several days a week. Theo had described Vincent's illness to the doctor, who formed the opinion from what he had been told that Van Gogh's attacks had nothing to do with madness and that he might well be able to cure him. 'He looks like a man who understands things very well,' Theo assured his brother. Once Vincent was in Paris the two of them would arrange to go and meet him. He wondered somewhat anxiously if Vincent had yet spoken to Dr Peyron about the proposed move once he had fully recovered.

As for the Salon des Indépendants, Theo assured his brother that Pissarro took himself to the exhibition every day and reported back that 'you are enjoying a real success there among the artists'. But there were still no sales and the newspapers remained silent. Critics had still not got round to appreciating the Impressionists, even after nearly twenty years, 'but you know very well what they are worth'.

Theo's sour comment illustrated that the gulf between the views of the art establishment and those of the younger generation was still as unbridgeable as ever. Even if the President of France could honour the Indépendants with his presence, the taste of most Parisian art-lovers remained as inflexibly conventional as ever. It was to take the arrival of a new generation of American self-made millionaires hungry for the new art of the old world to open their eyes to the incomparable richness that lay around them.

Sadly for Van Gogh, it would be just too late.

The birthday greetings for Vincent that arrived at the asylum from Theo and Jo stirred Dr Peyron to communicate about his patient's protracted breakdown. It had persisted since late-February. Peyron had earlier predicted a speedy recovery and now wrote somewhat guardedly on April 1st that 'M. Vincent has not yet recovered his full clarity of mind and for the time being is unable to reply to your letters. This attack,' he admitted, 'has taken more time to wear off than the previous ones.'

The doctor went on to explain why Van Gogh's condition was so hard to deal with. 'At times one is inclined to believe he is coming to his senses. He explains the feelings he has been experiencing. But then a few hours later a complete change has taken place and the patient once again becomes despondent and suspicious and ceases to respond to any questions I put to him. But I remain confident that he will regain his sanity again, just as he has before…As soon as he is capable of writing you will undoubtedly hear from him.'

This report on Van Gogh's erratic shifts of mood and behaviour explains why in mid-March, in the depths of his breakdown, he had still been capable of writing a cool and lucid letter to his brother, only to be followed by a further stretch of silence lasting five more weeks. During that time there were no further medical reports from

Dr Peyron and no letters from Theo or from anyone else. The monastery walls of the asylum might have enclosed members of a silent order.

Finally, on April 23rd Theo ventured a cautious letter to his brother. 'Your continued silence suggests to us that you are still suffering,' he began. Not knowing whether Vincent would be in any state to read the letter, he nonetheless continued in an optimistic vein, reassuring him that his paintings in the Salon des Indépendants were being considered a triumph. Theo related the story of how he was stopped in the street the other day by a colleague who urged him to send his 'warmest congratulations to your brother and to tell him that his paintings are quite remarkable'. What was more, Theo continued, Claude Monet had personally assured him that Vincent's canvases were the best things in the exhibition. This from the most esteemed landscape painter of the day was a compliment to be savoured.

What Theo did not know when he wrote his hopeful letter was that just one day earlier, on April 22nd, Vincent had quite suddenly emerged from his two-month despair. The darkness had lifted at last and not merely for a few hours as it had previously. The sun had re-emerged. Vincent had even started to paint again. There had been periods during his illness when he had felt well enough to work a little, but only painting from nostalgic memories of scenes from his younger days in Holland. Now for the first time since painting the blossoming almond tree for his young nephew more than two months before, Vincent went out of doors and opened his eyes to the world of plants and trees, to the small intimate things in a landscape he had always particularly cherished.

On April 29th he wrote a long-overdue letter to his brother to explain what he had been doing now that at last he could celebrate the return of the sun and his sanity. 'I haven't been able to write to you until now,' he began. 'But since I'm beginning to feel better I didn't want to delay wishing you a happy birthday.' His brother's birthday was due on May 1st, a little over a month after Vincent's own. He went on to explain how at last he felt able to paint again. 'I've just finished a sunlit canvas of a meadow which I think is fairly strong.' The painting, *Pine Trees and Dandelions in the Asylum Garden,* is one of Van Gogh's throw-away masterpieces. The subject is nothing more than the lower trunk of two trees amid a rough carpet of wildflowers; yet it has the same rich attention to detail and texture as the almond blossom he had painted before his breakdown. The roughness of the tree-bark contrasting with the lushness of the meadow is the real subject of the painting. This combined with Van Gogh's familiar ability to detect subtleties of colour in materials, such as bark, which to the untrained eye would appear to be monochrome or even colourless. Like the almond blossom painting it represents one extreme of Van Gogh's vision of nature. It is the very opposite of his dramatic account of mountains and wild skies described in bold, vigorous strokes of the brush. Tiny flowers and wild skies: they are the twin poles of his art and perhaps of his nature, a bipolarity of turbulence and calm, more prevalent at Saint-Rémy than at any other phase of his life.

He was proud of the painting. It represented the first fruits of his recovery and of his return to working directly from nature rather than from memory. Immediately after describing his progress to Theo he wrote a combined letter to his mother and sister Wil in which he stressed that as a measure of his recovery for several days now he had been busy

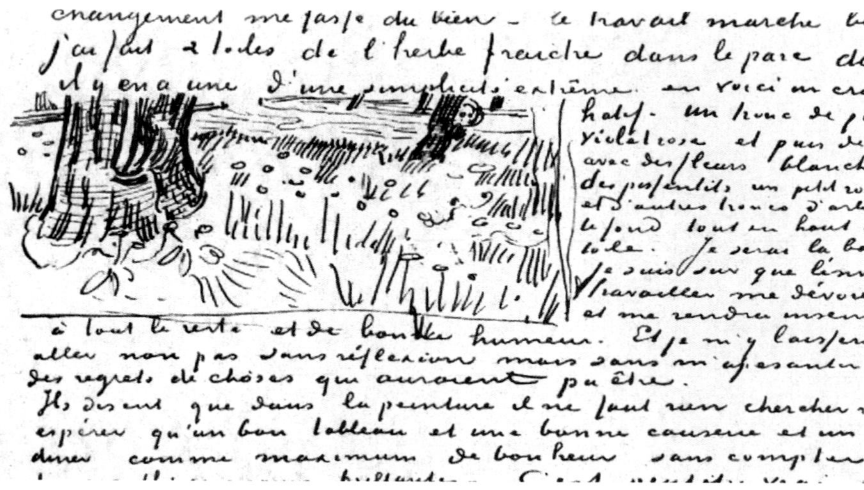

Sketch of *Pine Trees and Dandelions in the Asylum Garden* Ink on paper, Van Gogh Museum, Amsterdam

'painting a field in the full sunshine with yellow dandelions'. Then in a follow-up letter to Theo a few days later he elaborated on the experience: 'As soon as I got out into the park all my urge to work returned.' He had by now completed a second canvas, also of grasses in the asylum garden, 'and now the brushstrokes do their job like clockwork'.

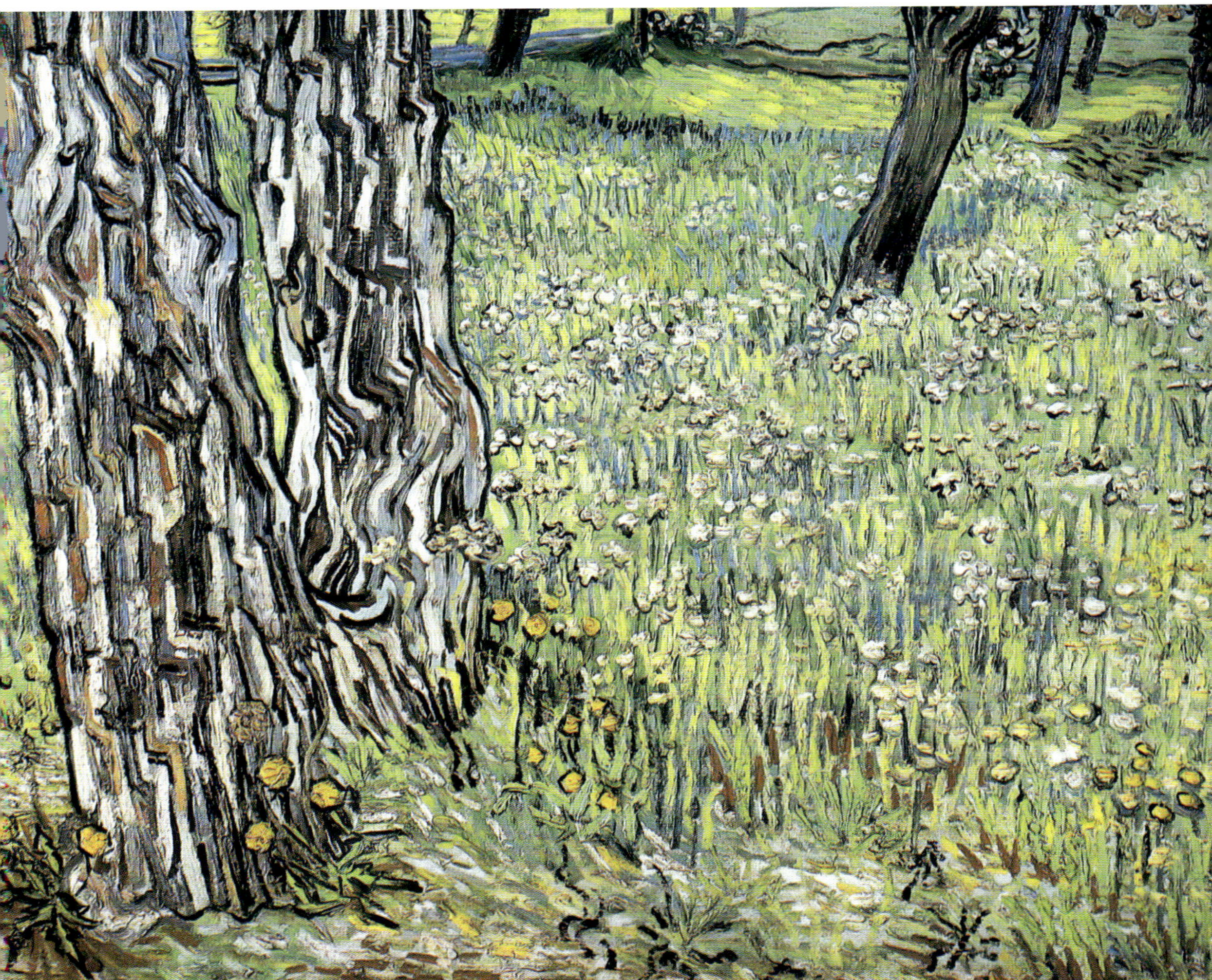

Pine Trees and Dandelions in the Asylum Garden Oil on canvas, 72 x 90 cm
Kröller-Muller Museum, Otterlo

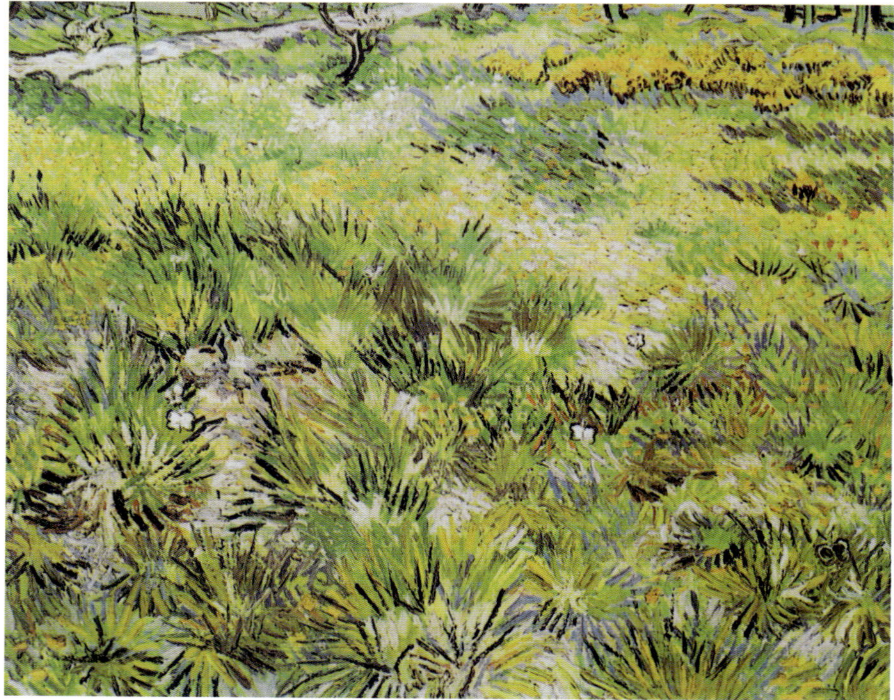

Butterflies in the Long Grass Oil on canvas, 64.5 x 80.7 cm
National Gallery, London

The return of energy brought with it a feeling of urgency. 'I'm very behindhand, not having been capable of working for two months until now,' he explained to his brother in the long letter of April 29th. 'I hardly know what to do or think,' he added, 'but I have a huge desire to leave this place.' The desire to move north had lingered on throughout his illness, finding expression in the canvases he had chosen to paint of cherished scenes in Holland as he remembered them. Now the growing desire to draw a line under his period of time at Saint-Rémy stirred him into action. He arranged, we do not know precisely how, to pack up all the remaining paintings he had done and to send them by train to Theo in Paris. 'Please accept the various paintings I'm sending you, with my thanks for all the many kindnesses you have shown me,' he wrote.

There was an air of finality about the statement. He was getting ready to move out. He proceeded to forewarn Theo by itemising the paintings he was sending him. This was to be the seventh consignment of canvases to his brother since his arrival at the asylum almost a year ago. It was by far the largest, about seventy paintings altogether, almost half the total number he had painted. Vincent was especially pleased to be able to include the canvas of almond blossom painted specially for his new nephew and which had satisfactorily dried during the months he had been ill. Now he wanted it to be a birthday gift for Theo.

The first group of paintings he mentioned, perhaps surprisingly, were his 'copies' after Millet which he had done intermittently throughout the year, generally when confined to the asylum. He valued them highly, regarding them as interpretations rather than copies, capturing the spirit of Millet while making them his own.

The second group consisted of the series on the theme of the olive orchards, which Vincent had always held to be among the most important canvases he painted at Saint-Rémy. He felt it necessary to tell Theo that 'you'll find the olive trees with the pink sky are the best', and they would look good as pendants 'to those with a yellow sky'. As always Van Gogh was deeply conscious of how his work should be displayed, repeatedly anxious to issue instructions to Tanguy in Paris on how they must be framed. This letter to his brother, even though he had only recently recovered from his long illness, shows him already anticipating a day when his work would be exhibited together. Self-denigration accompanied by a fierce pride in his work were Van Gogh's twin voices constantly vying with one another to be heard. Theo must often have wondered whether his brother's ambition was to be escorted down the hall of fame or to be left alone to brood on his own inadequacies.

The third category of paintings sent to Theo consisted of four versions of a portrait of Vincent's friend in Arles, the café-owner's wife Mme Ginoux. The portrait was done, not from life but from a drawing Gauguin had made of her at the time when Van Gogh and he had shared the Yellow House and would sit and drink in the Ginoux' café next door. The painting was therefore a gesture of homage to his friend, but also to Gauguin. The four versions differ only in the colour of the background and of Mme Ginoux' jacket and neck-scarf. Van Gogh invariably made second versions of paintings he valued, especially portraits, one of which he generally presented to the sitter. In this case he painted four versions because he had hoped to give one to Mme Ginoux. Another he had promised to Gauguin himself, instructing Theo 'to see that he gets it'. The third was for Theo and one he presumably kept for himself as a memento of a cherished friendship and of a time when he and Gauguin were painting in harness and in harmony.

The final canvas in the consignment described to Theo was the study of cypress trees which he had painted specially for the critic Albert Aurier in gratitude for the article Aurier had written about him in the *Mercure de France*. The painting was at last dry. 'I would have liked to redo (the trees) with a little less impasto,' he told Theo, 'but I don't have the time.' Van Gogh was now in a hurry. He needed to get the huge consignment of paintings on the train to Paris, then, all being well, he dreamed of getting on that train himself as soon as he felt strong enough.

There was a final instruction about the cypress trees to his brother: 'they must be washed a number of times in cold water, then a strong varnish applied once the impasto has dried right through so that the blacks won't get dirty when the oil has finally evaporated.' Then, without a break in the paragraph Vincent went straight on to instruct his brother what he required 'right now…I urgently need colours, part of which you could get from Tanguy's shop…at least half of them straightaway because I've already lost too much time…Here's the list of the colours I need.' And so the letter continues: 'twelve zinc white, three cobalt, five Veronese green, one ordinary lake, two emerald green, four chrome 1, two chrome 2, one orange lead, two ultramarine. All large tubes.' He then added that he needed brushes too, as well as canvas – 'seven metres, or even ten.' Vincent was back in business.

The brisk business-like tone of the letter promptly changes to one of introspection and melancholy as the clouds of self-doubt roll in once again. 'What can I tell you of these past two months?' he goes on, 'I'm more sad and bored than I can say and I no longer know what stage I'm at.' Then he returns to the theme of Aurier's article about him which had dominated his mind before the recent breakdown. This time a note of paranoia has entered his thoughts on the subject. 'Please ask M. Aurier not to write any more articles about my paintings,' he insists. 'Tell him in all earnest that he is quite wrong about me, then that I feel far too damaged by grief to be able to face publicity.'

The emphasis on 'publicity' is revealing, as if a single article was likely to inspire crowds of admirers to beat on the gates of the asylum. Though Van Gogh had always been unhappy with some of Aurier's more romantic interpretations of his paintings the real substance of his hostility to the critic's article was a feeling of horror about his paintings being written about at all. 'If I hear talk of them,' he goes on, 'this gives me more pain than he can possibly know.' It was not so much that he felt it inappropriate to apply words to paintings. Vincent himself always enjoyed doing so at some length in his letters, as did Gauguin. What he seems to have found unbearable was that Aurier's words were expressed in the public forum of a newspaper. Van Gogh felt exposed to the point of panic.

The mounting hysteria which Aurier's article had aroused in Van Gogh over the past months became vividly expressed in the combined letter he wrote to his mother and his sister Wil on the same day, April 29th. 'I wrote to Theo today and sent him seventy paintings,' he began. After describing his illness and his determination to leave the asylum he then ended the letter with the customary warm wishes to both of them and 'Believe me, I think of you so often and embrace you in my thoughts.' There follows a brief postscript about the subject lodged most firmly in his mind. 'When I heard that my work was having some success and I read that article, I was immediately afraid that I would be made to pay for it, it's nearly always the case that success is the very worst thing that can happen in a painter's life.'

What did Van Gogh imagine success would do to him? Did he really believe success was the worst thing that ever happened to Michelangelo or his beloved Delacroix? The line of argument seems scarcely worth pursuing. Yet his bleak view of an artist's destiny could hardly be clearer, or at least his own destiny. Much of Vincent's damaged psyche, with its distorted puritanical demand for punishment, seems exposed in the few simple lines of his letter to Wil and his mother. Any form of publicity was a sign of a painter achieving success, which was the worst thing that could happen and for which he would be punished. The payment Van Gogh felt would be required of him as a result of Aurier's article was his two-month illness. He had become convinced that it was his due punishment.

It was Puritanism gone mad. What an artist should work towards in Van Gogh's philosophy is unclear. Maybe an entirely anonymous success might be acceptable. He had enjoyed being acclaimed by his peers in Brussels and at the Salon des Indépendants, perhaps because he had not been present at either venue but safely behind his asylum walls far removed from the public glare.

Perhaps the roots of Van Gogh's paranoia lie here, in the dread of exposure. However deeply he professed to hate his life at Saint-Rémy he could feel unthreatened in the seclusion of the former monastery with its overgrown garden and its enclosed wheat field within the embrace of the Alpilles mountains under the watchful eye of the sun and stars. This was the secure world he needed and could record with a love that was constantly recharged. While his dream was to be free of his prison, his nightmare was the threat of the outside world and the challenge of ordinary life but that is what success entailed, re-entering ordinary life and being embraced by it.

Those few lines written to Wil and to his mother may well be the most revealing postscript in the history of art. What they suggest, which subsequent events bear out, was that Van Gogh was caught in an impossible trap from which he could never escape.

Yet, even in injury time the hunger to reach out to the beautiful world he could never inhabit remained as powerful as ever. That huge order of paints and canvas sent to Theo as an accompaniment to his draft of seventy paintings was proof that there was still much of that beautiful world to be recorded in the final three weeks he was to spend in this land of the sun.

MAY 1890

Van Gogh's yearning to leave the asylum as soon as possible was matched by a determination to make full use of his final days, painting from dawn to dusk, then occupying his evenings despatching a volley of letters to his brother almost daily. The letters exude a sense of urgency, along with a lament at so much time lost through illness, particularly his favourite months of spring. By now most of the blossom was over, he commented ruefully, just as it had been a year earlier in Arles following his first breakdown.

The flood of correspondence was also Vincent's response to a backlog of letters he had been unable to read until now because Dr Peyron had been away for some weeks. It was a rule of the asylum that all incoming mail could be passed to patients only through him. 'Today, as M. Peyron has returned I've been able to read your kind letters… which have done me no end of good', Vincent wrote to Theo on May 1st. They had lifted his spirits, reminding him that it was for him 'to climb up from the pit of depression I've been in'.

At Vincent's request Theo had sent him a number of etchings mainly by Rembrandt which he had acquired during his time in Paris. As always whenever Van Gogh felt unable (or unwilling) to go out and find subjects to paint he turned to the work of artists he admired and threw his energies into making interpretations of their work. They were his experiences of the wider world at second-hand. Now, in his recovery period following two months of illness, he expressed his delight to Theo at being able to paint scenes based on the prints his brother had sent him. The biblical themes he particularly enjoyed copying were those that clearly struck a personal chord at this time of recovery from 'the pit of depression', notably Rembrandt's *The Raising of Lazarus* and his study of David in prayer before going out to fight Goliath. Equally pertinent to his state of mind was the comment to his brother that he was painting a version of Delacroix's study of the Good Samaritan.

Every page of this letter to his brother and of the one he wrote to him the following day (May 2nd), expressed his longing to leave Saint-Rémy and to see Theo again, as well as Jo and the new baby. 'I'm all but convinced that I'll get better in the north…at least for quite some time,' he added cautiously. By now Van Gogh had become realistic enough to admit the likelihood of an attack returning, though not for two years, he hoped. His time here in the asylum has been a kind of 'shipwreck', he explained. But he had survived; and he even 'dared to believe that in the north I shall re-discover my self-confidence', The stricken vessel could be re-floated, he hoped, at least until the next reef.

His brave words, perhaps only half-believed, are repeated constantly throughout these letters to Theo. Much as he was looking forward to Paris, the prospect of city life also frightened him. He had by now warmed to the plan of being placed under the care of Dr Gachet in the village of Auvers, north-east of Paris and sooner he could get there the better. Because the doctor liked artists, according to Pissarro, Vincent also felt confident that 'a good friendship might develop'. It was now more than a year since Van Gogh had enjoyed any kind of friendship with fellow artists or with anyone remotely interested in art, except by correspondence; and his isolation and sense of frustration had become painful to him. Dr Gachet and a new working life in the countryside of northern France, had become a bright beacon for which he could hardly wait.

Theo responded immediately to the barrage of letters from his brother. He was delighted to tell him that the huge consignment of paintings he had sent had just arrived safely. It included the study of almond blossom which Vincent had painted specially for Theo's child, as well as the painting of cypress trees he intended to give to Albert Aurier in gratitude for the critic's article about him (even while continuing to insist that Aurier write nothing further about him). In Theo's view the painting had 'all the richness of a peacock's tail'. This was unusual language for Theo, who clearly felt delighted that such an outstanding painting should go to a critic who had already done much to draw people's notice to Vincent's work and might well be encouraged to do more in spite of his brother's paranoia. Theo's letter also enclosed a photograph of the infant Vincent, which he hoped might inspire his brother to paint a portrait of the child. As for the proposed departure from Saint-Rémy, Theo agreed that his brother should come to Paris 'as soon as possible', but insisted that Vincent should be accompanied by an attendant from the asylum on the entire journey.

This final injunction from an anxious Theo had the effect of sparking off a dismissive rant from Van Gogh in yet another letter, the third he had written to his brother within four days. There was no question of needing someone to accompany him on the train to Paris, he insisted. He was not 'a dangerous animal'. All he asked was that Theo be prepared to meet the train at the Gare de Lyon station at ten in the morning on whatever day was agreed. What was most important, he went on, was that he should be able to take full advantage of the 'three of four months of complete calm' which he anticipated he was likely to enjoy. After so many breakdowns Van Gogh was becoming almost coldly pragmatic about his mental condition, though his earlier prediction of having two further years of peace seems to have shrunk dramatically. As always his optimism varied, often dramatically, from mood to mood.

What remained constant in his thoughts was his urgent need to leave the asylum, he hoped within two weeks. 'I need air,' he wrote, 'I feel damaged by boredom and grief here.' But Paris would only be a temporary stay, he assured his brother. It was Auvers he was looking forward to in the long term; and he was now drafting a letter which he would like Theo to forward to Dr Gachet making absolutely clear his situation and his needs. They were all the things the asylum had been quite unable to provide. 'My patience is utterly exhausted, my brother,' he ended the letter after a further diatribe about the destructive atmosphere of the asylum. 'I can't continue here. I must move, even if it's only somewhere temporary.'

There followed a pause in the torrent of letters before Theo replied on May 10th that he accepted Vincent's assurance that he could travel to Paris alone. It was a risk worth taking. Theo had now written to Dr Peyron about Vincent's proposed departure, hoping for his approval. At the same time he had written to Dr Gachet in Auvers, reminding him of his offer of help and assuring him that Vincent was 'very well at present and writes me very reasonable letters.'

All now seemed in place and Theo enclosed 150 francs in cash to pay for his brother's railway ticket. Vincent responded immediately with copious thanks. Now it was just a matter of packing up his last belongings and organising his departure. An attendant from the asylum, possibly Trabuc, would accompany him as far as the mainline railway station. Then he would be on his own, heading for Paris. 'The whole horrible experience has vanished like a passing thunderstorm,' he wrote, referring particularly to his long breakdown, but also undoubtedly to his year-long incarceration within the walls of the asylum.

Yet even now, at the eleventh hour, Van Gogh was driven to work. He had received the canvas and paints he had requested from Theo and for the past few days had been working 'with calm and unremitting energy', he assured his brother. (How often in his correspondence over the past year had Van Gogh used the word 'calm' to describe the state of mind of this least calm of men?) He went on to describe the new canvases he was working on, 'roses on a bright green background' and another of irises – 'a violet-coloured bouquet standing out against striking lemon-yellow background, with other yellow tones.' Even in these final days, in the midst of packing up his possessions and despatching them to Paris Vincent felt it important to describe the precise colour-tones of the subjects he was painting.

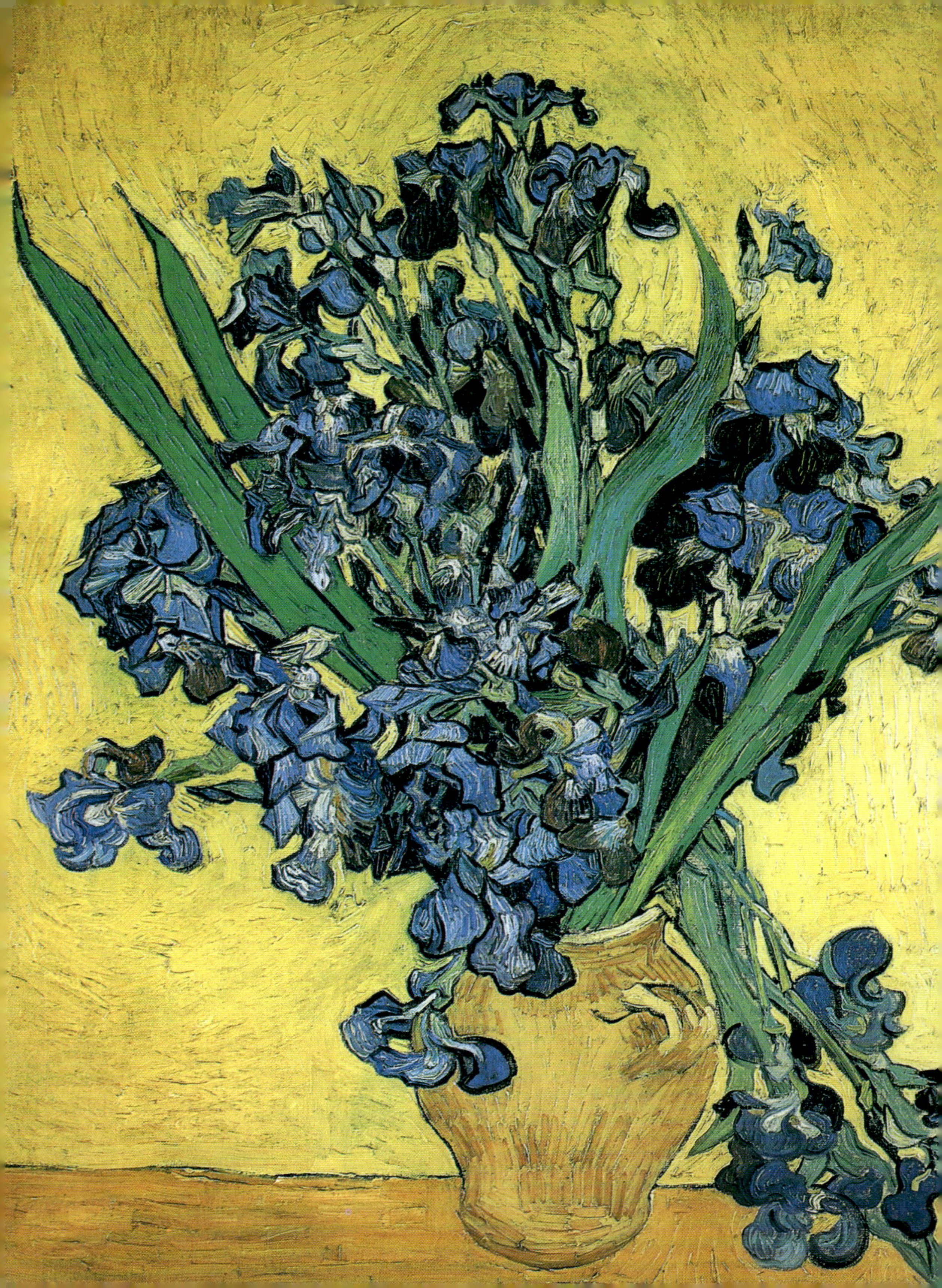

In fact there were four canvases in this final group of flower-paintings – two of roses and two of irises, all of them executed with the same attention to fine detail as had characterised his recent study of almond blossom. Until now he had virtually neglected still-life subjects during his year at Saint-Rémy. Why he chose to paint still-lives now he never explained, though it may be no accident that he chose to round off his year as a patient here just as he had begun it, with a study of irises that grew in the overgrown asylum garden. All he mentioned, to his sister Wil, was that in his last few days he had worked 'like a man in a frenzy'; in other words, very far from 'calm'.

Even in his urgent desire to leave the asylum at the first possible moment, Vincent could still say to his brother that the actual day he could depart would depend on when he had finished these last paintings. They of course would have to be left to dry and the chief attendant Trabuc had promised to take care of them. That said, he could scarcely wait to leave this place and between his final frenzy of work he was busy packing up all his things and feeling excited amid a whole jumble of emotions. 'Yes, it seems to me too,' he wrote towards the end of his long response to Theo, 'that there has been a terribly long gap between the day we said goodbye to one another at the railway station and today.' Then, on an optimistic note he went on: 'My dear brother, I feel I have so much more confidence in my own work now than I did before I left (Paris) and it would be ungrateful of me to speak ill of the south and I must confess to you that it is with deep sorrow that I am now turning my back on it.'

So, after months of longing to return to his roots in the north, Van Gogh finally felt overwhelmed by everything the south had given him. He was left with powerful images in his head which for him symbolised the character of Provence as he had experienced it; and he felt the need to paint them a final time. Probably his very last painting before leaving for Paris is one he never mentioned in his letters to Theo, as if it was too private and personal to be explained at this moment. The painting is *Road with Cypress and Star*. A single cypress tree rises into a dark sky, with a crescent moon on one side and the whirling image of

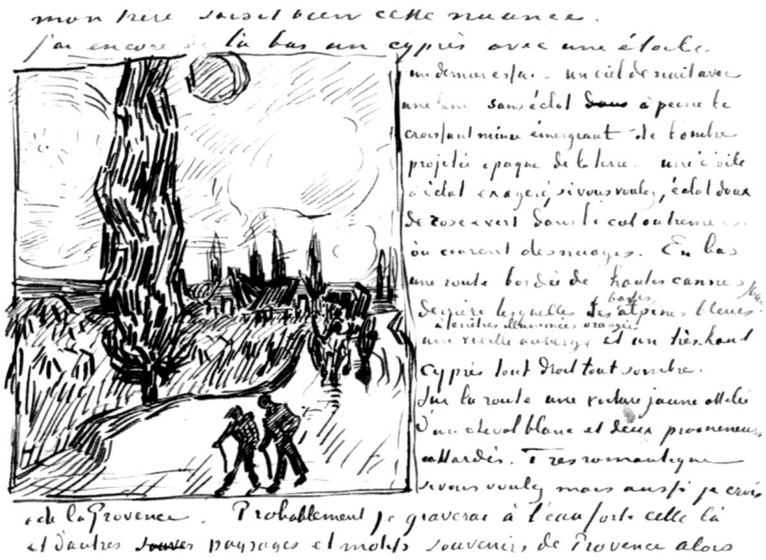

Sketch of *Road with Cypress and Star* Ink on paper,
Van Gogh Museum, Amsterdam

a star on the other, echoing the dramatic sky of *The Starry Night* painted nearly a year earlier. Two figures stand in the foreground on the moonlit road beside the shadow cast by the cypress tree. Approaching them on the road is a small horse-drawn carriage with another figure half-concealed beneath its canopy. The whole painting seems to be telling a story. It is a compilation of images drawn from other canvases, brought together to create a pictorial metaphor for his most deeply-felt experiences during his time at Saint-Rémy. It was Van Gogh's salute to Provence and his farewell to it.

Not until he had finally left the south did he make any reference to the painting. Then, five weeks after his departure, Vincent wrote to Gauguin: 'I still have a cypress with a star from down there. It's a final attempt…very romantic, if you like, but very Provençal, I think.' In fact the canvas was still at Saint-Rémy, drying out under the care of Trabuc along with the other late paintings and the sketch Van Gogh

Road with Cypress and Star Oil on canvas, 92 x 73 cm
Kroller-Muller Museum, Otterlo

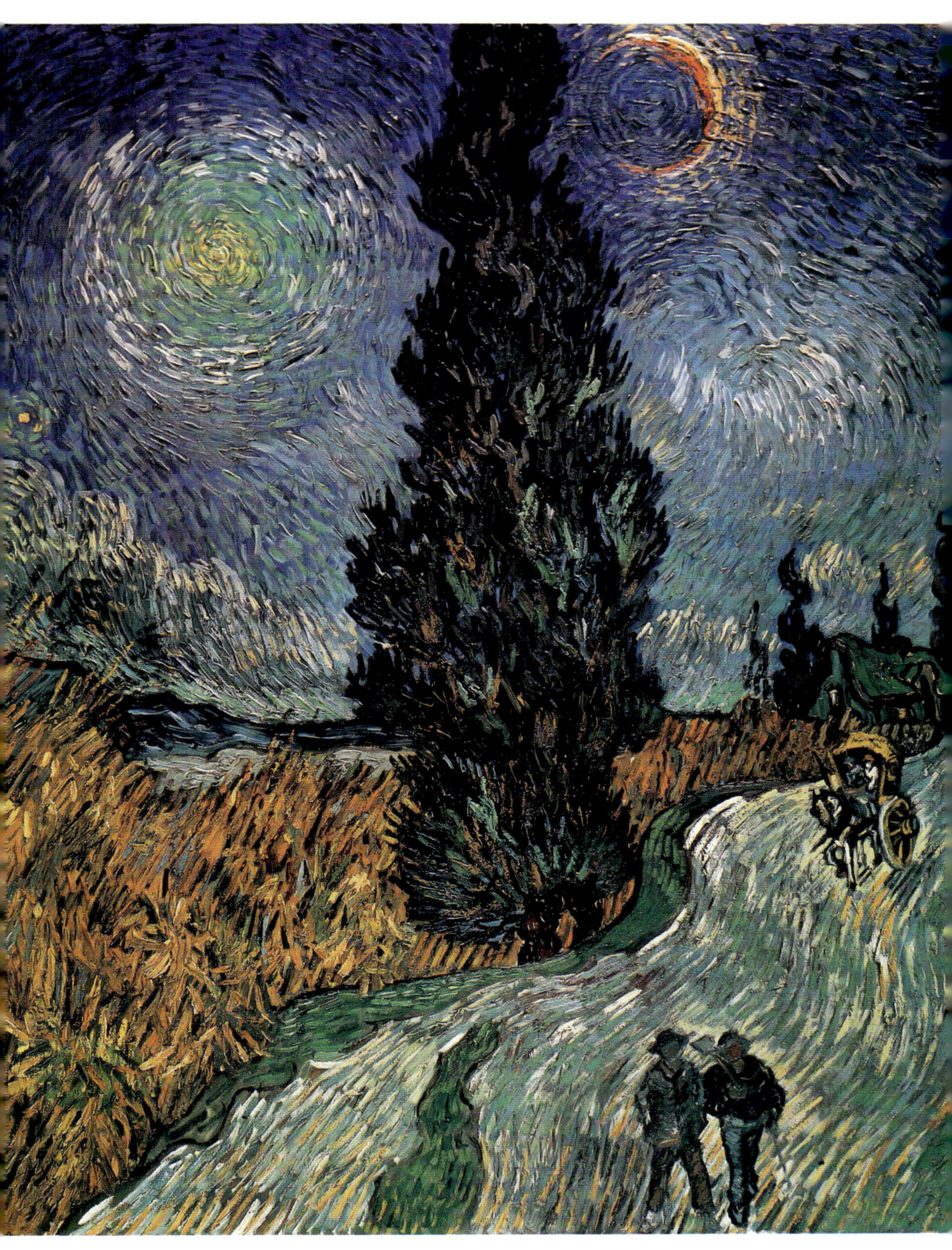

included in his letter to Gauguin was done from memory. It may be no accident that he decided to describe it to Gauguin. The painting was exactly the kind of composition pieced together from his imagination rather than directly from life which Gauguin had so often advocated and which Van Gogh so often claimed to reject.

On May 12th Vincent wrote to his friend Ginoux in Arles who had been storing his furniture from the Yellow House. He asked if his two beds, a mirror and a few other personal items could be crated up and sent to Paris by goods train. He expressed his deep regret at having been unable to see him on his last visit to Arles and explained that he was about to leave the region and was making plans to work in the countryside near Paris. The letter was Vincent's regretful goodbye to the city where he had first discovered the light and colours of the south more than two years earlier.

The following day Van Gogh wrote a final letter to his brother. Dr Peyron had given him permission to leave the asylum, he explained. Strictly speaking, Vincent being a voluntary patient he could not have done otherwise. Nonetheless the doctor's verdict would have given reassurance to Van Gogh himself and above all to Theo. Dr Peyron, for his part, however sympathetic and forbearing he had been towards his patient, had always been far out of his depth in dealing with Van Gogh and was surely glad finally to wash his hands of him. His last entry in the asylum register was a careful summary of his patient's period of time under his care, with a concluding comment which spoke more of profound relief than professional judgment. 'Cured' he wrote.

Meanwhile Van Gogh was still unsure of the precise date when he would leave. He hoped it would be by the following week-end so that he could spend Sunday with Theo on his brother's day off. His paintings of roses and irises were now finished, he explained; and he had also been to the station in Saint-Rémy to send off his trunk in advance. There was a final note of nostalgia in his letter. 'I saw the countryside again, wonderfully fresh after the rain and it was covered in wild flowers – Oh, how many more things I would have done if I had been able,' he wrote. Then, turning his attention to the immediate days ahead he suddenly reminded his brother of his desire to paint a yellow bookshop while he was in Paris.

So, 'until Sunday AT THE LATEST' he concluded.

In fact he departed a day earlier. On Friday May 16th he left the asylum for good. Accompanied by an attendant, probably the faithful Trabuc, Van Gogh caught the local train from Saint-Rémy, the same train on which he had arrived just as a year and eight days earlier. This time he planned to catch the Paris train not at Arles but at Tarascon, a short distance further north. Here he telegraphed Theo to confirm that he would shortly be on his way and that he would be arriving at the Gare de Lyon at ten o'clock the following morning, where Theo had promised to meet him.

There is no account of Vincent's departure; but as he boarded the train his friend and guardian, Trabuc, would certainly have given the warmest of handshakes. Trabuc had watched over and come to know and respect this troubled and endearing foreigner, who had even painted his portrait. It would have been a touching farewell.

The train headed north into the night. Van Gogh's Asylum Year was over.

In the Preface I described Van Gogh's Asylum Year as a play within a play but it was a play without a last act. The final scenes occupied little more than two months after Vincent's departure from Saint-Rémy in May 1890. In July he shot himself in a field at Auvers where he had been living under the care of Dr Gachet.

Shortly before leaving Saint-Rémy, Van Gogh referred to his time in the asylum as a 'shipwreck'. The vessel on the rocks was of course himself. Throughout his year-long stay as a patient there, he lived with the constant fear of the ship breaking up completely. Indeed there were entire months when he felt this to be taking place. It is hard to imagine a state of mind less congenial to a study of the wonders of nature and the colours of the South, which was Van Gogh's *raison d'être* for being in Provence.

I began this account of his Asylum Year as an exploration, a journey of discovery – to explore the relationship between his illness, his isolation here and his art. I had read numerous books on Van Gogh over the years, biographies as well as works of criticism. His year in Saint-Rémy has tended to be treated in rather general terms as a single episode along a dramatic path to self-destruction. In fact a study of his letters and of the paintings he produced during those twelve months, reveal startling shifts of mood, of intent and of vision throughout that time, sometimes within a matter of days. It was a year filled with extremes of light and dark, with little in between. There was no such thing as an 'ordinary day'. I have tried to imagine what it would have been like for so brilliant and damaged a person to find himself compelled to spend a year struggling to survive, simply to cope day by day, at the same time to paint whenever he could, to understand himself and his demons and always be driven to communicate, sending letters to the outside world like doves released in the hope of finding home.

Tracing his passage through those desperate months in the asylum helped put in perspective the remarkable productivity he achieved during his time here. He produced an estimated 150 canvases, the more remarkable since at least four of those months saw him incapacitated and either forbidden or unable to paint. Apart from writing letters to his family, painting was his entire life. There were no friends; he had no social life; he was too frightened to go into Saint-Rémy itself to sit in a café or watch the world pass by. Often he was too disturbed to go out at all, even in search of fresh subjects to paint. He was locked up within himself and within the safe confines of his studio or his bedroom. In consequence a surprisingly high proportion of those 150 canvases are either copies of his own work, or studio variations of landscapes he had once painted out of doors, or else interpretations of the work of other artists he admired, in particular Rembrandt, Delacroix and Millet.

What seems to have mattered most to him was the physical act of painting. This, as he repeatedly stated in his letters, was his 'profession' – like being a carpenter or a farmer – and he needed to practice it. This distracted him from dwelling on his demons and was in his view the best cure for his illness. Painting was a therapeutic exercise as much as a creative act, or rather, it enabled him to be creative at second-hand when direct exposure to his subject was unavailable or too daunting.

The distinction is not always clear between canvases which are a direct response to nature and those which are studio variations: several of the olive orchards series, for example, are clearly versions based on precisely the same configuration of trees, shadows and patterns of soil. They are like a pianist playing the same tune in different keys, exploring its possibilities. Other canvases, particularly in the cypress tree series, are made up of images, pieced together from details in other paintings, sometimes with added figures to supply a human touch. Only he could have transformed the Provençal night sky into a whirling dance of Catherine Wheels to give us his most celebrated painting of the Asylum Year, *The Starry Night*. As for the sleeping village below, Saint-Rémy was only a short distance from the asylum but was invisible from Van Gogh's room; in any case this huddle of cottages round the church bears little resemblance to the stately 19th century buildings lined with massive plane trees which was the imposing place he knew and painted. The sleepy hamlet he painted, with its welcoming lights, is more a memory of his boyhood in Holland than a record of Saint-Rémy. The contrast is dramatic and moving, giving the painting an extra depth of meaning between the comforts and safety of a remembered past and the overbearing turbulence of his present life.

Circumstances contrived to make Van Gogh a changed painter in Saint-Rémy. With movements so severely restricted he was compelled to mix images recorded directly from the landscape with those borrowed from other sources, either his own work or that of other artists. This new path has been attributed to the influence of Gauguin, who remained a continual support in his letters to Van Gogh in spite of the break-up of their relationship in Arles. Yet, much as he valued Gauguin's allegiance and judgment of his new work Van Gogh was adamant about the fundamental distinction between his own 'inventions' and those of his friend. Whatever he pieced together from different sources needed to be rooted in something he had observed directly from nature and not spun out of his own imagination. Expressing truth to nature was never more rigorously pursued than by Van Gogh; even the whirling constellations of *The Starry Night* were phenomena of nature which in his unsettled state of mind he saw as real. To him that was what stars did. Again the boundary between reality and invention became blurred.

I come away from this journey through Van Gogh's Asylum Year with the conviction that the intensity of his eye for the natural world and especially for the colours of the natural world, is the strongest characteristic of his work during this chapter of his life. This sharpness of vision is as true of the compositions put together from memory in his studio-retreat as it is of canvases painted out of doors directly from nature. Often it is an analytical eye, especially when he is searching for the most elusive subtleties of colour which he has perceived in a plant or a landscape – colours which constantly change as the light changes. This is when representing truth to nature grips him most intensely: he becomes a man bewitched, obsessed. It is an obsession that distracts him from his illness, directing his attention away from himself and, since there is no one to share his passion, he is driven to convey his thoughts to his family and to friends in letters – and now, by extension, to us.

They are letters which express his thoughts with extraordinary lucidity and intelligence for a man often described as 'mad'. They supply a literary commentary on his paintings of incomparable value. There is no more eloquent an example than the account he gave to the Dutch critic Isaacson, written after his departure from Saint-Rémy, of what had driven him to undertake his series on the olive orchards. 'The effect of daylight, of the sky, makes it possible to extract an infinity of subjects from the olive trees. I sought contrasting effects in the foliage, forever changing with colours of the sky.' They were words written towards the end of Van Gogh's own journey, as his own sky darkened.

FURTHER READING

Books on Van Gogh can fill a library. The most recent biography (by Steven Naifeh and Gregory White Smith) runs to more than 900 pages, including a 'selected' biography of twenty-three pages. Take your pick. I feel I should apologise for adding one more to the crowded shelves.

I have absorbed a number of these tomes but my principal concern has been with Van Gogh's remarkable and effusive correspondence which provides a running commentary on his life in Saint-Rémy. This consists of an exchange of letters with his brother Theo in Paris, with other members of his family in Holland, with the few critics who had written articles about his work and with a number of friends with whom he remained in touch, in particular Paul Gauguin. There are a number of editions of these letters, both complete and selected. The one I used is the magnificent version in six volumes, *The Letters, the Complete, Illustrated and Annotated Edition* (Thames and Hudson, 2009).

As for commentaries of the paintings executed during Van Gogh's Asylum Year, the catalogue accompanying the 2010 exhibition *The Real Van Gogh, the Artist and his Letters* at the Royal Academy in London has been invaluable, while the best study I came across of the artist's work during this period is the publication based on the exhibition *Van Gogh in Saint-Rémy and Auvers*, by Ronald Pickvance (Metropolitan Museum of Art, New York, 1986).

INDEX